Flutter in 7 Days

Build user-friendly apps with widgets and navigation

Ipsi Patro

bpb

www.bpbonline.com

First Edition 2024

Copyright © BPB Publications, India

ISBN: 978-93-55516-091

To View Complete
BPB Publications Catalogue
Scan the QR Code:

Dedicated to

*To my beloved husband, **Sanat Patro**,
and my two sons, **Arnav Patro** and **Vivaan Patro***

About the Author

Ipsi Patro is a software engineer with extensive experience in mobile platforms, excelling in both native and hybrid environments. She graduated with a B.Tech degree and has since worked at renowned companies such as Tata Consultancy Services in India, Vitality, and OvalMoney in the UK, among several others. Currently serving as the Head of Engineering at Twyn in the UK, Ipsi has consistently showcased outstanding leadership and managerial skills, effectively guiding mobile development teams with proficiency.

Motivated by an insatiable curiosity and a dedication to remaining at the forefront of technology, Ipsi immersed herself in mastering Flutter and Dart, swiftly achieving proficiency in both. Her technical expertise spans various programming languages, frameworks, and tools, complemented by a deep understanding of software architecture, agile methodologies, and DevOps practices. These capabilities have empowered her to successfully oversee complex projects from conception through deployment.

Beyond her technical accomplishments, Ipsi is passionate about knowledge-sharing. Her extensive hands-on experience with Flutter projects, coupled with a natural talent for teaching, enables her to articulate complex concepts clearly and accessibly. She firmly believes in the transformative impact of education and is committed to empowering aspiring developers to fulfill their potential.

When not deeply engaged in coding or teaching, Ipsi enjoys pursuits such as listening to music, gardening, cooking, and exploring the outdoors. Actively involved in developer communities, she collaborates with peers to exchange insights and deepen her knowledge.

Ipsi's book, **Flutter in 7 Days**, reflects her deep expertise and passion for Flutter development. She hopes this guide will empower readers to embark on their own Flutter journey and create exceptional mobile applications.

About the Reviewer

SriSindhu Pydimukkala is a seasoned software engineer with a strong foundation in Android development and a burgeoning expertise in Flutter. With seven years of experience in Android development, SriSindhu brings a wealth of knowledge and a fresh perspective to the world of cross-platform mobile app development.

Graduating with a B.Tech degree from Jawaharlal Nehru Technological University, SriSindhu embarked on a dynamic career journey, collaborating with industry-leading companies such as *OvalMoney* and presently serving as a Staff Software Engineer at *BlueYonder*. Throughout her professional tenure, SriSindhu has demonstrated exceptional leadership skills, having led mobile development teams with finesse and efficiency.

SriSindhu's proficiency spans a wide spectrum of Android development, encompassing frameworks, app architecture, memory management, multi-threading, development tools, debugging, problem-solving, Test-Driven Development (TDD), Pair Programming, and deployment strategies. Her commitment to excellence and knack for taking ownership of projects have propelled her to success in delivering high-quality Android applications that meet and exceed client expectations.

Outside of her professional endeavors, SriSindhu enjoys cooking up culinary delights in the kitchen, embarking on adventures to new destinations around the globe, and cherishing quality time with family. Her passion for technology is matched only by her love for exploring new flavors, cultures, and experiences, making her a well-rounded individual with a thirst for knowledge and a zest for life.

Acknowledgement

I would like to express my deepest gratitude to my family and friends for their unwavering support and encouragement throughout the writing of this book. A special thanks to my beloved husband, Sanat Patro, and my two sons, Arnav Patro and Vivaan Patro, whose love and patience have been my greatest source of strength.

I am also profoundly grateful to BPB Publications for their guidance and expertise in bringing this book to fruition. This journey involved numerous revisions and benefited immensely from the participation and collaboration of reviewers, technical experts, and editors.

I would like to acknowledge the valuable contributions of my colleagues and co-workers during my many years in the tech industry. Their insights and feedback have significantly shaped my understanding and approach to mobile app development.

Finally, I extend my heartfelt thanks to all the readers who have shown interest in my book. Your support and enthusiasm have been invaluable in making this book a reality. Thank you for embarking on this journey with me.

Preface

Welcome to *Flutter in 7 Days!* If you are holding this book, you have taken the first step towards mastering one of the most versatile and powerful frameworks for building cross-platform applications. Whether you are a seasoned developer looking to expand your skill set or a newcomer eager to dive into the world of mobile app development, this book is designed to be your comprehensive guide to learning Flutter in just seven days.

In today's fast-paced world, the demand for high-quality mobile applications is ever-increasing. Flutter, with its robust set of features and unparalleled flexibility, has emerged as a frontrunner in the realm of cross-platform development. With Flutter, you can create stunning user interfaces, leverage a single codebase to deploy apps on multiple platforms, and enjoy blazing-fast performance – all without compromising on quality or user experience.

Flutter in 7 Days is structured to provide you with a step-by-step journey through the fundamentals of Flutter development. Each day is carefully crafted to build upon the concepts learned in the previous days, ensuring a smooth and progressive learning experience. From setting up your development environment to building complex UI layouts, handling user input, and integrating with backend services, this book covers everything you need to know to become proficient in Flutter development.

Throughout this book, you will find a balance of theoretical explanations, practical examples, and hands-on exercises to reinforce your learning. Whether you prefer to read through concepts, follow along with code examples, or roll up your sleeves and dive into coding challenges, you'll find something here to suit your learning style.

As you embark on this seven-day journey, remember that learning Flutter – like any new skill – takes time, patience, and practice. Do not be discouraged by challenges or setbacks along the way. Embrace them as opportunities to deepen your understanding and grow as a developer.

By the end of *Flutter in 7 Days*, you will have the knowledge and confidence to tackle real-world Flutter projects with ease. Whether you are building your own apps, contributing to open-source projects, or launching your career as a Flutter developer, this book will serve as your trusted companion on your Flutter journey.

So, without further ado, let us embark on this exciting adventure into the world of Flutter development. Get ready to unleash your creativity, build amazing apps, and take your skills to new heights. The next seven days are going to be both challenging and rewarding – let us make the most of them!

Chapter 1: Day 1– Getting Started with Flutter and Dart

This chapter introduces Flutter and Dart, guiding you through setting up your development environment and creating your first Flutter project. You will gain an understanding of the Flutter project structure and write your first Dart code.

Chapter 2: Day 2– Basic Programming Concepts

In this chapter, you will learn about variables and data types in Dart, control flow mechanisms such as loops and conditionals, and the fundamentals of functions and methods. Additionally, you will explore object-oriented programming basics in Dart and engage in hands-on exercises to reinforce these concepts.

Chapter 3: Day 3– First Flutter App

This chapter delves into the Flutter widget tree, teaching you how to create layouts with widgets and handle user input through gestures and interactions. You will learn to navigate between screens and build a simple app from scratch.

Chapter 4: Day 4– Flutter Widgets

Here, you will get an overview of commonly used Flutter widgets, including container widgets for layout and styling, and text and image widgets for displaying content. The chapter also covers ListView and GridView for creating scrolling lists and grids, as well as exploring advanced widgets and customizing their behavior.

Chapter 5: Day 5– Prep Up with Advanced Flutter

This chapter focuses on state management in Flutter, understanding the widget lifecycle, and using packages and plugins to extend Flutter's functionality. Additionally, you will explore Flutter's animation capabilities and learn techniques for optimizing performance and debugging.

Chapter 6: Day 6– Fetching Data Internet

In this chapter, you will learn how to make HTTP requests in Flutter and handle asynchronous operations using Futures and Streams. You will also learn to parse JSON data, display remote data in your Flutter app, and implement error handling and loading indicators.

Chapter 7: Day 7– Firebase Integration to Flutter App

This chapter introduces Firebase and its services, guiding you through setting up Firebase for your Flutter project. You will learn to integrate Firebase Authentication, store and retrieve data with Cloud Firestore, and implement real-time updates with Firebase Cloud Messaging.

Chapter 8: Miscellaneous

The final chapter offers tips and best practices for Flutter development, guidance on deploying your Flutter app to different platforms, and resources for further learning and exploration. It also addresses troubleshooting common issues and exploring advanced topics and next steps in your Flutter journey.

Code Bundle and Coloured Images

Please follow the link to download the
Code Bundle and the *Coloured Images* of the book:

https://rebrand.ly/077b4d

The code bundle for the book is also hosted on GitHub at
https://github.com/bpbpublications/Flutter-in-7-Days.
In case there's an update to the code, it will be updated on the existing GitHub repository.

We have code bundles from our rich catalogue of books and videos available at
https://github.com/bpbpublications. Check them out!

Errata

We take immense pride in our work at BPB Publications and follow best practices to ensure the accuracy of our content to provide with an indulging reading experience to our subscribers. Our readers are our mirrors, and we use their inputs to reflect and improve upon human errors, if any, that may have occurred during the publishing processes involved. To let us maintain the quality and help us reach out to any readers who might be having difficulties due to any unforeseen errors, please write to us at :

errata@bpbonline.com

Your support, suggestions and feedbacks are highly appreciated by the BPB Publications' Family.

Piracy

If you come across any illegal copies of our works in any form on the internet, we would be grateful if you would provide us with the location address or website name. Please contact us at **business@bpbonline.com** with a link to the material.

If you are interested in becoming an author

If there is a topic that you have expertise in, and you are interested in either writing or contributing to a book, please visit **www.bpbonline.com**. We have worked with thousands of developers and tech professionals, just like you, to help them share their insights with the global tech community. You can make a general application, apply for a specific hot topic that we are recruiting an author for, or submit your own idea.

Reviews

Please leave a review. Once you have read and used this book, why not leave a review on the site that you purchased it from? Potential readers can then see and use your unbiased opinion to make purchase decisions. We at BPB can understand what you think about our products, and our authors can see your feedback on their book. Thank you!

For more information about BPB, please visit **www.bpbonline.com**.

Join our book's Discord space

Join the book's Discord Workspace for Latest updates, Offers, Tech happenings around the world, New Release and Sessions with the Authors:

https://discord.bpbonline.com

Table of Contents

CHAPTER 1
Getting Started with Flutter and Dart

Introduction

Hello readers welcome onboard to the journey of becoming a Flutter developer. In this chapter, first we will go through the installation steps to bring your machine ready for Flutter development and then we will go through some basic concepts of Flutter and Dart.

Structure

The chapter covers the following topics:

- Introduction to Flutter and Dart
- Understanding Flutter
- Defining Dart
- Installation in Windows
- Installation in Mac
- IDEs for Flutter
- Compilation logic of flutter
- Dartpad
- Function
- Dart data types

- Dart Variables
- Dart Classes and Objects
- Dart List
- Dart Map
- Null Safety in Dart
- String Interpolation

Objectives

By the end of this chapter, your machine must be ready for Flutter development, and you will get a good understanding of which IDE to pick and some important features provided by the IDE to make your development easier and faster. Along with that, some important and fundamental Flutter and Dart concepts will also be discussed.

Introduction to flutter and dart

In this book, we will learn Flutter from scratch to build fast, beautiful, native-quality iOS and Android Apps using just one code base and one programming language called **Dart**. **Flutter** is a tool developed by Google that can be used to build cross-platform iOS, Android, and web apps. It comes with loads of pre-built widgets, which makes it easier to layout any app. Flutter widgets are built using a modern framework inspired by Web Design.

Flutter just asks for a blank window and draws the widgets in it. Everything in a Flutter app is a widget, so we build a widget upon a widget. You can create your own widget or customize the pre-built widgets as per your requirements. One good thing about Flutter is when you are working with it, you get access to the original source code because it is open-source. If you want to know how an App bar is implemented, just click on the widget, and you can view it. If you are from an iOS development background, you must have noticed that the same thing is not possible in iOS. In iOS, many components are proprietary, so you will not be able to access them.

The term Flutter refers to two major things:

- The SDK contains many tools to compile the dart code to native machine code, which can run on iOS and Android platforms.
- It is a widget library that helps build beautiful apps.

In addition to Flutter, Dart is a fundamental aspect of app development with Flutter. Dart is the programming language utilized for writing code in Flutter. It was developed by Google and is designed for building fast, scalable, and efficient applications. Dart is a statically typed language with a syntax that is familiar to those who have experience with languages like Java or JavaScript.

Here are some key features of Dart:

- **Object-oriented**: Dart is an object-oriented language, which means it supports concepts like classes, objects, inheritance, and polymorphism. This makes it easy to organize code and build complex applications.

- **Strongly typed**: Dart is a statically typed language, meaning that variables are explicitly declared with their data types. This helps catch errors at compile-time and improves code robustness.

- **Asynchronous programming**: Dart provides built-in support for asynchronous programming using features like async and await. This allows developers to write code that can handle multiple tasks concurrently, such as making network requests or performing file I/O operations, without blocking the main execution thread.

- **Garbage collection**: Dart includes automatic memory management through garbage collection. Developers do not need to manually allocate and deallocate memory, making memory management less error-prone.

- **Package management**: Dart has a robust package management system called Pub. Developers can use Pub to easily manage dependencies and share their own packages with the community.

- **Cross-platform development**: While Dart is primarily associated with Flutter for mobile app development, it can also be used for server-side and web development. This versatility allows developers to use Dart for a wide range of projects beyond just mobile apps.

Understanding Dart is essential for effectively utilizing Flutter's capabilities to build powerful and feature-rich mobile applications. By mastering Dart, developers can leverage their strengths to write clean, efficient code that powers Flutter apps across multiple platforms.

Let us delve into a comprehensive comparison between Flutter and other popular frameworks to understand their respective strengths, weaknesses, and unique features in the realm of cross-platform mobile app development.

- **Flutter vs. React Native**
  - React Native, developed by *Facebook*, allows developers to build cross-platform mobile apps using JavaScript and React.
  - In Flutter, everything is a widget, which provides a more consistent and streamlined development experience compared to React Native's mix of native components and JavaScript.
  - Flutter uses a compiled programming language (Dart), which can result in better performance and more predictable behavior compared to React Native's JavaScript runtime.

- o Hot Reload in Flutter offers a faster development cycle compared to React Native's Hot Reload, as it updates the entire UI tree rather than just the JavaScript code.

- **Flutter vs. Xamarin**
  - o Xamarin, owned by *Microsoft*, enables developers to build cross-platform mobile apps using C# and .NET.
  - o Flutter's UI is rendered using Skia, a high-performance 2D graphics library, which can result in smoother animations and transitions compared to Xamarin's native UI approach.
  - o Flutter offers a more consistent development experience across platforms since it uses a single codebase, while Xamarin requires separate UI code for each platform.
  - o Dart's **Ahead-of-Time (AOT)** compilation in Flutter can lead to faster startup times and reduced runtime overhead compared to Xamarin's **Just-in-Time (JIT)** compilation.

- **Flutter vs. Native Development (iOS/Android)**
  - o Native development involves using platform-specific languages (Swift/Objective-C for iOS, Java/Kotlin for Android) and APIs to build apps.
  - o Flutter offers faster development cycles and a more productive workflow compared to native development, thanks to features like Hot Reload and a single codebase for multiple platforms.
  - o While native development provides access to platform-specific APIs and features, Flutter's extensive widget library and platform channels allow developers to achieve native-like behavior and performance.
  - o Flutter's UI is rendered using Skia, which may result in slightly different visual rendering compared to native components, though Flutter's customizable widgets can often achieve the desired look and feel.

In summary, Flutter's use of a single codebase, fast development cycles, high-performance rendering engine, and customizable widgets make it a compelling choice for cross-platform mobile app development, offering unique advantages over other frameworks like React Native, Xamarin, and native development. Additional advantages of Flutter, such as Hot Reload and strong community support, can provide further insights into its appeal. Here is an expanded comparison with these advantages:

- **Hot Reload for Rapid Development:**
  - o Flutter's Hot Reload feature allows developers to instantly see changes made to the code reflected in the app's UI without restarting the app or losing its current state.

- o This iterative development process significantly reduces development time by enabling developers to experiment, iterate, and refine UI elements and features rapidly.

- o In contrast, other frameworks like React Native and Xamarin offer similar features, but Flutter's Hot Reload is often praised for its speed and reliability, making the development experience smoother and more efficient.

- **Strong community support:**
  - o Flutter benefits from a large and active community of developers, enthusiasts, and contributors who provide extensive support, resources, and collaboration opportunities.
  - o The Flutter community actively shares knowledge, best practices, libraries, packages, and plugins through platforms like GitHub, Stack Overflow, Medium, and various forums and meetups.
  - o This vibrant community ecosystem fosters innovation, accelerates learning curves, and addresses challenges faced by developers, making it easier to find solutions and resources for building Flutter apps.
  - o Additionally, Google's continued investment in Flutter and its commitment to open-source development further bolster community engagement and contribute to the framework's growth and evolution.

Understanding Flutter

Google has introduced Flutter for native mobile app development on Android, iOS, and Windows. Flutter is a mobile app SDK, complete with framework, widgets, and tools, that gives developers a way to build and deploy mobile apps written in Dart. So, before moving ahead with learning Flutter, we will cover Dart basics later in this chapter. If you have prior experience of software development with any language, you must be familiar with these basics, but if you do not have any, it will be helpful for you in this journey.

Defining Dart

Dart is a programming language designed for client development, such as for the web and mobile apps. It is developed by Google and can also be used to build server and desktop applications. It is an object-oriented, class-based, garbage-collected language with C-style syntax.

Flutter Architecture

With UI as code, there is no visual editor in Flutter like native iOS and Android development. Therefore, no drag and drop of widgets; instead, write the code for adding and updating widgets. But it is extremely straightforward and easy to understand. We will introduce you to different concepts as we go. Throughout this book, we will build multiple apps. Many important links for deep diving into topics for extra support will also be provided in this book.

Now, without delay, let us go through the installation process.

Installation in windows

Installation in windows is a two steps process:

1. Installing Flutter SDK
2. Installing Android Studio

Installing Flutter SDK

Let us start with the Installation of Flutter SDK:

System requirements are:

- **Windows version**: Windows 10 or later
- **Disk Space**: While 1.64 GB of disk space is the minimum requirement, it is advisable to allocate more space for future project developments. Additionally, if you are considering installing Android Studio alongside Flutter, the combined space requirement should be at least 10GB to accommodate both tools effectively.
- **PowerShell**: Windows PowerShell 5.0 (This is preinstalled)
- **Git for Windows**: Git for Windows is an additional tool that Flutter uses under the hood for version control and managing project dependencies. It enables developers to track changes, collaborate with others, and revert to previous versions if needed. Having Git installed ensures smoother integration with Flutter and facilitates efficient project management.
- **Verification of Git installation**: After installing Git for Windows, you can verify its installation by running a simple command in your terminal or command prompt. Simply type `git --version` and press *Enter*. If Git has been installed successfully, you should see the installed version of Git displayed in the output. This step ensures that Git is set up correctly and ready to be used with Flutter for version control purposes.

Now let us move on to Git installation:

1. Let us start with Git installation. For that, navigate to this link: **https://git-scm. com/download/win**
2. Then, click the appropriate link and download the installable file.

3. Once downloaded, click and go ahead with the installation with the default selected options. Make sure to Use Git from the Windows Command **Prompt** option is selected, as shown in the following figure:

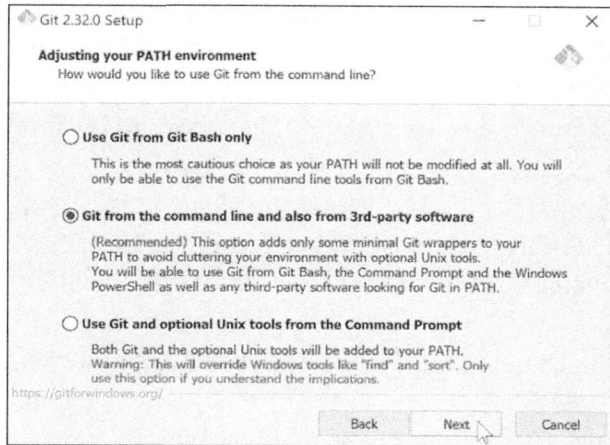

Figure 1.1: *Adjusting your PATH environment for Git*

4. Continue and finish the installation as shown in the following figure:

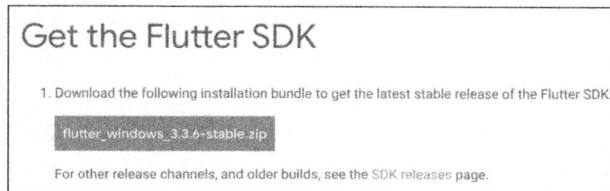

Figure 1.2: *Completing the Git installation process*

5. Once finished, move on to installing Flutter (*Figure 1.3*).

Figure 1.3: *Download Flutter SDK*

6. Go ahead and click on the button. While you are doing this, there are chances the version might have changed. But do not worry and continue downloading. This is a big file, so it will take a while.

7. Once the download is completed, you can extract the zip file and place the contained flutter folder in the desired installation location for the Flutter SDK (for example, `C:\src\flutter`).

8. Do not install it in a directory like `'C:\Program Files\'` or any folder that has restricted access.

Flutter is not a tool we double-click on to start, but a tool that we typically involve through the command prompt. For that, we must update the path of Flutter, which we just installed, so that it is globally available inside the command prompt no matter where in our system we execute this.

We need the Flutter and Dart commands, which are inside the `'bin'` folder of Flutter, to install the Android Studio:

9. First, type `'env'` on the search bar of your Windows machine and select `'Edit environment variables for your account.'`

10. Under User variables just look for Path. If you do not have one, just add a new one with the same name, `'Path,'` and add a new entry with the full path to Flutter/bin folder. By doing this, it becomes a part of the path environment variable, and we will be able to invoke the Flutter command from the command prompt.

11. After this, open the command prompt and type 'Flutter,' it should show a list of available commands for 'Flutter,' and it should not show any error. After that, you can run the flutter doctor command; it is an analysis command that will analyze if the system is ready to build a Flutter app or not. At this point, it will show some errors, as we have not set the development environment for Android yet. You may also get errors for Visual Studio, but that is only required if you are planning to build a desktop app. So, we can ignore that error for now.

Installing Android Studio

As a next step, we will install Android Studio by following these steps:

1. Flutter can be used as a tool to build cross platform apps but under the hood Flutter needs extra tool to develop apps that can run on iOS and Android devices. Due to the restrictions by Apple, you cannot build cross platform apps for iOS on windows, For iOS build, you need a mac. However, you can build the app for Android on windows.

2. For android setup, as the document says we need to install 'Android Studio' which is the official development environment by Google for building Android apps (*Figure 1.4*). So, download the Android Studio from the link given in the official doc **https://developer.android.com/studio**.

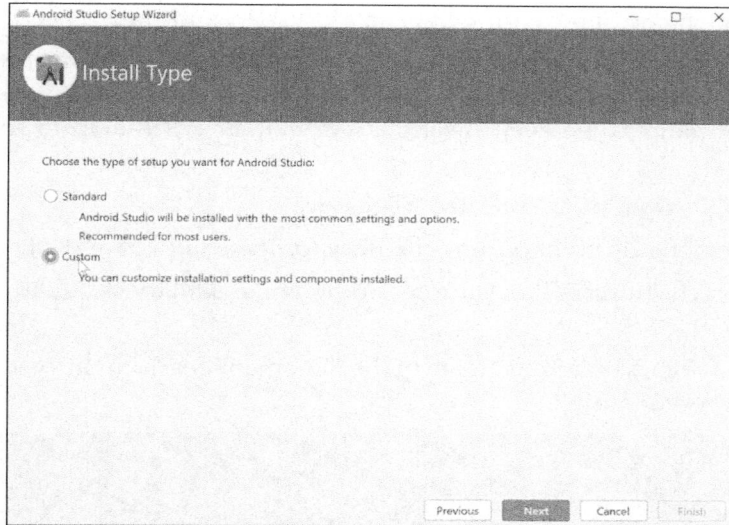

Figure 1.4: *Download Android Studio*

3. Click on the download button to start downloading the installable file. It may take a couple of seconds, depending on your internet speed. But once downloaded go ahead with all default settings and install both Android Studio and Virtual device which we need for Flutter app development.

4. Once the installation is finished, we can also start it immediately by keeping the 'Start Android Studio' check box checked. By default, when you open Android Studio for the first time, you will see a setup Wizard; we should go through that as we need certain tools and settings to be set up. As shown in the following figure, just select custom as the installation type to customize everything:

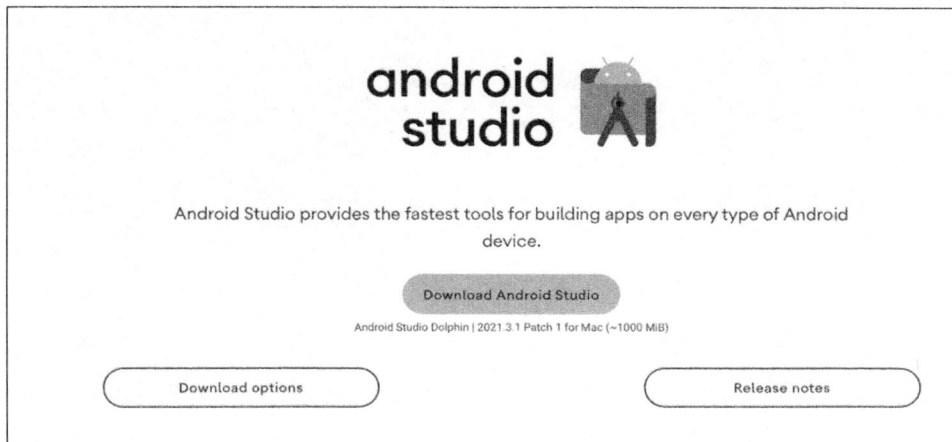

Figure 1.5: *Android Studio Setup Wizard*

5. Try to keep the default path for JDK.

6. Select the theme of the editor, light/dark, as per your preference.

7. Next step is selecting the check box for an Android version whichever is the latest version available, Android SDK, Android virtual device and if you have the option of Performance, then keep it selected as well as it will help to speed up virtual emulator.

8. Once all the options are selected, click next.

9. Keep the defaults for allocating memory for the emulator and click next.

10. Once you click finish, the Android Studio will install the required tools under the hood.

11. Once installed, you can navigate to the SDK manager from the welcome screen, by clicking on 'configure'.

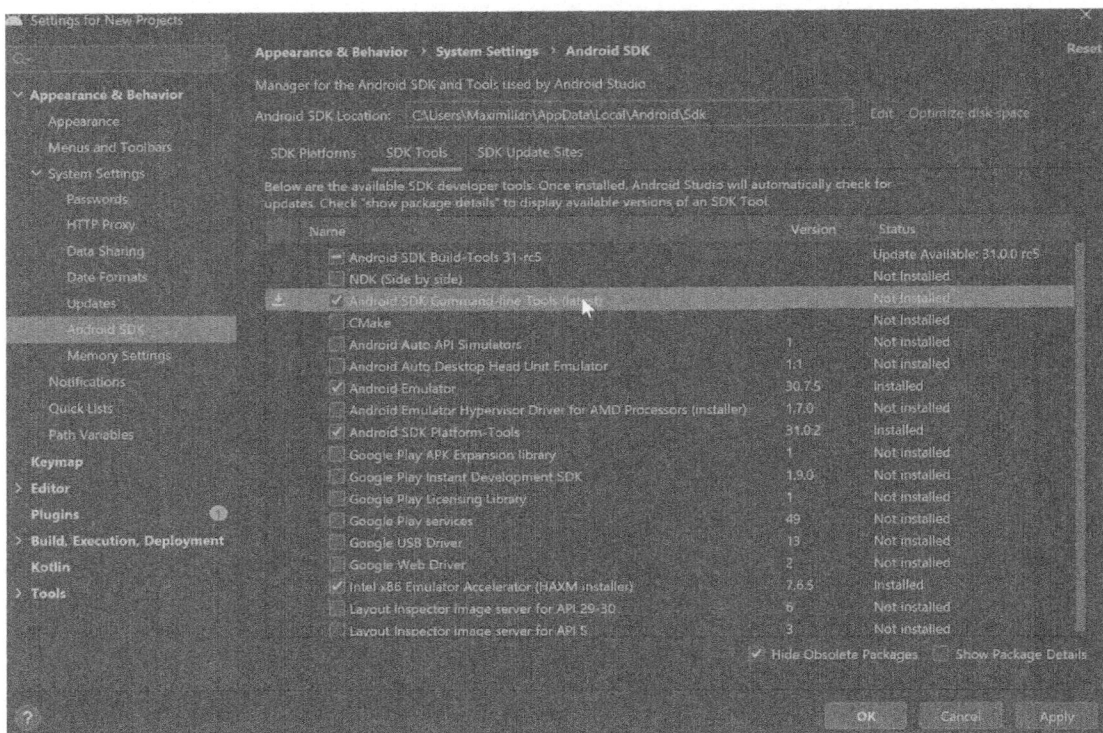

Figure 1.6: Android Studio Welcome Screen

12. To install any missing software that you might need, we recommend navigating to SDK tools, inside **tools | SDK Manager,** and selecting the check box for Android-SDK command line tools, to avoid some unnecessary errors, as shown in the following figure:

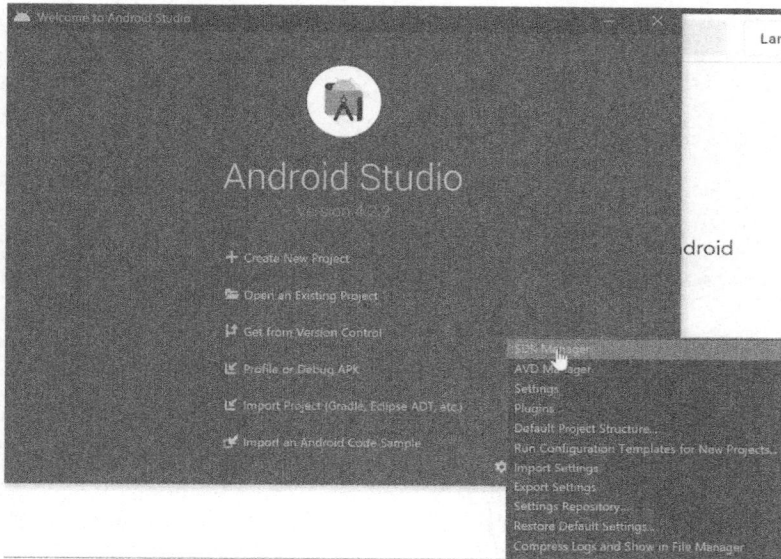

Figure 1.7: Android Studio SDK Manager

13. Click **OK**.

14. Accept the license agreement, and Android Studio will download the necessary utility software. Once the download is complete, go to the 'Configure' option on the welcome screen and select **AVD Manager**.

15. At this point, try and run **Flutter doctor** again in the command prompt, and you may get an alert to accept the terms and conditions, to do so try running this command 'flutter doctor --android-licenses' in your terminal. After that, if you run 'Flutter doctor' again, we should have a working Android Setup.

16. With that, if you open Android studio, you should be able to see the option of **Start a new Flutter Project**. This means the installation process is successful.

If you have any queries or need more support, please refer to the installation guide by Flutter **https://docs.flutter.dev/get-started/install/windows.**

Installation in Mac

Now, we will go through the installation process in a mac. As a system requirement to install Flutter, you should have:

- A minimum of 10GB free space.

- You must install 2 large applications Xcode and Android Studio along with Flutter SDK, for a smooth experience.

Before you start with the installation process, we advise you to update your MacOS to the latest available version, because to run the latest iOS version, you need latest XCode version and that has a dependency on MacOS version. If you are not concerned about the iOS version, you can just continue as it is.

Installing Flutter SDK

As a first step, select the appropriate button (Intel/Apple M1) and download the Flutter SDK by following these steps (*Figure 1.9*):

Figure 1.8: *Download Flutter SDK*

1. Download and unzip the file which you downloaded. You can see a **Flutter** folder.

2. Move this folder from downloads to the right location. We feel the best place is to create a new folder like **developer**, under the home folder, which is your username inside the users list, something like this **/Users/ipsipatro/developer**. You can use *Command* + up arrow button to go to the root folder if you are not sure where your user folder is located.

3. As a next step, we will update the path of Flutter for our terminal. For that open your terminal and verify if you have z shell enabled (*Figure 1.9*). You should see **zsh** on the top.

Figure 1.9: *Mac Terminal Window*

4. We have to find the path of a file **.zshrc**. It lives in our home folder.

5. To open it, you can type vim **~/.zshrc**. This command will basically open **the .zshrc** file using a text editor called '**vim**' which is installed by default in mac.

6. Then enable editing by pressing '**i**'.

7. Then, you must add the Flutter/bin folder path to this file. Navigate to the dart file or any other file inside '**bin**' folder, right click and tap '**Get info**' which will give you the full path of the file.

8. In our case, it is **'/Users/ipsipatro/Developer/flutter/bin'**. So, we are going to insert this line into our .zshrc file

```
export PATH="$PATH:/Users/ipsipatro/Developer/Flutter/bin"
```

9. Once done, press esc and then type ':**wq**', then just hit enter. This will save our changes and close the file.

10. After this, quit and restart a new terminal window. Type Flutter in the new window. If it shows the list of available commands in Flutter, that means you have updated the Flutter path successfully.

11. After that, you can run the 'flutter doctor' command; it is an analysis command that will analyze if the system is ready to build a flutter app or not. At this point, it will show some errors, as we have not set the development environment for Android or iOS yet. You may also get errors for Visual Studio, but that is only required if you are planning to build a desktop app. So, we can ignore that error for now.

Installing Android studio

Once you are ready, as the document says, navigate to **https://developer.android.com/ studio**. It is intelligent to detect and show the right downloadable file for Android Studio:

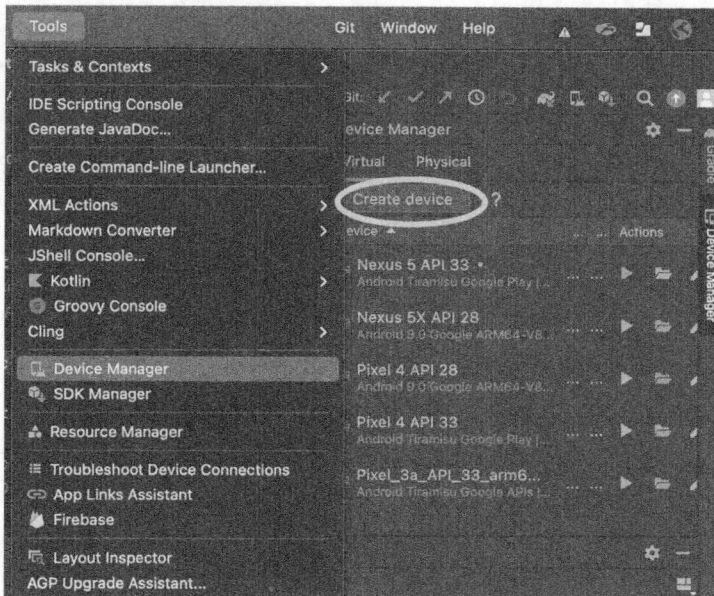

Figure 1.10: *Android Studio download link*

Follow these steps to successfully install Android Studio:

1. Click on the **Download Android Studio** button to start downloading.

2. Once that is done just launch Android Studio and go through the setup wizard by selecting yes to everything, which will keep the default settings. That will install Android SDK, Android platform tools and build tools, which we need for development of Android app using Flutter.

3. From the welcome screen, click on **configure** | **Preferences**. If you have already installed Android studio, you can open **Android Studio** | **Preference** | **Plugins**.

4. Then, search for **Flutter** and click **install**. If it asks you to install dart alongside, then click yes, otherwise search for **Dart** and install that as well.

5. Once both 'Flutter' and 'Dart' plugins are added, click **ok** to close the preferences and restart your Android Studio.

6. If you can see the option for 'Start a new Flutter Project', that means this step is successful and your Android Studio is ready for Flutter app development.

To run the Flutter app, you will need an emulator. To set up an emulator, navigate to the 'Device Manager' under the tools menu. You can add a new device by selecting 'Create Device'. Choose the device you prefer to use as the emulator. If the system image (API level) is not installed, you will have the option to download and install it using the available button. After installation, continue creating the virtual device. Once done, finish the setup, and the emulator should be ready to use:

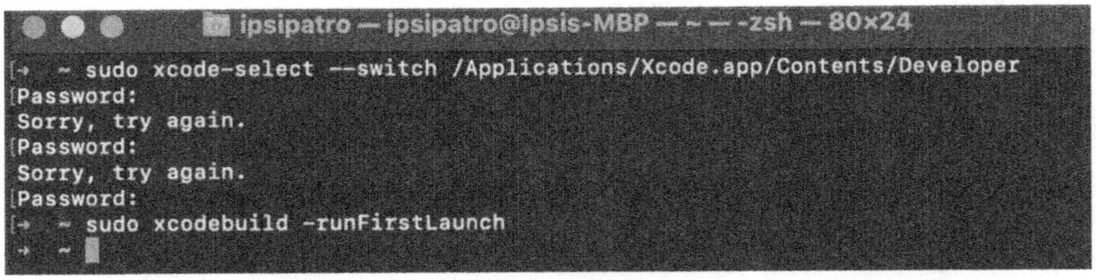

Figure 1.11: Android Studio tools menu device manager

iOS Setup

As the next step, let us do the iOS setup. To do so, follow these steps:

1. Go ahead and download Xcode from the link given in the doc for Mac App Store:

   https://apps.apple.com/us/app/xcode/id497799835

2. Then, click on **View in Mac App Store**, open and download Xcode. It will take a while to download as the file size is huge.

3. After finishing downloading, it is important to open it, as the first time, it will ask you a bunch of things like agreeing to the terms and conditions and some other questions. Just click yes to everything and continue.

4. After that, you have to set up the Xcode command line tool, for that you have to run two commands in the terminal:

   ```
   sudo xcode-select --switch/Applications/Xcode.app/Contents/Developer
   sudo xcodebuild -runFirstLaunc
   ```

5. As you are running 'sudo' command, which is a super user command, the terminal will ask you to enter the password. You need to enter the password you use to

login to the computer. Until you get it right, it will prompt you to try again, as shown in the following figure:

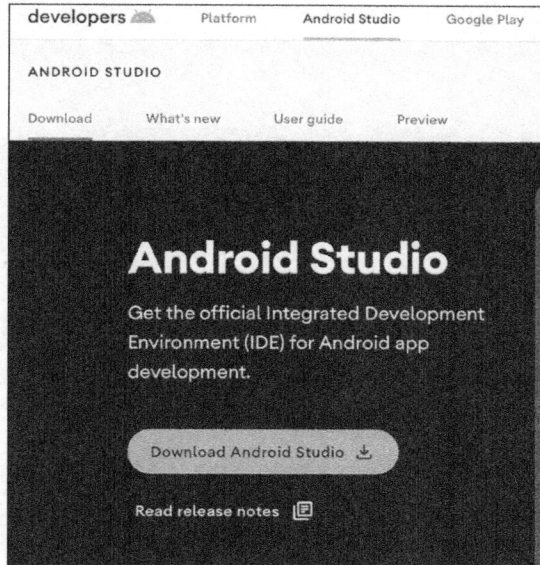

Figure 1.12: Terminal window

6. After that, quit both terminal and Xcode.

7. Now you are all set with both Android and iOS setups.

If you get stuck anywhere just try to find the help online, type your error in google, you will find some help. Also, you can refer to the Flutter doc installation guide link **https:// docs.flutter.dev/get-started/install**, as it is possible things might have changed slightly when you are installing Flutter than mine.

Updating some configurations for Android Studio

Let us update some configuration for Android Studio by following these steps:

1. Open Android Studio, click on the new Flutter Application, or from the file menu, select 'New Flutter Project'

2. Android Studio will show you the path for Flutter SDK. If it is correct, then click next.

3. Enter values as shown in the following figure, or feel free to name the app according to your preference. Then, select the required project location and organization name.

4. On clicking **finish**, it will launch the app (*Figure 1.13*):

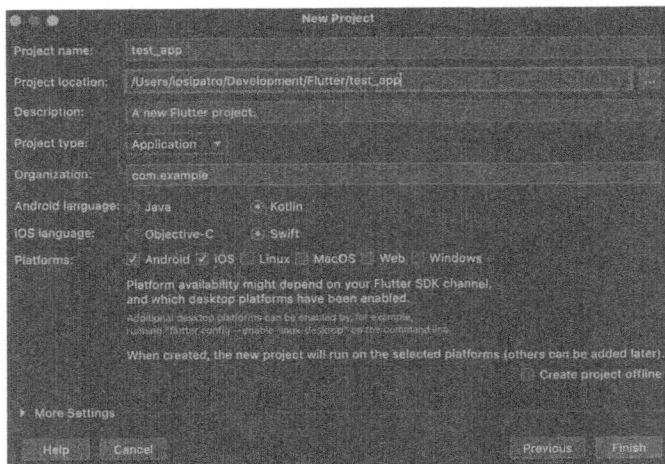

Figure 1.13: Android Studio new project creation window

5. Once the project is open, go to **Android Studio | Preference** in mac or on Windows, you can go to **File | Settings** and there you can select **Appearance** under **Appearance and Behaviour** to update Theme.

6. Since we prefer a dark theme, we would like to keep **Darcula** as our Android Studio theme.

7. Next, navigate to Language and Framework and check if both **Perform hot reload on save** and **Format code on save** are checked.

8. Click **ok**.

9. For now, we are good to go with configurations:

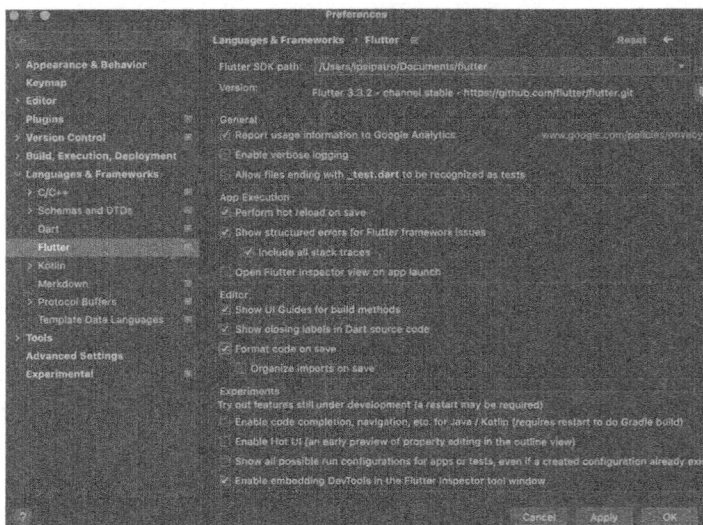

Figure 1.14: Android Studio preferences for Flutter

IDEs for Flutter

There are several popular **Integrated Development Environments (IDEs)** and code editors that are commonly used for Flutter development. Here are some of the most popular ones:

1. **Android Studio**: Android Studio is the official IDE for Android app development, and it offers robust support for Flutter development with features like Flutter plugin, emulator integration, and debugging tools.

2. **Visual Studio Code (VS Code)**: VS Code is a lightweight and highly customizable code editor developed by Microsoft. It has a rich ecosystem of extensions, including the Flutter and Dart extensions, which provide excellent support for Flutter development.

3. **IntelliJ IDEA with Flutter Plugin**: IntelliJ IDEA is a powerful IDE developed by JetBrains. It offers extensive support for Flutter development with the Flutter plugin, providing features like code completion, debugging, and integration with Flutter tools.

Feel free to decide which IDE you would like to go with. In this book, we will use Android Studio.

Features of IDE

Now, we are all set with the installations and ready for Flutter development. Let us take a tour of our 'Android Studio' IDE, what it offers, and how we can best utilize the tools it offers. It is important to familiarize ourselves with different areas of our IDE and know what it can do. We will discuss some important ones here, which will make our lives easier:

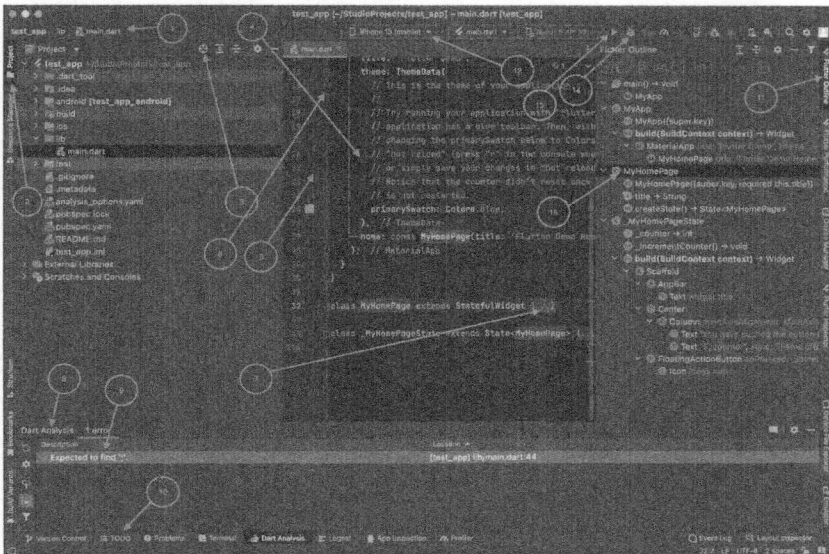

Figure 1.15: Android Studio Tools

1. **Navigation Bar**: It shows the location of currently opened file relative to your project.

2. **Project Pin**: Click on it to open and close the project files. It contains the iOS and Android folders along with others, but we will mainly work on lib folder.

3. **Locate File**: If your project folders are collapsed and you would like to know where your opened file is located, use this button.

4. **Editor Pin**: This is the place we write all the code.

5. **Margin**: Where you get a chance to preview colors you set, like you can see a blue color in the image. It also shows the line numbers and you can click at that area to add a breakpoint while debugging the app.

6. It is a button in margin, using which you can collapse the block of code which you do not want to work on at any point of time.

7. If you would like to expand or open the collapsed code, use the 3 dots button shown in number 7.

8. **Dart Analysis**: It is placed underneath the Editor panel. If you have any error in the code, you can find it in dart analysis as shown in number 9. If you double-click the error, it will take you to the line which has the error.

9. If you have any **TODO,** like you would like to add some unit test later or try some different color, you can add a TODO using '**// TODO:** '. Then, at any point of time you can go to the place shown in number 10, to check your to do list for the app.

10. **Flutter Outline**: This is where you can find a tree like structure of your whole app.

11. Device list: This is the place where you can select the available device list using which you can run the app.

12. The button to run the app.

13. The button to debug the app.

14. When you click on any part, like in the image, where we clicked on 'MyHomePage', shown as number 15, it takes you where exactly it is located in the app and highlights it.

15. **Flutter Inspector:** To view the stuff inside Flutter inspector, you must run the app first. Once the app is running, you can view widgets. It is very similar to Chrome developer tools.

16. **Widget Details Tree**: If you select any of the widgets in the widget tree like I have selected a Text widget, then as shown in the following figure, it will show all the properties of the selected widget.

17. **Layout Explorer**: In the bottom section in Layout explorer, it will show how and where the selected widget is laid out.

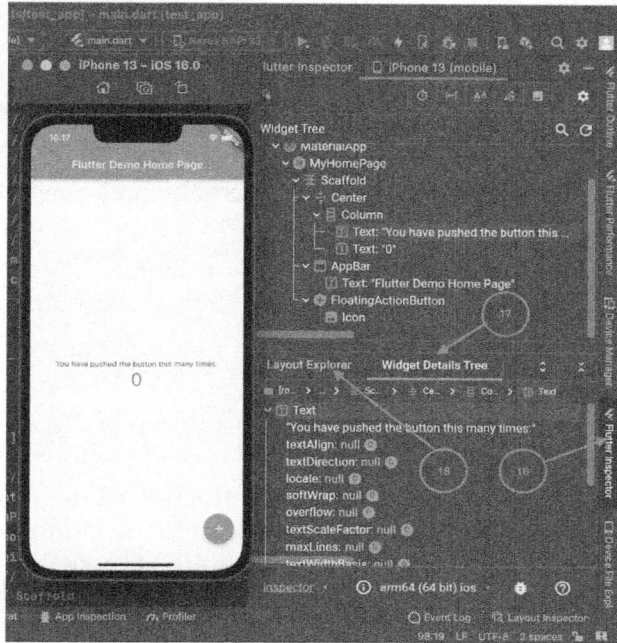

***Figure 1.16**: Android Studio Tools*

18. Show and Hide Debug Point: When the app is running, select **Flutter Performance** and tap on the little blue button marked as number 19. Then, the view inside the emulator will change too, as shown in the following figure, by adding more layout details of each widget, how it is being padded, and other minute details.

***Figure 1.17**: Android Studio debug points tool*

There are many more features integrated in the IDE, which you will learn as you start using it more.

Compilation logic of Flutter code

Let us understand how Flutter and Dart work internally and how your Flutter app gets converted to a native app.

1. We write the code in DART language using Flutter API, which provides us a collection of functions and widgets to build our application.

2. Then, we have our own code with some pre-existing and some of your own widgets.

3. Then Flutter compiles flutter code to optimized and high-performance native iOS and Android code, and that happens with the help of Flutter SDK.

4. High performance is one of the benefits of using Flutter. Flutter does not use platform primitive, which means it does not translate Flutter widgets to platform-specific views or widgets. But instead, Flutter has its own implementation. Flutter does not translate code to its native equivalent but controls every pixel in the device. We don't have to know it, but it is better to understand how Flutter has more control and no fear of any translation issue.

Dartpad

DartPad is an open-source tool that lets you play with Dart language in any modern browser. You can also say that it is a web-based playground that allows you to write some Dart code and run it in the browsers. So, it is easy to practice some dart syntax using Dartpad. For that, just type Dartpad in Google, and you will be able to get a link to it.

Function

Functions are crucial in any programming language. Functions are code snippets, which you can execute multiple times or anytime you want. In the following figure, there are two functions `'main'` and `'multiplyNumbers'`. You can give any name to a function but main is a special function, which is an entry point for any dart application. Dart automatically looks for and calls the main function when the app starts. You should always give the function name in camel case, just like our second function `'multiplyNumbers'`. Function names always start with lowercase followed by other words that start with a capital letter. When you click the **run** button, dart will look for the entry point 'main' function, execute the code and print the result in console.

Code:

```
1. multiplyNumbers(arg1, arg2) {
2.    return print(arg1 * arg2);
3. }
4.
5. void main() {
6.    multiplyNumbers(3, 5);
7. }
```

Code 1.1: *Example of Function Implementation*

Output will be: 15

Dart data types

Dart is a strongly typed language. So, if you do not define any explicit type, dart will compile it as a dynamic type. That is the reason you can see in the preceding figure, that the documentation section is showing dynamic types. But it is better to avoid that. It is good to define the type of object so that Dart will throw an error if you try to pass something of the wrong data type as an argument or expect the wrong data type for the return of a function. It is better for cleaner and safer code to define explicit type. String, int, and double are all examples of dart data types.

> *Tip:* **Click on any part of the code in Dartpad and you will get some information about it, in the documentation section.**

Dart variables

Variable is a core feature in dart. It can hold any value. In the following example, we have created a variable **'result'**, which holds the value returned by **'multiplyNumbers'** function. You can simply define it with **'var'** keyword. Dart has a feature call type inference, using which dart can infer the type of var to the type returned by the method, which is a good practice to use dart type inference feature and leave it to the dart by declaring a variable with var keyword. In our case, the result will be inferred to double. But sometimes, we may need to create a variable whose value can be assigned later. For example:

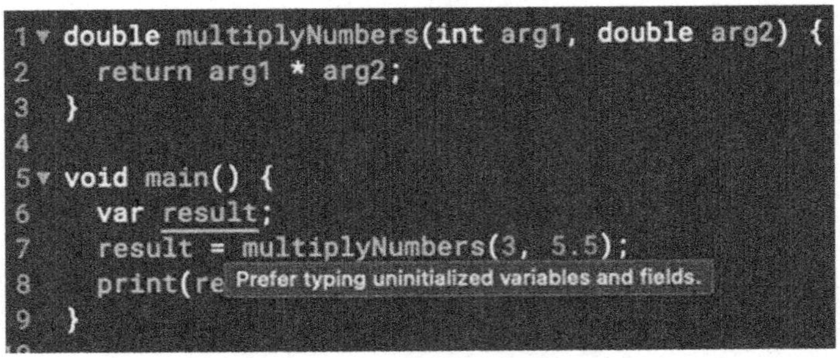

```
1 ▼ double multiplyNumbers(int arg1, double arg2) {
2     return arg1 * arg2;
3 }
4
5 ▼ void main() {
6     var result;
7     result = multiplyNumbers(3, 5.5);
8     print(re Prefer typing uninitialized variables and fields.
9 }
```

Figure 1.18: Variable type inference with warning

In this case, it is better to define the type of var, so that dart compiler will know which type of value it should allow the '**result**' object to hold. That is the reason if you run this code in Dartpad, it will show a blue underline for result object and suggests preferring typing as shown in above figure. If you replace it with double, the underline will disappear.

Code:

```
1. double multiplyNumbers(int arg1, double arg2) {
2.    return arg1 * arg2;
3. }
4.
5. void main() {
6.    double result;
7.    result = multiplyNumbers(3, 5.5);
8.    print(result);
9. }
```

Code 1.2: Dart Variable Usage in a Function

Output will be: 16.5

Dart classes and objects

Dart is an object-oriented programming language, so everything in dart is an object. This result is an object, 3 is an object of type int and so on. In real world also, if you imagine everything is an object. Your house is an object, it has 4 rooms, rooms are also objects but for the house object, number of rooms is a property of it. Similarly, in object-oriented programming we have something called 'class' which allows you to define a blueprint of an object as shown in the following code.

Code:

```
1.   class Employee {
2.     String name = 'Ipsi';
3.     int age = 30;
4.   }
5.
6.   void main() {
7.     var employee1 = Employee();
8.     var employee2 = Employee();
9.     employee2.name = 'Oscar';
10.    print(employee1.name);
11.    print(employee2.name);
12.  }
```

Code 1.3: *Dart Classes and Objects Demonstration*

Output will be:

Ipsi

Oscar

In the preceding example, we have created a blueprint of an **'Employee'** object which has 2 properties, name and age. We have created 2 objects of the class **employee1**, **employee2**.

Dart List

A very commonly used collection in programming is an array. Dart represents arrays in the form of List objects. A List is simply an ordered group of objects. The dart core library provides the List class that enables the creation and manipulation of lists:

Code:

```
1. void main() {
2.    var numbersList = [];
3.    numbersList.add(1);
4.    numbersList.add(2);
5.    print(numbersList);
6. }
```

Code 1.4: *Dart list Demonstration*

Output will be: [1, 2]

Dart map

The dart map is a dynamic collection object where you can save key value pairs of any type of data. Dynamic because, maps can grow and shrink at runtime. Please look at the following code to understand Dart Map and some important methods of it which will be useful for you at some point of time in Flutter development.

Code:

```
1. void main() {
2.    var user = {'name': 'Ipsi', 'surname': 'Patro'};
3.    print('Map is: $user');
4.
5.    user.addAll({'gender': 'F', 'email': 'ipsi@xyz.com'});
6.    print('Map after adding keys: $user');
7.
8.    user.remove('surname');
9.    print('Map after removing keys: $user');
10.
11.    user.forEach((k, v) => print('$k: $v'));
12.
13.    user.clear();
14.    print('Map after clearing entries: $user');
15. }
```

Code 1.5: Dart Map and methods Demonstration

Output will be:

```
Map is:{name: Ipsi, surname: Patro}
Map after adding keys:{name: Ipsi, surname: Patro, gender: F, email: ipsi@
xyz.com}
Map after removing keys:{name: Ipsi, gender: F, email: ipsi@xyz.com}
name: Ipsi
gender: F
email: ipsi@xyz.com
Map after clearing entries:{}
```

Null safety in Dart

Null Safety in Dart means a variable cannot contain a 'null' value unless it is a nullable type of variable.

Non-nullable types

When we use null safety, all the types are non-nullable by default in dart. For example, when we declare a variable of type int, the variable will contain some integer value.

Nullable types

To specify a variable as a nullable variable, just add a '?' mark after the name of the variable. Thereafter, you can assign a null value to it anytime you need to.

For better understanding, let us look at the following figure:

```
1  void main() {
2    String name = null; // Non-nullable String type     ☰     ▶ Run
3    print(name);
4
5    // Assigning null to nullableName is valid
6    String? nullableName = null;
7    print(nullableName);
8  }
9
                                                                    1 issue
   ⓘ A value of type 'Null' can't be assigned to a variable of type 'String'.    line 2, col 17
     Try changing the type of the variable, or casting the right-hand type to 'String'.
```

Figure 1.19: Nullable type example code with error

Dart gives compile time error. A value of type null cannot be assigned to the value of type String in line number 2 because the '**name**' object is declared as a non-nullable type String. If you try to assign null to a non-nullable type of variable, you will get an error as shown in *Figure 1.19*. Whereas there is no error in assigning null to '**nullableName**' object as it is a nullable type of object.

String Interpolation

String interpolation is the process of inserting variable values into placeholders in a string literal. To concatenate strings in Dart, we can utilize string interpolation. We use the $ {} symbol to implement string interpolation in our code. To interpolate the value of Dart expressions within strings, use $ {}. The curly braces {} are skipped if the expression is an identifier.

Code:

```
1. void main() {
2.   List<int> numbers = [1, 2, 3, 4];
3.   print('List is: $numbers');
4.   print('First element of the List is: ${numbers.first}');
5. }
```

Code 1.6: String interpolation demonstration

Output will be:

List **[1, 2, 3, 4]**

First element of the List is: 1

Further reading

- Flutter official docs: **https://docs.flutter.dev**
- Installation Guide for Window: **https://docs.flutter.dev/get-started/install/windows**
- Installation Guide for mac: **https://docs.flutter.dev/get-started/install/macos**
- Android Studio: **https://developer.android.com/studio/**
- Visual Studio Code: **https://code.visualstudio.com**

Conclusion

Dart is a programming language developed by Google. It is an object-oriented language similar to Java and C#, that can be used to build web, mobile, and desktop apps. It's also the main language for the Flutter framework, which allows for creating high-performance, cross-platform mobile applications.

If you're interested in learning Flutter, it's important to first set up your development environment, which includes installing the necessary software on your computer. Once that's done, you can begin learning the basics of Dart by using DartPad, an online tool that allows you to experiment with the language. As you work through different projects, you'll get a chance to see how these concepts are used in practice. If you encounter any issues or have questions, you can look for solutions online, 'flutter doctor' to check for any errors. If you see any issues, make sure to fix them before moving forward with development.

Questions

1: What is Dart?

2: What is the starting point of execution of a Dart programming?

3: Is Dart case sensitive?

4: What are data types in Dart language?

5: What warning you will get in the following code?

```
1. void main() {
2.   var roomNumber = 102;
3.   print('Your roomNumber is ${roomNumber}');
4. }
```

Answers

Answer 1: Dart is an object-oriented programming language, which can be used to build web, mobile, and desktop applications. It is also used as the language for the Flutter framework, which allows for the creation of high-performance, cross-platform mobile apps.

Answer 2: main()

Answer 3: Yes

Answer 4: Dart is a statically typed language, meaning that variables are declared with a specific data type. Here are the basic data types in Dart:

- **Numbers (int, double)**
- **Strings (String)**
- **Booleans (bool)**
- **Records ((value1, value2))**
- **Lists (List, also known as arrays)**
- **Sets (Set)**
- **Maps (Map)**
- **Runes (Runes; often replaced by the characters API)**
- **Symbols (Symbol)**
- **The value null (Null)**

Answer 5: Avoid using braces in interpolation when not needed

Multiple choice questions

1. **Dart is developed by?**

   a. Facebook

   b. Google

   c. Apple

   d. Amazon

2. **Which of the following statement does not use string interpolation correctly?**

   a. `var roomNumber = 102;`

   b. `print("Your roomNumber is $roomNumber");`

   c. `print('Your roomNumber is ${roomNumber}');`

   d. `print('Your roomNumber is {roomNumber}');`

Answers

Answer 1: b

Answer 2: d

Join our book's Discord space

Join the book's Discord Workspace for Latest updates, Offers, Tech happenings around the world, New Release and Sessions with the Authors:

https://discord.bpbonline.com

CHAPTER 2
Basic Programming Concepts

Introduction

By now, we trust that you have completed the necessary software installations and that your machine is prepared for Flutter development. In this chapter, we will discuss fundamental programming concepts and explore how they can be applied in Dart language. This is a crucial step to take before progressing further.

Structure

In this chapter, we will cover the following topics:

- Object Oriented Programming
- Introduction to Git
- Async await

Objectives

By the end of this chapter, you will gain an understanding of the key concepts in **Object-Oriented Programming (OOP)**, its benefits, and how Dart supports OOP. You will learn about encapsulation, inheritance, polymorphism, and abstraction and how they contribute to the design of software systems. Additionally, you will understand how OOP can enhance code modularity, reusability, and maintainability. Finally, you will explore how Dart's syntax and features facilitate OOP principles.

Object oriented programming

Dart is an object-oriented programming language that fully supports all the fundamental concepts of OOP, including classes, objects, inheritance, encapsulation, and abstraction. OOP facilitates the implementation of polymorphism and data-hiding, leading to reduced complexity and more structured code. OOP provides greater control over accessibility, allowing developers to hide the complexity of implementation details from users. For instance, users of a mobile phone may only be interested in using the call feature and need not be aware of the intricate network selection mechanisms. The core OOP concepts include:

- Class
- Object
- Inheritance
- Interface
- Abstract class
- Polymorphism

Class

In the first chapter, we went through some dart-provided data types like int, double, String, and so on. Classes are examples of a user-defined data type. Using classes, you can define your own custom data type. Class supports encapsulation. Encapsulation means binding data and methods in a single unit. A class can contain constructors, getters, setters, and methods. By using a getter and setter, we can make variables or properties either editable or read-only as per our requirements. Using 'class' followed by the class name keyword, you can create a class. Do not forget the curly braces {}, which hold the members of the class.

Syntax:

```
class className {
  <variables>
  <constructor>
  <getters/setters>
 <functions>
}
```

Example:

```
1. //class
2. class Student {
3. //variable
4.    String name;
5.    int age;
6.
7. //private variable
8.    int _score;
9.
10. //constructor
11.    Student(this.name, this.age, this._score);
12.
13. //getter
14.    int getScore() {
15.      return _score;
16.    }
17.
18. //setter
19.    void setScore(int newScore) {
20.      _score = newScore;
21.    }
22. }
```

Code 2.1: Dart class demonstration

Object

In Dart, everything is an object. However, for creating an object you need a blueprint, same as before making a house, anyone needs an architecture or a plan diagram of it. Similarly, class is the plan diagram of an object using which you can specify, what are object's properties and behavior. To access methods of a class, we need to create an object first.

Syntax:

```
var objectName = ClassName(arguments);
```

We should use **objectName** followed by '.' operator to access the properties and methods of a class.

Example:

```
1.  // class
2.  class Employee {
3.    var name = 'Tom';
4.    var designation = 'Developer';
5.  }
6.
7.  void main() {
8.    // Object of Employee
9.    var employee1 = Employee();
10.   print('${employee1.name}, ${employee1.designation}');
11.
12.   // Object of Employee
13.   var employee2 = Employee();
14.   employee2.name = 'Arnav';
15.   employee2.designataion = 'Team Lead';
16.   print('${employee2.name}, ${employee2.designation}');
17. }
```

Code 2.2: Demonstrating Class Objects

The output will be:

Tom, Developer

Arnav, TeamLead

Key points to note in the above code:

- This is a Dart code that defines a class called **Employee** and creates two instances of the class, **employee1** and **employee2**.
- On *Lines 2-4*, the **Employee** class defines two member variables, name, and designation, which are both initialized to specific string values.
- In **main()** function, on *Line 9*, an instance of **Employee** class called **employee1** is created using the default constructor. Then, the name and designation of **employee1** object are printed using string interpolation.
- On *Lines 13-16*, another instance of the **Employee** class called **employee2** is created using the default constructor. After that, the name and designation of **employee2**

are changed to '**Arnav**' and '**Team Lead**' respectively using dot notation. Finally, the new values of employee2's name and designation are printed.

- So, the first print statement will output the default values of name and designation for employee1, and the second print statement will output the updated values of name and designation for **employee2**.

Inheritance

Inheritance is one of the most important and useful features of the OOP concept, where one class can inherit any property of another class. This feature is very useful when the developers try to follow the **Don't Repeat Yourself** (**DRY**) principle. If you know the number of classes that need some common properties or methods in it, you can extract the common code to a separate class and all the other classes that need those properties and methods that can extend the extracted class. The extracted class is called the parent or superclass, and all the other classes, which just extend from the parent class, are called child or subclass. In dart, we use 'extends' keyword for inheritance. Child classes can inherit all methods by the constructor of the parent class.

Syntax:

```
class ChildClassName extends ParentClassName {…}
```

Code:

```
1.  class Human {
2.    void walk() {
3.      print('Humans walk!');
4.    }
5.  }
6.
7.  // Inheriting the parent class i.e. Human
8.  class Man extends Human {
9.    void speak() {
10.     print('That man can speak');
11.   }
12. }
13.
14. void main() {
15.   var man = Man();
16.   man.speak();
```

```
17.   man.walk(); // Invoking the parent class method calls the
      inherited method from Human.
18. }
```

Code 2.3: Inheritance code example

The output will be:

That man can speak

Humans walk!

In the above example, Human is a parent class, and Man is a child class. Dart does not support multiple inheritance, which means you cannot extend more than one class.

Polymorphism

Polymorphism means the ability of anyone to take many forms, and it can be achieved using inheritance. For example, a person can be a doctor, a teacher, or an engineer. So, if you use inheritance a **Person** can be a super class and all others sub classes are **Doctor**, **teacher** and **Engineer**. A person can take any one of these forms of sub classes. We should use **@override** keyword to notify that you are overriding. It is a good practice to use **@override** but it is not mandatory, the program will still run without that as well.

Syntax:

```
class SubClassName extends SuperClass {…}
```

Code:

```
1. class Employee {
2.   void salary() {
3.     print("Employee salary is £3000.");
4.   }
5. }
6.
7. class Manager extends Employee {
8.   @override
9.   void salary() {
10.     print("Manager salary is £4000.");
11.   }
12. }
13.
14. class Developer extends Employee {
```

```
15.    @override
16.    void salary() {
17.      print("Developer salary is £5000.");
18.    }
19. }
20.
21. void main() {
22.    Manager manager = Manager();
23.    Developer developer = Developer();
24.
25.    manager.salary();
26.    developer.salary();
27. }
```

Code 2.4: *Polymorphism demonstration*

The output will be:

```
Manager salary is £4000.

Developer salary is £5000.
```

Advantage of polymorphism in Dart

Polymorphism is a powerful concept in object-oriented programming that allows objects of different classes to be treated as if they are objects of the same class. This has several advantages in Dart, including:

- **Code reusability**: With polymorphism, you can reuse code across multiple classes, reducing code duplication and making your codebase more efficient and maintainable. This is because you can define a common interface or superclass that multiple classes can inherit from, and then use that interface or superclass to write generic code that works with any object that implements or extends it.

- **Flexibility and extensibility**: Polymorphism allows you to write code that is flexible and extensible, making it easier to adapt to changing requirements. Because polymorphic code can work with any object that implements or extends a common interface or superclass, you can easily add new classes to your codebase without having to modify existing code.

- **Simplification of code**: Polymorphism can simplify your code by allowing you to write generic code that works with any object that implements or extends a common interface or superclass, rather than having to write separate code for each class. This can make your codebase more concise and easier to understand.

- **Improved maintainability**: Polymorphism can make your codebase easier to maintain by reducing the amount of code duplication and increasing the clarity and organization of your code. By using common interfaces or superclasses, you can create a clear hierarchy of classes that is easy to understand and navigate.

In summary, polymorphism provides a range of benefits in Dart, including code reusability, flexibility and extensibility, simplification of code, and improved maintainability. By allowing objects of different classes to be treated as if they are objects of the same class, polymorphism can make your codebase more efficient, maintainable, and adaptable to changing requirements.

Interface

In Dart, there is no special keyword to declare an object as an Interface, but any implementing class or inherited class makes one class an Interface. If a class inherits an interface, it must implement all the methods defined in the interface. Usually, an interface does not implement any method but just defines them so that any class that implements the interface must redefine all the methods inside the interface. You must be thinking then, what is the difference between a superclass and an interface, and why do we need both? The answer is that a subclass does not have to override all methods inside a superclass, but in the case of interface, the implementing class must do that. Coming to why we need an interface, dart does not support multiple inheritance, but it is achievable by using an Interface. One class can implement multiple interfaces. A class needs to use '`implement`' keyword to implement any interface.

Syntax:

```
class InterfaceName1 {…}


class InterfaceName2 {…}


class ImplementingClass implements InterfaceName1, InterfaceName2 {…}
```

Code:

```
1. //class Example1 (Interface1)
2. class Example1 {
3.   void printdata1() {
4.     print("Hello Example1!!");
5.   }
6. }
7.
8. //class Example2 (Interface2)
```

```
9. class Example2 {
10.   void printdata2() {
11.     print("Hello Example2!!");
12.   }
13. }
14.
15. //class Example implementing Example1, Example2.
16. class Example implements Example1, Example2 {
17.   @override
18.   void printdata1() {
19.     print("Hello Example1, welcome!");
20.   }
21.
22.   @override
23.   void printdata2() {
24.     print("Hello Example2, welcome!");
25.   }
26. }
27.
28. void main() {
29.   // Creating object of the class Example
30.   var example = Example();
31.
32.   // Calling method (After Implementation)
33.   example.printdata1();
34.   example.printdata2();
35. }
```

Code 2.5: Interface Implementation Sample Code

The output will be:

Hello Example1, welcome!

Hello Example2, welcome!

Key points to note in the above code:

- The code above defines three Dart classes: **Example1**, **Example2**, and **Example**.

- **Example1** and **Example2** are two separate classes that define a single method each: **printdata1()** and **printdata2()**, respectively. These methods simply print a message to the console.
- Example is a class that implements both **Example1** and **Example2**, which means that it provides an implementation for all of the methods defined in those two classes. In this case, Example overrides the implementation of **printdata1()** and **printdata2()** to print a different message to the console.
- In the **main()** function, an instance of Example is created using the var keyword for type inference. The **printdata1()** and **printdata2()** methods are called on this instance, which will invoke the overridden implementations defined in Example.

Note that the **Example** class is not an interface, but rather a concrete class that implements two interfaces (**Example1** and **Example2**). When a class implements an interface, it must provide an implementation for all the methods defined in that interface.

Abstract class

At any point of time, if you want no one to create an object of a class, abstract is the keyword. Some important points about abstract class are:

- To declare an abstract class, we use '**abstract**' keyword.
- Any class which has an abstract method in it, must be declared as an abstract class
- An abstract class may not have any abstract method.
- An abstract class cannot be initialized.
- Any class that extends an abstract class, must implement or override all abstract methods of that class.

Syntax:

Abstract class AbstractClassName {…}

Example:

```
1.  //abstract class
2.  abstract class Language {
3.    //abstract methods
4.    void write();
5.    void read();
6.
7.    //concrete method
8.    void understand() {
9.      print('I can understand');
```

```
10.   }
11. }
12.
13. class English extends Language {
14.   @override
15.   void write() {
16.     print('I can write English!');
17.   }
18.
19.   @override
20.   void read() {
21.     print('I can read English!');
22.   }
23. }
24.
25. void main() {
26.   //object of English class
27.   var english = English();
28.
29.   //Accessing property using object
30.   english.write();
31.   english.read();
32. }
```

Code 2.6: Abstract class implementation sample code

The output will be:

I can write English!

I can read English!

In the above example:

- The Language class is an abstract class with two abstract methods: **write()** and **read()**. The English class extends Language and provides implementations for the **write()** and **read()** methods using the **@override** annotation. The **main()** function creates an instance of the English class and calls its **write()** and **read()** methods.

.erstand() method in the Language class is a concrete method, which
it has a default implementation that can be used by any subclass that does
verride it.

.y, this code demonstrates the use of an abstract class and its implementation in a
subclass. It shows how to use abstract methods to define a contract for subclasses
.w and how to provide default behavior for concrete methods.

Data encapsulation

In Dart, data encapsulation means data hiding; it means hiding the implementation details
from the outside world. In Dart, we do not have access specifiers like public, private, and
protected. But, if we would like to declare something as private, just add an underscore in
Infront of the name of the object or property. For example:

```
String name;
```

In the above example, the name is a public property:

```
String _name;
```

Now that the name has become private, we cannot access this property outside the class.

So, Dart gives us the power to hide some data from the outside world. By using
encapsulation, we can make any property read-only or write-only. For making a property
read only we need to add a getter method of the private property. For example, to make
the name read only, we must add this method:

```
String getName() {

    return _name;

}
```

To make the property write only, we need to implement setter method like this:

```
void setName(String newValue) {

    _name = newValue;

}
```

So, if you would like to make any property private, you can achieve it by adding an
underscore to the name and just adding a public getter and setter to access them outside
the library. That is how implementation can be hidden, but still, the field is accessible by
using the public getter and setter. Private properties are accessible only inside the library
or the class. We can also make a property read-only by making it final. To make a variable
final, we should use the 'final' keyword. A property that is declared as final must initialized
and can never update its value after declaration.

Example:

```
1.  class YearGroup {
2.      //public property
3.      var students = ['Arnav', 'Vansh', 'Oscar'];
4.      //final and a private property
5.      final _teacher = 'Mr. Sanat';
6.    //public property
7.      String topper = 'Freya';
8.
9.      String getTeacher() {
10.       return _teacher;
11.   }
12. }
13. void main() {
14.     //object of YearGroup class
15.     var year1 = YearGroup();
16.     year1.topper = 'Ipsi';
17.
18.     //Accessing property using object
19.     print(year1.getTeacher());
20.     print(year1.topper);
21. }
```

Code 2.7: Encapsulation illustration

The output will be:

Mr. Sanat

Ipsi

Key points to note in the above code:

- The **YearGroup** class has a public property student that is an instance variable initialized with a list of student names. The **_teacher** property is a private instance variable initialized with the value **'Mr. Sanat'** using the final keyword. The **topper** property is a public instance variable initialized with the value '**Freya**'.

- The **getTeacher()** method is a public method that returns the value of the private **_teacher** instance variable.

- In the **main()** function, an instance of the **YearGroup** class is created, and the topper property is modified to have the value **'Ipsi'**. The **getTeacher()** method and the topper property are accessed using the **year1** object.
- The **print()** statements in the **main()** function demonstrate the use of the **getTeacher()** method to retrieve the private **_teacher** property and access the modified topper property.

In summary, this code demonstrates the use of public, private, and final properties in a Dart class, a getter method to access the private property, and modifying and accessing public instance variables using an object.

Dart mixins

A mixin is a class with methods and properties utilized by other classes in Dart. It is a way to reuse code and write code clean. To declare a mixin, we use the mixin keyword.

Syntax:

```
mixin MixinName {…}
```

Mixins, in other words, are regular classes from which we can grab methods (or variables) without extending them. To accomplish this, we use the with keyword. A mixin cannot be instantiated, meaning you cannot create an object from a mixin directly. Instead, mixins are used to augment the functionality of a class by adding methods and properties.

In Dart, mixins provide a way to reuse a class's code in multiple class hierarchies, promoting code reuse and modular design. They are particularly useful when you need to share behavior across multiple classes that are not necessarily in the same inheritance tree. Let's look at some

Example:

```
1.  //creating a Laugh Mixin
2.  mixin Laugh {
3.    void laugh() => print('Laughing');
4.  }
5.
6.  //creating a Talk Mixin
7.  mixin Talk {
8.    void talk() => print('Talking');
9.  }
10.
11. //creating super class
```

```
12. class Human {
13.   void think() => print('Thinking');
14. }
15.
16. //creating sub class
17. class Boy extends Human with Laugh, Talk {
18.   @override
19.   void think() => print('No more thinking');
20.
21.   @override
22.   void laugh() => print('Smiling');
23. }
24.
25. void main() {
26.   var boy = Boy();
27.   boy.laugh();
28.   boy.talk();
29.   boy.think();
30. }
```

Code 2.8: Mixin Sample Code

Output will be:

Smiling

Talking

No more thinking

First, two mixins **Laugh** and **Talk** are defined. Each mixin provides a single method, **laugh()** and **talk()** respectively.

Next, a superclass Human is defined with a single method think().

Then, a subclass Boy is defined, which extends Human and mixes in the Laugh and Talk mixins using the with keyword. The Boy class overrides the **think()** method from the Human class and provides a new implementation. It also overrides the **laugh()** method from the Laugh mixin and provides a new implementation.

In the **main()** function, an instance of the Boy class is created, and its **laugh(), talk(),** and **think()** methods are called. The **laugh()** and **talk()** methods are called from the

Laugh and Talk mixins, respectively, while the **think()** method is called from the Boy subclass, which overrides the implementation in the **Human** superclass.

Boy is a subclass of **Human**. It extends the functionality of **Human** by inheriting from it and also mixes in behavior from the Laugh and Talk mixins.

In summary, this code demonstrates the use of mixins in Dart to provide additional functionality to a class hierarchy. Mixins can be used to extend a class without creating a new subclass and can be combined with other mixins and inheritance to create complex class hierarchies.

Enum

Enums are enumerated type. Which is a collection of named values or constants. We mainly use them to create a type of object or list of constants, for example, user state, it might be pending, authorized, or temp authorized. Creating an Enum for user state is beneficial to avoid using string values directly. Enums are particularly helpful in switch cases. The keyword to create an enum is 'enum'.

Syntax:

```
enum EnumName{

    option1, option2, option3

}
```

As you can find in the syntax:

- Enum name should start with a capital letter.
- Options should be separated by a comma.
- Each Enum option has an assigned int value by default, which starts with 0 and is followed by 1,2,3…
- No need of a comma or semicolon after the last option

Example:

```
1.  // Creating enum UserState
2. enum UserState {
3.   //Inserting data
4.   authorised,
5.   pending,
6.   rejected
7. }
8.
```

```
9. void main() {
10.    // Printing the values present in the UserState
11.    for (UserState state in UserState.values) {
12.      print(state);
13.    }
14. }
```

Code 2.9: *Enum sample code*

Output will be:

UserState.authorised

UserState.pending

UserState.rejected

Key points to note in the above code:

- The **UserState** enum has three possible values: authorized, pending, and rejected. These are defined using the **enum** keyword followed by the names of the values separated by commas.

- In the **main()** function, a for loop is used to iterate over the values of the **UserState** **enum** using the values property. The **print()** function is used to output the value of each **UserState** value in the console.

In summary, this code demonstrates the use of enum in Dart to create a new type with a fixed set of possible values. Enums are useful for defining a set of related constants and can be used to provide more readable and self-documenting code.

In the preceding example, you can see how the string options look as an Enum. Enum can only hold string values. Let us look at another example of using Enums for switch case.

```
1. // Creating enum UserState
2. enum UserState { authorised, pending, rejected }
3.
4. void main() {
5.    // Using Late variable with enum type
6.    late UserState lateEnumVariable;
7.
8.    // Assigning an enum value to the late variable later in the code
9.    lateEnumVariable = UserState.authorised;
10.
11.    // Using const variable with enum type
```

```
12.   const UserState constEnumValue = UserState.authorised;
13.
14.   // Using switch-case with enums
15.   switch (lateEnumVariable) {
16.     case UserState.authorised:
17.       print("This is an authorised user.");
18.       break;
19.     case UserState.pending:
20.       print("This is a pending user.");
21.       break;
22.     case UserState.rejected:
23.       print("This is a rejected user.");
24.       break;
25.   }
26.
27.   // Using .name property of enums (not available in Dart)
28.   // Instead, use toString() to get the enum's name as a string
29.   // Here, we use toString() and split('.') to extract the enum name
30.   print("The state is ${constEnumValue.toString().split('.').last}");
31.
32.   // Using index getter of enums
33.   // The index getter returns the index of the enum value in the
         enum declaration
34.   print("The index of state is ${constEnumValue.index}");
35.
36.   // Using .name property of enums (not available in Dart)
37.   // Instead, use toString() to get the enum's name as a string
38.   // Here, we use toString() and split('.') to extract the enum name
39.   print("The name of lateEnumVariable is ${lateEnumVariable.
         toString().split('.').last}");
40.
41.   // Using index getter of enums
42.   // The index getter returns the index of the enum value in the
         enum declaration
```

```
43.    print("The index of constEnumValue is ${constEnumValue.index}");
44. }
```

Code 2.10: *Enum Usage Sample Code*

Output will be:

This is an authorised user.

The state is authorised

The index of state is 0

The name of lateEnumVariable is authorised

The index of constEnumValue is 0

Key points to note in the above code:

- We define an **enum** called **UserState** with three possible states: authorised, pending, and rejected.
- We demonstrate the usage of a late variable (**lateEnumVariable**) of type **UserState**, which is assigned a value later in the code.
- We demonstrate the usage of a **const** variable (**constEnumValue**) of type **UserState**, which is assigned a value at compile-time.
- We use a switch statement to handle different cases based on the value of **lateEnumVariable**.
- We explain that Dart **enums** do not have a built-in name property, so we use **toString()** to get the enum's name as a string. We split the result by '.' and extract the last part, which represents the enum's name.
- We explain that the index getter returns the index of the enum value in the enum declaration.
- We provide similar explanations for accessing the name property and index getter for both **constEnumValue** and **lateEnumVariable**.

Enums are like classes with a few limitations:

- We cannot subclass or use mixins for Enums.
- We can never instantiate an Enum.

Type inference

Type inference in Dart is the ability of the Dart compiler to determine the type of a variable at compile-time, without the need for the programmer to explicitly specify the type.

Dart uses the **var** keyword for type inference. When **var** is used to declare a variable, the compiler infers the variable's type based on the value that is assigned to it. For example:

```
var x = 10; // x is inferred as an integer

var y = 'hello'; // y is inferred as a string
```

In the above code, the type of the variables **x** and **y** is inferred based on the value that is assigned to them. In the first line, **x** is inferred as an integer because **10** is an integer. In the second line, **y** is inferred as a string because '**hello**' is a string.

Dart also supports type inference for function return types, using the => operator. For example:

```
int add(int x, int y) => x + y;
```

In the above code, the return type of the **add()** function is inferred as int because the => operator is used to return an integer value.

```
dynamic z = 10;      // z can hold any type of value

z = 'hello';         // Now z holds a string
```

The main difference between var and dynamic is that var is statically typed but with type inference, whereas dynamic is explicitly declared as a dynamic type.

In summary:

- Use **var** when you want the compiler to infer the type of a variable based on the assigned value but still want static typing benefits.
- Use dynamic when you want maximum flexibility and are willing to sacrifice some of Dart's static typing benefits.

Type inference can make code more concise and easier to read by reducing the amount of type annotations needed. However, it is important to note that explicit type annotations can still be used when necessary for clarity or to enforce type constraints.

Generics

Generics in programming is a way to code that makes any class or function work for a range of data types. For example, in Dart, with all collection types, streams, and futures, you can use generics. Do not worry if you are not aware of what streams and futures are; we are going to cover them in upcoming chapters. By using generics, you can avoid duplicate code and increase code reusability. For example, you can write a method for adding two numbers. By using generics, you can avoid rewriting the same code for int, double, and float by allowing generic type arguments.

Usually, we denote T to use generic type. Generics can be used:

- As a function argument type.
- A local variable type.
- A function's return type.

```
1.  //This generic function prints and returns the itemat the required
    index of a list
2.  T getElement<T>(List<T> genericList, int index) {
3.      T element = genericList[index];
4.      print(element);
5.      return element;
6.  }
7.
8.  void main() {
9.      //Lists of three different datat types declared
10.     List<int> ageList = [9, 3, 16];
11.     List<double> heightList = [4.4, 3.6, 5.8];
12.     List<String> nameList = ['Arnav', 'Oscar', 'Sanat'];
13.
14.     getElement(ageList, ageList.length - 1);
15.     getElement(heightList, heightList.length - 1);
16.     getElement(nameList, nameList.length - 1);
17. }
```

Code 2.11: Generics demonstration

The output will be:

16

5.8

Sanat

In the preceding example:

- The **getElement()** function is a generic function that takes two arguments: a list of type T and an integer index. The function returns an element of type T from the list at the specified index.

- Within the **getElement()** function, the generic type T is used to declare a new variable element, which is assigned the value of the list element at the specified index. The **print()** function is then used to output the value of the element variable to the console.

- In the **main()** function, three lists of different data types are declared: **ageList, heightList**, and **nameList**. Each list is then passed to the **getElement()** function along with the index of the last element in the list. The output of the function for each list is printed to the console using the **print()** function.

- The use of generics in this code allows the **getElement()** function to be reused with different data types. The code demonstrates how to declare and use generic functions in Dart, which can improve code reuse and maintainability.

Anonymous functions

Anonymous functions, also known as lambda expressions or closures, are functions without a name. These functions can be assigned to variables or constants and can be passed as parameters to other functions or methods. Anonymous functions can accept parameters and contain a block of code to be executed. In Dart, they are often used as closures or in places where a function is required but defining a named function would be excessive.

Syntax:

```
(parametersList)

{

    statement(s)

}


// closure or lambda expression

(parametersList) => {

    return statement;

}
```

Example:

```
1.  void main() {
2.  //Assigning an anonymous function to a variable
3.  var addNumbers = (int x, int y) {
4.    return x + y;
5.  };
6.
7.  //Calling the anonymous function using the variable
8.  var result = addNumbers(3, 4);
9.  print(result);
10.
11. //Passing an anonymous function as an argument to another function
```

```
12.    var multiplyNumbers = (int x, int y) {
13.      return x * y;
14.    };
15.
16.    doCalculation(5, 6, multiplyNumbers);
17. }
18.
19. void doCalculation(int x, int y, Function operation) {
20.    var result = operation(x, y);
21.    print(result);
22. }
```

Code 2.12: *Anonymous function sample code*

Output will be:

7

30

Key points to note in the above code:

- In this example, an anonymous function is assigned to a variable called **addNumbers**. The function takes two integer arguments, x and y, and returns their sum.
- The **addNumbers** function is then called using the variable and its return value is stored in a variable called result. The result variable is then printed to the console using the **print()** function.
- Next, another anonymous function is defined and assigned to a variable called **multiplyNumbers**. This function takes two integer arguments, **x** and **y**, and returns their product.
- Finally, the **doCalculation()** function is called with three arguments: two integer values and the **multiplyNumbers** function as an argument. The **doCalculation()** function calls the **multiplyNumbers** function with the two integer arguments, and the result is printed to the console using the **print()** function.

Loops

Loops in any programming language means looping some statements, loops are used to repeat statements based on certain conditions until those conditions are met or no longer met. There are different types of loops and most programming languages supports them:

- **for** loop
- **for in** loop

- **while** loop
- **do while** loop

For loop

It is a special kind of loop, where we can initialize an object, which can be used for checking the condition also. We can specify an expression with which we can update the value of initialised object.

Syntax:

```
for (initialization; condition; increment) {…}
1.  void main() {
2.    for (int i = 0; i < 5; i++) {
3.      print('i is $i');
4.    }
5.  }
```

Code 2.13: for loop sample code

Output will be:

```
i is 0
i is 1
i is 2
i is 3
i is 4
```

In the preceding example, int i=o is the object initialization, i < 5 is the condition and i++ is the expression to update i.

for in

This loop is another form or an advanced form of a for loop, where you can directly access the object at each index in the condition itself. You should use for looping, this way when you do not need an expression.

Syntax:

```
for (var item in itemList) {…}
1. void main() {
2.    List<String> namesList = ['Arnav', 'Oscar', 'Sanat'];
```

```
3.
4.    for (String name in namesList) {
5.       print(name);
6.    }
7.  }
```

Code 2.14: for in sample code

The output will be:

Arnav

Oscar

Sanat

While loop

In this kind of loop, the body will be executed unless the condition is satisfied.

Syntax:

```
While(condition) {…}
1.   void main() {
2.     var count = 4;
3.     int i = 1;
4.     while (i <= count) {
5.       print('Hello Ipsi');
6.       i++;
7.     }
8.  }
```

Code 2.15: while loop sample code

The output will be:

Hello Ipsi

Hello Ipsi

Hello Ipsi

Hello Ipsi

Do while loop

There is one thing that makes this loop special. In do while loop, the body will be executed at least once, as it checks the condition only after going through the loop once. And keep on looping the body until the condition is satisfied. We can use break and continue inside do while loop. The "**break**" statement is used to exit the loop when the condition is met. The "**continue**" statement is used to skip the current iteration and move to the next iteration when the condition is met.

Syntax:

```
do {

    ...

} while(condition);
```

Example:

```
1.  void main() {
2.    var count = 4;
3.    int i = 1;
4.    do {
5.      // Print statement inside the loop
6.      print('Hello Ipsi!');
7.
8.      // Increment i
9.      i++;
10.
11.     // Check a condition and break out of the loop
12.     if (i == 3) {
13.       break;
14.     }
15.
16.     // Check a condition and continue to the next iteration
17.     if (i == 2) {
18.       continue;
19.     }
20.
```

```
21.  } while (i <= count);
22. }
```

Code 2.16: do while demonstration

The output will be:

Hello Ipsi!

Hello Ipsi!

In this example:

- We use the "**break**" statement to exit the loop when i reaches the value of 3.
- We use the "**continue**" statement to skip the iteration when i equals 2.

These statements alter the flow of the loop according to the conditions provided.

VoidCallBack

VoidCallbacks are functions or methods, that we can pass as an argument or make them as void type and call from another methods or widgets as needed. These functions mostly do not take any argument or return any value but still plays an important role and helps in communication between parent and child widget.

Syntax:

```
typedef VoidCallback = void function();
```

For example, you have a child widget, which contains a button, and you want to notify Parent widget when the button is clicked in the child widget. This is an ideal scenario for using VoidCallback, as demonstrated in the example code below:

```
1.  import 'package:flutter/material.dart';
2.  import 'Count.dart';
3.
4.  class CounterPage extends StatefulWidget {
5.    @override
6.    State<CounterPage> createState() => _CounterPageState();
7.  }
8.
9.  class _CounterPageState extends State<CounterPage> {
10.   int count = 0;
11.
```

```
12.   @override
13.   Widget build(BuildContext context) {
14.     return Scaffold(
15.       appBar: AppBar(title: Text("Widget Communication")),
16.       body: Center(
17.         child: Count(
18.           count: count,
19.           onCountSelected: () {
20.             print("Count was Selected");
21.           },
22.         ),
23.       ),
24.     );
25.   }
26. }
```

Code 2.17: VoidCallBack sample code for Parent widget CounterPage

```
1. import 'package:flutter/material.dart';
2.
3. class Count extends StatelessWidget {
4.   final int count;
5.   final VoidCallback onCountSelected;
6.
7.   const Count({
8.     super.key,
9.     required this.count,
10.    required this.onCountSelected,
11.  });
12.
13.  @override
14.  Widget build(BuildContext context) {
15.    return MaterialButton(
16.      child: Text("$count"),
17.      onPressed: () => onCountSelected(),
18.    );
```

```
19.   }
20. }
```

Code 2.18: VoidCallBack sample code for Child widget Count

In the preceding example,

- Count is a child widget, which has been added to the parent widget **CounterPage**.
- **onCountSelected** is a property of the Count widget of type **VoidCallback**.
- Whenever a button is clicked inside the Count Widget, it will call **onCountSelected** of the parent class.

Function(n)

A function can be defined as Function(n), where n is the return data type of the function. Function(n) is similar to VoidCallback, with the key difference being that it returns a value to the parent widget. When a callback function needs to return a value to the parent widget, Function(n) should be used.

Let us revisit the example by replacing VoidCallback with Function(int), where int represents the value of the count. In this updated example, the parent widget CounterPage will send count updates to the child widget Count using the onCountChanged callback.

```
1.  import 'package:flutter/material.dart';
2.  import 'Count.dart';
3.
4.  class CounterPage extends StatefulWidget {
5.    const CounterPage({super.key});
6.
7.    @override
8.    State<CounterPage> createState() => _CounterPageState();
9.  }
10.
11. class _CounterPageState extends State<CounterPage> {
12.   int count = 0;
13.
14.   @override
15.   Widget build(BuildContext context) {
16.     return Scaffold(
17.       appBar: AppBar(title: const Text("Widget Communication")),
```

```
18.        body: Center(
19.          child: Count(
20.            count: count,
21.            onCountSelected: () {
22.              print("Count was Selected");
23.            },
24.            onCountChanged: (int value) {
25.              setState(() {
26.                count += value;
27.              });
28.            },
29.          ),
30.        ),
31.      );
32.    }
33. }
```

Code 2.19: Parent widget CounterPage sending count updates to child widget Count.

In the above code, the CounterPage widget represents a page that manages the count state internally. It utilizes the Count widget to display the count value and allows users to interact with it. When the count changes, this widget updates the Count widget by invoking the onCountChanged callback. Additionally, it handles the callback triggered when the count value is selected. Now let's look at the code for the child widget Count.

```
1.  import 'package:flutter/material.dart';
2.
3.  class Count extends StatelessWidget {
4.    final int count;
5.    final VoidCallback onCountSelected;
6.    final Function(int) onCountChanged;
7.
8.    const Count({
9.      super.key,
10.     required this.count,
11.     required this.onCountChanged,
12.     required this.onCountSelected,
```

```
13.   });
14.
15.   @override
16.   Widget build(BuildContext context) {
17.     return Row(
18.       mainAxisAlignment: MainAxisAlignment.center,
19.       children: [
20.         IconButton(
21.           onPressed: () {
22.             onCountChanged(1);
23.           },
24.           icon: const Icon(Icons.add)),
25.         TextButton(onPressed: () => onCountSelected(), child:
              Text("$count")),
26.         IconButton(
27.           onPressed: () {
28.             onCountChanged(-1);
29.           },
30.           icon: const Icon(Icons.remove)),
31.       ],
32.     );
33.   }
34. }
```

Code 2.20: Child widget Count receiving count updates from parent widget CounterPage.

The Count widget is the child widget that displays the count value along with buttons to increment and decrement it. It receives the current count value and callback functions for count updates from its parent widget (CounterPage). The onCountChanged callback is invoked when the count is incremented or decremented, while the onCountSelected callback is triggered when the count value is selected.

VoidCallback is typically used for functions that do not take any arguments or return any values. It is suitable for callbacks where only the invocation of an action is needed without any specific data passing or return expectation.

On the other hand, Function(int) specifies a function type that takes an int parameter and does not necessarily return void. This type is useful when a callback function needs to receive and possibly utilize an integer parameter, and it may return a value of any type.

Arrow functions

Arrow functions are also called lambda expressions. In a function where the body is just one statement, the cleaner way is to replace the function with a lambda expression or an arrow function. As the name says, it contains a fat arrow, '=>' before the return statement.

Syntax:

```
returnType functionName(parameters) => statement;
```

Where **returnType** is a data type like **int**, **String**, **void**.

functionName is the name of the arrow function.

Parameters are a list of parameters that are required by the arrow function.

Statement is the returned statement.

Example:

```
1.  void main() {
2.    addNumbers(15, 20);
3.  }
4.
5.  void addNumbers(int i, int j) {
6.    var result = i + j;
7.    print('The result of addition is $result');
8.  }
```

Code 2.21: Function without Arrow Syntax

The output will be:

The result of addition is 35

In the preceding example, **addNumber** is a function which calculates the value of addition of two numbers and prints it. Let us see in the next example how this **addNumbers** can be replaced with an arrow function.

```
1.  void main() {
2.    addNumbers(15, 20);
3.  }
4.
5.  void addNumbers(int i, int j) => print('The result of addition is ${i
      + j}');
```

Code 2.22: Function with Arrow Syntax

The output will be:

```
The result of addition is 35
```

Both examples return the same value, but the arrow function looks much cleaner.

> **Note:**
> - **Arrow functions are a cleaner way to write code.**
> - **Arrow functions don't have statements body {...}**
> - **Arrow functions can have only one statement.**
> - **In the case of the arrow function, the statement should finish with a semicolon ';'.**

Ternary operator

Ternary Operator is a shorthand version of if-else condition. There are two types of ternary operators:

- Conditional statement,
- Null safety condition.

Syntax 1:

```
condition ? statementOne : statementTwo;
```

In the above case, if the condition evaluates to true, **statementOne** will be executed otherwise **statementTwo**.

Example:

```
1.  void main() {
2.    var age = 20;
3.    age >= 18 ? print('Eligible') : print('Not Eligible');
4.  }
```

Code 2.23: Ternary Operator type 1 sample code

The output will be:

```
Eligible
```

In the preceding example, we have declared and initialized a variable with name, age, and, value 28. Then, we have a statement with a ternary operator, where the condition of if age is greater than or equal to 18, then **statementOne** will be executed and '**Eligible**' is printed; otherwise **statementTwo** will be printed as '**Not Eligible**'.

Syntax 2:

```
object ?? statement
```

In this kind of ternary operator, first dart evaluates if object is null, statement will be executed, otherwise not.

Example:

```
1. void main() {
2.    dynamic age;
3.    print(age);
4.    age ?? print('age is null');
5. }
```

Code 2.24: Ternary Operator type 2 sample code

The output will be: **null**

age is null.

```
1.    void main() {
2.       dynamic age = '10';
3.       print(age);
4.       age ?? print('age is null');
5. }
```

Code 2.25: Ternary Operator type 2 demonstration

The output will be:

```
10
```

In the first example age is null, so dart executes the print statement, whereas, in the second example age is not null with value 10, print statement is not executed.

Introduction to Git

Git is a modern, open-source version control system. It is vastly used by developers in their day-to-day work for managing the source code repositories. There are some old version control systems like svn and cvs, which are centralized, as compared to Git, which is a distributed version. In a distributed system, there is less risk of failure, as developers have multiple copies, and they clone to their local distributed version control workstations. Git gives a complete history of code changes performed by the developer. The initial clone of the repository could be slower, but subsequent operations are faster. The different operations that we perform using Git are commit, merge, push, and pull.

Git supports the branching and merging mechanism. So, every developer can create their own branches and work on them independently. If many developers work on the same branch, there are chances of getting conflicts if they try to update the same file that needs to be resolved before merging. Pull requests or merge requests can be used to merge branches in Git, which can be reviewed by other developers easily. Git is a kind of standard for software development now.

Let us **look** at the fundamental outline of Git's functionality:

1. **Create project repository**: Start by creating a project repository on a Git hosting platform like Bitbucket, GitHub, or GitLab.

2. **Create Branch**: From the main or master branch, create a new branch to work on your changes.

3. **Clone repository:** Clone the repository to your local machine using Git commands.

4. **Checkout branch**: Switch to the newly created branch in your local repository using the git checkout command.

5. **Add and commit changes**: Add or update your code files in the local repository and then commit the changes with a descriptive message using git add and git commit commands.

6. **Push changes**: Push the committed changes from your local repository to the remote repository using the git push command.

7. **Open pull request**: Open a pull request on the Git hosting platform to request a review of your changes by a peer or reviewer.

8. **Merge changes**: After approval, merge your branch into the main or master branch using the pull request interface on the Git hosting platform.

Difference between Git and Git hosting tool

The following are the differences between Git and Git hosting tools:

- Git is a popular version control system used by software developers to manage their source code. Git provides a range of features and tools to help developers manage their code, including:

  o **Committing changes**: Git allows developers to commit changes to their codebase, creating a snapshot of the code at a specific point in time. This allows developers to track changes and easily roll back to earlier versions of the code if needed.

  o **Branching and merging**: Git provides powerful branching and merging capabilities that allow developers to work on multiple versions of the code simultaneously and then merge changes back into a single codebase when ready.

- o **Collaboration**: Git enables collaboration between developers by allowing them to share their code with each other, track changes made by others, and easily merge changes back into their own codebase.

- o **Remote repositories**: Git allows developers to store their code in remote repositories, making it easy to collaborate with others and access their code from anywhere in the world.

- There are many Git hosting tools available, including popular platforms like GitHub, GitLab, and Bitbucket. These tools provide additional features and services on top of Git, such as issue tracking, continuous integration and deployment, and collaboration tools. They also provide a convenient platform for developers to share their code with others and contribute to open-source projects.

Overall, Git and Git hosting tools provide a powerful and flexible system for managing source code, enabling collaboration and version control in software development projects.

Async await

In any programming language, when we need to perform multiple tasks parallelly or together, we use asynchronous tasks. If we want all other operations to stop, we should use synchronous tasks. For making a method asynchronous we use asyn await keywords. The most common use cases where we use asynchronous operation in an app are:

- Updating database
- Reading data from a file
- Fetching data over a network

In Dart, asynchronous tasks typically return a Future object or a Stream if the result has multiple parts. You can only call an asynchronous method from another asynchronous method to wait for the result before proceeding to the next statement.

An asynchronous function allows other operations to execute before it completes, which can be useful in scenarios where you want to avoid blocking the execution of other code while waiting for the asynchronous task to complete. However, it's important to note that asynchronous programming can introduce additional complexity and requires careful handling of potential errors and race conditions.

Let us look at an example where we need async programming. We will look at what issue can come up if we do not use it:

```
1.  // This example shows how *not* to write asynchronous Dart code.
2.
3.  String getEmoployeeDetails() {
4.    var employee = fetchEmployeeName();
5.    return 'Employee name is: $employee';
```

```
6.  }
7.
8.  Future<String> fetchEmployeeName() =>
9.      //Imagine that this function is more complex and slow.ArgumentError
10.       Future.delayed(
11.         const Duration(seconds: 2),
12.         () => 'Tapsi',
13.       );
14.
15. void main() {
16.   print(getEmoployeeDetails());
17. }
```

Code 2.26: Sample code without async await

The output will be:

Employee name is: Instance of '_Future<String>'

The preceding example code fails to print the value that **fetchEmployeeName()** eventually produces because:

- **fetchEmployeeName()** is an asynchronous operation, which takes 2 seconds to return the employee name: '**Tapsi**'.
- The calling statement needs to wait for those 2 seconds to fetch the name.
- In this case, **getEmployeeDetails()** does not wait for those 2 seconds, so it fails to get the name value.
- This is why **getEmployeeDetails()** gets a representation of an uncompleted future and prints: Instance of '**_Future<String>**'

Understanding asynchronous programming is crucial for efficient Dart and Flutter development. Below are the essential concepts:

- Add async keyword before any function's body to mark it as asynchronous.
- Use await keyword to wait and get the completed result of an asynchronous expression.
- The await keyword only allowed within an async function.

Future

As mentioned above, in Dart, asynchronous task either returns a future or a stream. Future has two states one is completed or uncompleted. A future (starts with lower case f) is an instance of Future (starts with capital F) class.

Stream

In Dart, a stream is an asynchronous sequence of data commonly used for handling events or data that occur over time. Streams can be single-subscription or broadcast, and they are lazily evaluated, meaning data is processed only when a listener is actively listening. Streams are frequently used for scenarios such as receiving data over a network connection, processing user input or reading from a file.

Completed

Once an asynchronous operation is initiated, a future is returned. The future can return a value if the operation succeeds or an error if it fails. The future is of type '`Future<T>`', and when the operation is completed, it returns a value of type T.

Uncompleted

When you call an asynchronous function but do not wait for it to finish, it returns an uncompleted future.

> **Note: When you call a function that returns a future and do not wait, the function queues up work to be done and returns an incomplete future.**

To define an asynchronous function, add '`async`' before the function body. The await keyword is only allowed in an async function.

If an async function does not explicitly return a value, then the return type could be `Future<void>`.

Syntax:

```
void functionName() async {…}
```

Inside an async method, you can use the await keyword and wait for the async wait to finish.

```
1.  Future<String> getEmoployeeDetails() async {
2.    var employee = await fetchEmployeeName();
3.    return 'Employee name is: $employee';
4.  }
```

```
5.
6.  Future<String> fetchEmployeeName() =>
7.     //Imagine that this function is more complex and slow.ArgumentError
8.      Future.delayed(
9.        const Duration(seconds: 2),
10.       () => 'Tapsi',
11.    );
12.
13. Future<void> main() async {
14.   print(await getEmoployeeDetails());
15. }
```

Code 2.27: Sample code with async await

The output will be:

Employee name is: Tapsi

Key points to note in the above code:

- The given code defines two asynchronous functions - **fetchEmployeeName()** and **getEmoployeeDetails()**, and an asynchronous main() function.

- The **fetchEmployeeName()** function returns a Future that completes with the employee name '**Tapsi**' after a delay of 2 seconds. This function simulates a slow and complex operation that could involve fetching data from a database or making an HTTP request.

- The **getEmoployeeDetails()** function calls **fetchEmployeeName()** using the await keyword, which waits for the Future returned by **fetchEmployeeName()** to complete before continuing execution. Once the employee value is obtained, the function returns a string containing the employee's name.

- The **main()** function is marked as async and uses the await keyword to wait for the completion of **getEmoployeeDetails()**. When the Future returned by **getEmoployeeDetails()** completes, it prints the employee details to the console. Therefore, when you run the code, it will print the given output to the console after a delay of 2 seconds.

- The **main()** function is asynchronous, it needs to be run using the **runApp()** function or a similar function that is designed to run asynchronous code. **runApp()** is a function provided by the Flutter framework that is used to run the main entry point of a Flutter application. This function takes a widget as its argument, typically the root widget of your application, and starts the Flutter framework's execution process. You will find many practical examples in upcoming chapters.

Conclusion

As you continue your development journey in Dart, you will find that these fundamental concepts will be extensively used. It is highly recommended that you practice these concepts in DartPad by trying out different examples to solidify your understanding before moving forward.

In the next chapter, we will begin working with Flutter by developing our first app and examining the fundamental structure of a Flutter application. We can use Flutter's rich set of pre-built widgets and layout tools to create a beautiful, responsive UI, and leverage Dart's powerful programming features to add logic and functionality to our app.

Join our book's Discord space

Join the book's Discord Workspace for Latest updates, Offers, Tech happenings around the world, New Release and Sessions with the Authors:

https://discord.bpbonline.com

CHAPTER 3
First Flutter App

Introduction

After successfully completing the necessary machine setups and mastering the fundamentals of Dart, it is now time to start on our journey into Flutter development and begin constructing our very first Flutter application. This application, which we have chosen to name the "`hello_user`" app, marks our first step in this exciting endeavor.

Structure

This chapter covers the following topics:

- Build your first Flutter project
- Code formatting tips
- Folder structure
- Sample app
- Widget
- Run the app in the simulator
- Run the app in a physical device
- App icon
- Hot reload

Objectives

By the end of this chapter, you will have gained the necessary confidence to build a new Flutter application from scratch. You will also acquire a comprehensive understanding of the folder structure, become familiar with the significant files and their respective roles within the project, and successfully run the application on both emulators/simulators and real devices. Once you are prepared, launch Android Studio and let us commence our journey.

Build your first Flutter project

Let us begin and build your first Flutter project. Here are the steps to do so:

1. Once you are ready, open Android Studio and select the option 'New Flutter project' as shown by 1 in *Figure 3.1:*

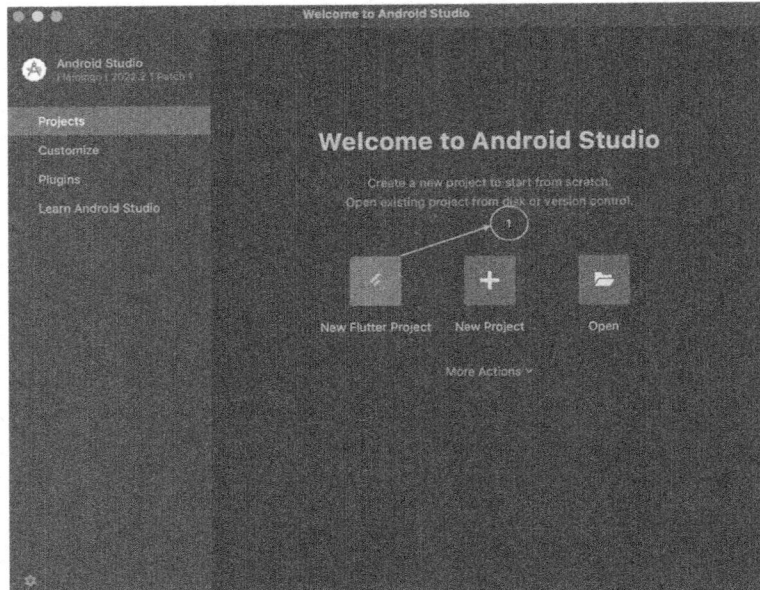

Figure 3.1: New Flutter project

2. If you have already opened a project in Android Studio, navigate to **File** | **New Flutter** project and then continue as shown in *Figure 3.2:*

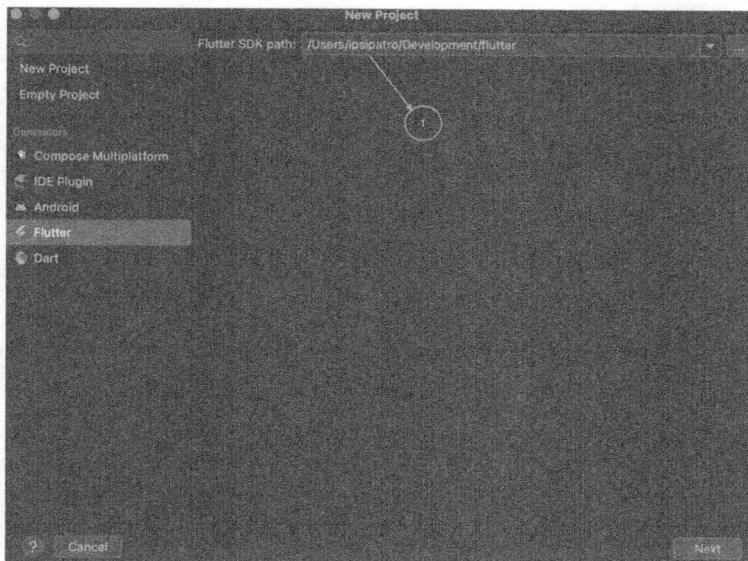

Figure 3.2: *Flutter SDK Path*

SDK path for Flutter should be auto populated, in case it is not, you can manually add the path where you have relocated the Flutter folder.

3. Then tap next, to move to the screen as shown in *Figure 3.3*:

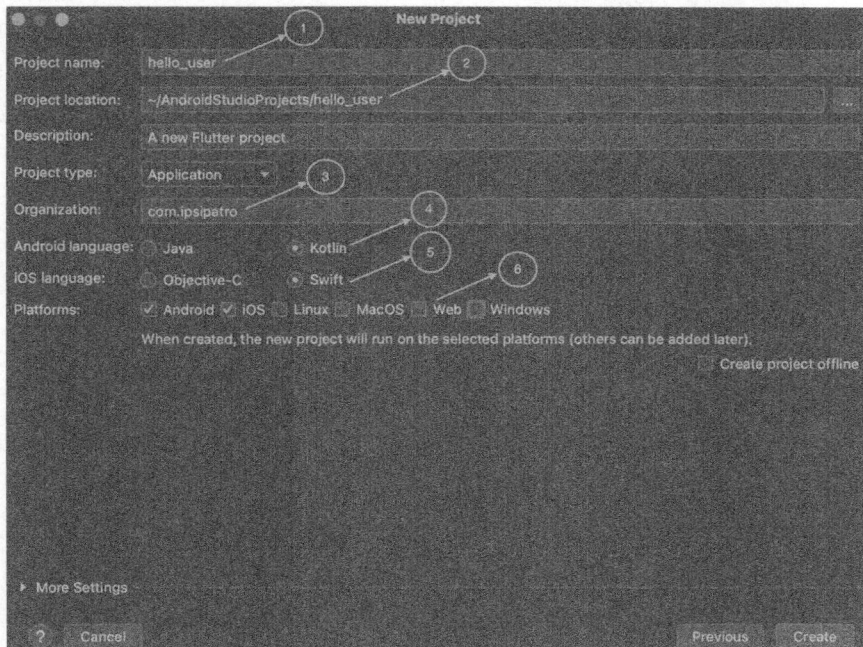

Figure 3.3: *New Flutter project details*

Let us now understand the various sections in *Figure 3.3:*

1. Ensure that the name of your project is in all lowercase with an underscore between each word.

2. Specify the path where you want to save the newly created project. By default, it will show a path like ~/**AndroidStudioProjects**, but you have the flexibility to update it to your preferred location. If desired, you can copy the path and search for it to locate it on your system.

3. Provide the organization name, which Flutter will use to generate a unique package name for your app by combining it with your project name. The format for the package name is going to be, organization name dot app name. For example, the package name for this app will be `com.ipsipatro.hello_user`.

   It is important that this package name needs to be unique for every app in the app store. Ideally, use your own company name or website name. If you do not have one, you can use your full name instead of "example." As long as no one else has the same organization and app name, Flutter will successfully generate a unique package name for your app.

4. Select the language for the Android app. You have the option to choose between Java or Kotlin.

5. Choose the language for the iOS app. You can select either Objective-C or Swift.

6. Please select the platforms you want to support (iOS, Android, Web, Windows, macOS, Linux) during the project creation process to ensure proper configuration and setup.

Then just tap on '**create**', then Android Studio will create a brand-new Flutter project for you, and it will set you up with some starting code. The starting code, which is a simple counter app, is created by the Flutter team. In this case, the counter app is created using a Scaffold, as shown in the following figure:

Figure 3.4: Running the default Flutter project.

4. Select the device in which you want to run the app, iOS or Android.

5. Click the **run** button to run it on the selected device.

As you can see, it is a simple app with a title on the screen, some text in the middle, and a button to increase the counter. This gives a good idea of how a basic Flutter app works and looks, but this is not what we are going to build; later in this chapter, in the '**Sampleapp**' section, we are going to build our very own first app.

Folder structure

Whenever you create a new Flutter project using Android Studio, these are the folders you are going to get:

*   **android**: This folder contains the Android-specific project files and configurations. It includes the AndroidManifest.xml file, **build.gradle** files, and other necessary files for building and running the app on an Android device.

*   **ios**: This folder contains the iOS-specific project files and configurations. It includes the **AppDelegate.swift** file, **Info.plist** file, and other necessary files for building and running the app on an iOS device.

*   **lib**: This folder is where you will spend most of your time developing the Flutter app. It contains the Dart code for your app, including the **main.dart** file that serves as the entry point of your application. You will create additional Dart files and organize them into folders based on your app's structure and functionality.

*   **test**: This folder is used for writing tests for your Flutter app. It contains test files that help ensure the correctness of your app's logic and behavior.

*   **images**: This folder is used to store static files, such as images, fonts, JSON files, or any other assets that your app may require. You can organize them into subfolders based on the asset type if needed. If this folder is not present, you can create one before adding any assets to your project.

Now let us look at some important files of any Flutter project:

pubspec.yaml

This file is meant to be a human-readable language file, which a machine can also understand to interpret how you want to configure your Flutter project.

The **pubspec.yaml** file is a configuration file used in Flutter projects to define dependencies, assets, and other metadata related to the project. It is located in the root directory of your Flutter project.

Whenever we create a new Flutter project, a basic pubspec file is generated. The default pubspec file has various commented lines, which is important for the initial understanding but makes the file difficult to read. So before we start working on it, it is a good idea to read and delete the unwanted sections or comments.

The code in this file relies heavily on the indentation. So, you can notice that every section inside the file is right next to the margin, without any gap or space on the left. If there is any gap, then it will be considered as a child of the above section. That means we need to be careful about the indentation of the code we are writing in this file.

To uncomment any section, you can use *command + forward slash* (/). Once you are done with your updates, you can tap on '**pub get**' from the top toolbar, so that Flutter will provide you with the resources available to use. Refer to the following figure for how the pubspec file looks after removing all the commented lines:

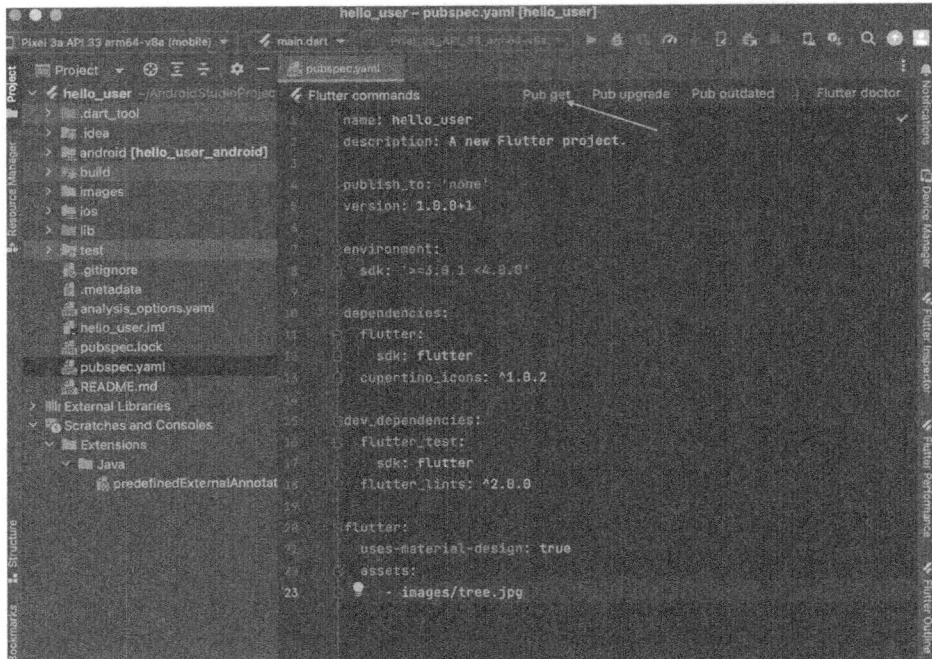

Figure 3.5: pubspec.yaml file

Now, let us go through the different sections of the **pubspec.yaml** file:

- **name**: Specifies the name of your Flutter project.
- **description**: Provides a brief description of your project.
- **publish_to**: This is used to specify the destination where you want to publish your package. It determines whether you want to publish your package to the official Dart package repository (**pub.dev**) or to a private package repository. It is perfectly fine to remove it at this point if you do not want to publish it anywhere.
- **version**: Specifies the version number of your project.
- **environment**: Specifies the minimum SDK version required for your project.
- **dependencies**: Lists the external packages that your project depends on. In the example above, **cupertino_icons**, http, and provider are listed as dependencies.

The version numbers are specified using the ^ symbol to allow updates within a compatible range.

- **dev_dependencies**: Lists the development dependencies required for testing and development purposes.
- **flutter**: Contains configuration specific to the Flutter framework. In this example, uses-material-design is set to true, indicating that the project uses Material Design as the design language.
- **assets**: Specifies the assets (such as images or fonts) that are bundled with the application. In the example above, the assets folder contains images and fonts subfolders, and their paths are listed under assets.

Make sure to update the **pubspec.yaml** file with the necessary dependencies, assets, and configurations specific to your Flutter project. Once you make all required changes to the **pubspec.yaml** file, click the "**Pub Get**" button to fetch the dependencies specified in the file.

pubspec.lock

This file is automatically generated by Flutter, when you run flutter pub get or flutter pub upgrade. It contains the exact versions of the dependencies used in your project.

Before going to build our own Flutter app, let us learn some useful code formatting tips, which are going to be useful in this Flutter journey.

Code formatting tips

Every Flutter application consists of a widget tree. When the code is not properly formatted, the readability becomes significantly lower. As an illustration, the code provided below, without any formatting, appears as a single line:

```
1. void main() {
2.    runApp(const MaterialApp(home: Center(child: Text("Hello User"))));
3. }
```

Code 3.1: Flutter code without formatting

In this code, there are three widgets in total. The topmost widget is a MaterialApp widget, holding a Center widget that, in turn, contains a Text widget. It is difficult to see which widget is present inside which one, so we need code formatting.

Let us format this code now.

While installing Flutter and Dart, we automatically got access to a code formatter called Dart format. To use the formatter, the Flutter team advises adding a comma after each widget's closing parenthesis and using the formatting option by right-clicking, as shown in *Figure 3.6*:

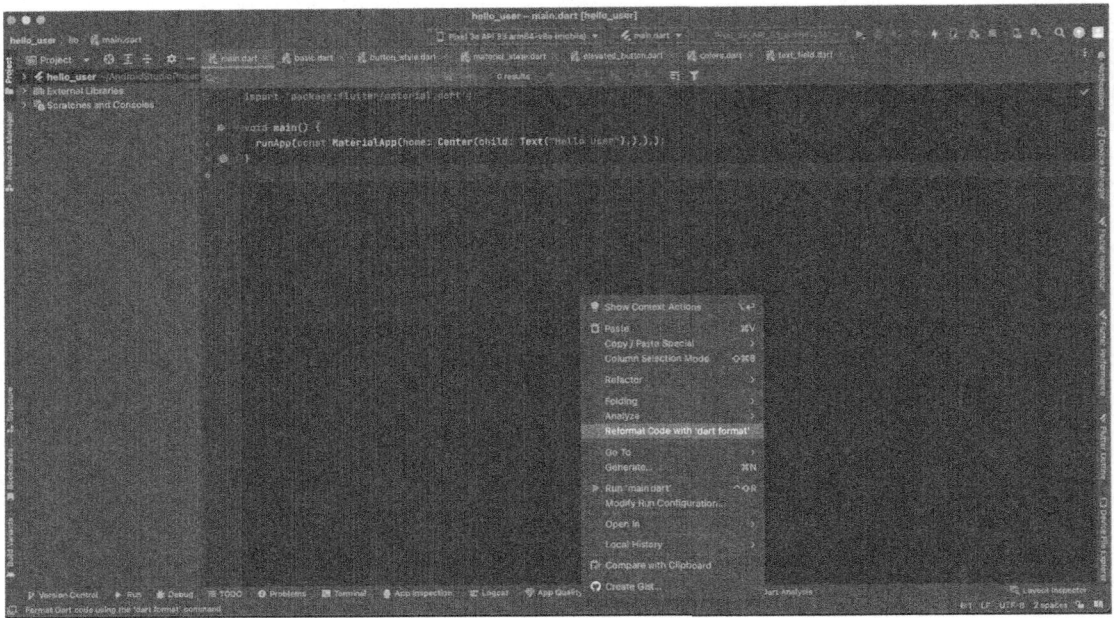

Figure 3.6: Code formatting option

After selecting the highlighted option, the code will be formatted automatically to an indented structure, and this is how it will look:

```
1.  void main() {
2.    runApp(
3.      const MaterialApp(
4.        home: Center(
5.          child: Text("Hello User"),
6.        ),
7.      ),
8.    );
9.  }
```

Code 3.2: Formatted code

Now it is so easy to say which widget goes inside which one.

Another useful feature is that just try the '*option + Enter*' key on any widget, and you will get a handful of useful options. Just for example, if you need to add some more widgets underneath the Text widget, then we need a column widget. The quickest way to add it is by trying '*option + enter*' key on my Text widget and selecting '**Wrap with column**' option, as shown in *Figure 3.7*:

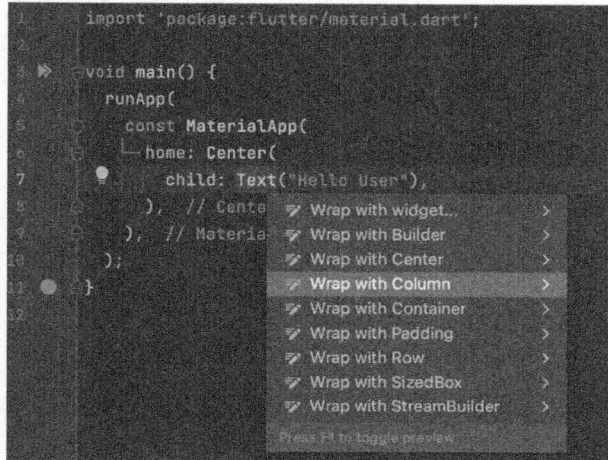

Figure 3.7: Code Formatting option

After selecting the option, the code will be changed as shown in *Code 3.3*:

```
1.  import 'package:flutter/material.dart';
2.
3.  void main() {
4.    runApp(
5.      const MaterialApp(
6.        home: Center(
7.          child: Column(
8.            children: [
9.              Text("Hello User"),
10.           ],
11.         ),
12.       ),
13.     ),
14.   );
15. }
```

Code 3.3: Code after updating.

Closing labels

You must have noticed already that the dart code formatter adds a comment of the widget name after each widget as shown in *Figure 3.8*:

Figure 3.8: Flutter code with closing labels

If the settings are not upto your standards, you can update them. For that, click on **Android Studio | Settings** and toggle the setting as shown in *Figure 3.9*:

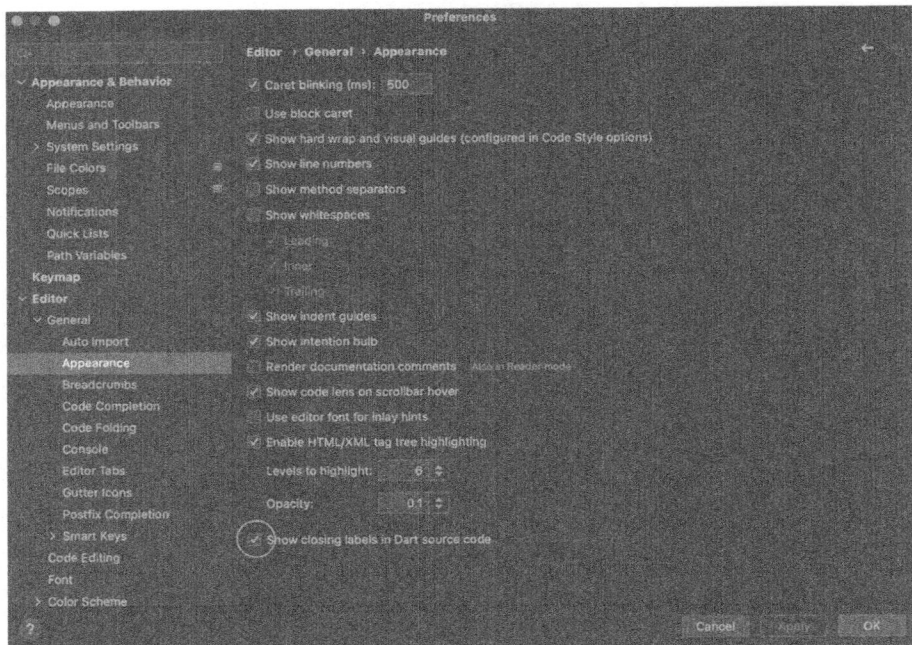

Figure 3.9: Toggle closing labels settings.

After updating the setting, you need to reformat the code to remove/add the comments.

Debug banner

When you run the app in the simulator or emulator, you must notice a banner in top right corner, as shown in *Figure 3.10:*

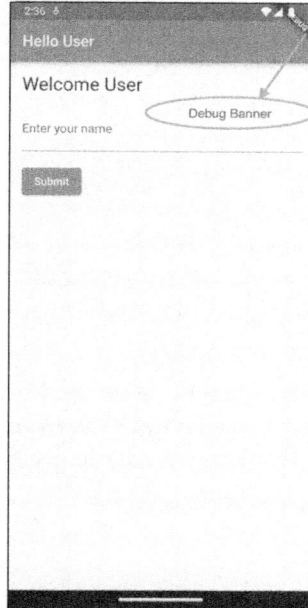

Figure 3.10: Emulator running on debug mode.

It is there to indicate, whatever is running is not the final version of the app. When you finally build your app and run it on a real device, this banner will disappear. When it is there, it says it is not the fastest version of the app; there may be a few lacks. It is not optimized, and it is just for debugging and development. If you don't like the banner to be shown, it can be removed easily. To remove the debug banner, set the **debugShowCheckedModeBanner** property to false, as shown in the code below:

```
1. void main() {
2.   runApp(
3.     MaterialApp(
4.       debugShowCheckedModeBanner: false,
5.     ),
6.   );
7. }
```

Code 3.4: Code for removing debug banner.

Sample app

Now, let us jump and build our own first app, which is going to be a basic app. It is going to have an app bar with title '**Hello User**', and stack of widgets:

- Text widget with text '**Hello User**',
- Textfield with place holder text '**Enter your name**'
- Button with title 'Submit'.

Although at this point we are not going to make the button functional, we will cover it in the next chapter. For now, let us just focus on the UI.

First things, let us delete all the code from the **main.dart** file and just leave the main method. This is done since whenever we run the Flutter app, the compiler looks for a main method to start with and then at the instructions for what is to be done. So, the main method is the starting point for all of our apps.

Inside **runApp**, it will show an error, as we have deleted the Flutter provided **myApp** widget. So, let us remove that and replace it with a **MaterialApp** widget and place other widgets to achieve the required layout as shown in the code given below:

```
1.  import 'package:flutter/material.dart';
2.
3.  void main() {
4.    runApp(
5.      MaterialApp(
6.        home: Scaffold(
7.          appBar: AppBar(
8.            title: const Text('Hello User'),
9.          ),
10.         body: const Padding(
11.           padding: EdgeInsets.all(16.0),
12.           child: Column(
13.             crossAxisAlignment: CrossAxisAlignment.start,
14.             children: [
15.               Text(
16.                 'Welcome User',
17.                 style: TextStyle(fontSize: 24),
18.               ),
19.               SizedBox(height: 16),
```

```
20.                  TextField(
21.                    decoration: InputDecoration(
22.                      labelText: 'Enter your name',
23.                    ),
24.                  ),
25.                  SizedBox(height: 16),
26.                  ElevatedButton(
27.                    onPressed: submitButtonPressed,
28.                    child: Text('Submit'),
29.                  ),
30.                ],
31.              ),
32.            )
33.          ),
34.        ),
35.   );
36. }
37.
38. void submitButtonPressed() {
39.   // Add button click logic here
40.   print('Submit button pressed!');
41. }
```

Code 3.5: *First Flutter project code*

Before running the app, let us understand some important concepts which we have used in this code.

Widget

In Flutter, a Widget is a basic building block and fundamental concept of the framework. A widget represents a visual element or component in the user interface of a Flutter application.

Widgets are used to construct the user interface by assembling and nesting them together. They can be as simple as a text label or as complex as a custom interactive component. Examples of widgets include buttons, text fields, images, containers, rows, columns, and more.

Widgets in Flutter are categorized into two types:

- **Stateless widgets:** These widgets are immutable, meaning they cannot change their properties once created. They represent a static piece of UI and do not have any internal state. Stateless widgets are typically used for UI elements that do not change based on user interaction or external factors.

- **Stateful widgets:** These widgets are mutable and can change their properties or appearance over time. They have associated state objects that can be updated, triggering a rebuild of the widget. Stateful widgets are used for UI elements that need to maintain a dynamic state, handle user input, or update based on external data changes.

Widget tree

Widgets are organized in a tree-like structure called the widget tree. The parent-child relationship between widgets defines the layout and composition of the user interface. When a widget's state changes, Flutter's framework efficiently rebuilds only the affected widgets, updating the UI accordingly.

Overall, widgets are the core elements of Flutter that allow you to create rich, interactive, and responsive user interfaces for your applications. If we make a pictorial representation of the widget tree of our app, it will be as shown in *Figure 3.11:*

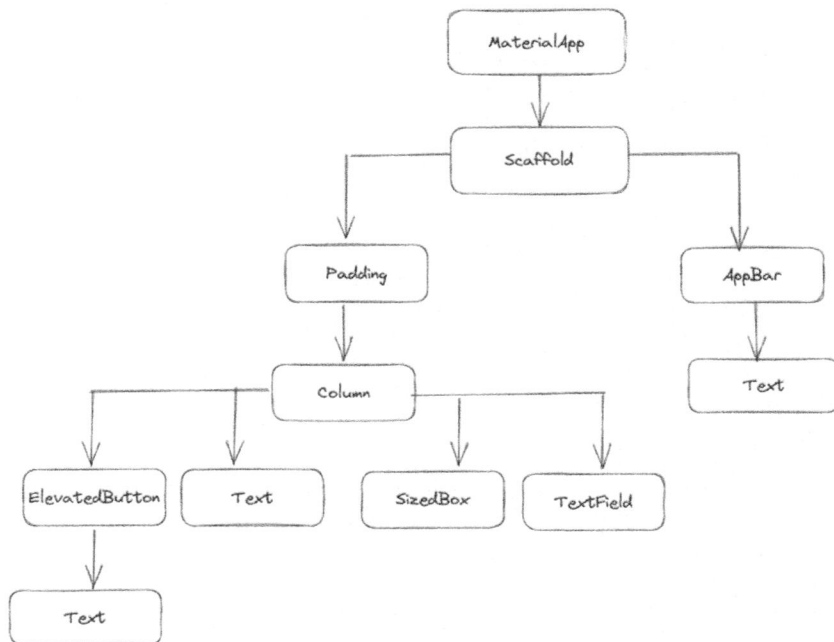

Figure 3.11: Widget tree

Now let us go through some important widgets of any Flutter application.

MaterialApp

The MaterialApp widget is a core component in the Flutter framework, providing a convenient way to set up and configure a Material Design-themed application. Serving as the root or top of the widget tree, it defines the overall theme, routing, and other configurations for the app. For a comprehensive list of properties and methods available for MaterialApp, please refer to the official documentation: **https://api.flutter.dev/flutter/material/MaterialApp-class.html**.

By using the MaterialApp widget as the root of your Flutter app, you establish the foundation for implementing material design principles, handling navigation, managing themes, and more.

Scaffold

In Flutter, applications are typically structured as a tree of widgets. The top-level widget, MaterialApp, serves as the root of the widget tree. Within MaterialApp, we commonly find the Scaffold widget, which forms the basic framework for building user interfaces.

In Flutter, the Scaffold widget is a fundamental component used to implement the basic structure and layout of a typical mobile application screen. It provides a framework for building material-design-style user interfaces.

The Scaffold widget represents a visual scaffold or container that encompasses the entire screen or a specific portion of the screen. It typically consists of multiple components, such as an app bar, body content, bottom navigation, and floating action buttons.

The key features of the Scaffold widget include:

- **App Bar**: The AppBar widget represents the topmost region of the scaffold and usually contains a title, actions, and navigation elements.
- **Body**: The body property of the Scaffold widget defines the main content of the screen, such as a scrollable list, a form, or any other widget hierarchy.
- **Bottom Navigation**: The `bottomNavigationBar` property allows you to add a bottom navigation bar to the scaffold, typically used for switching between different screens or views.
- **Floating Action Button**: The `floatingActionButton` property enables you to add a floating action button to the scaffold, which is typically used for prominent actions within the screen. Floating Action Button is placed at bottom right corner on the screen.

Additionally, the Scaffold widget provides other features like drawers, snack bars, and persistent toolbars, which can be used to enhance the user interface and navigation within the app. By utilizing the Scaffold widget as the main structure of your app's screens, you can quickly establish a standard layout and incorporate common UI elements.

Consider referring to the official documentation for the Scaffold class to acquire a comprehensive understanding of its properties and methods. Access the detailed information for the class through the official documentation available at the following link: **https://api.flutter.dev/flutter/material/Scaffold-class.html.** It is recommended to review the official documentation for any new widget before utilization to gain insight into its capabilities and functionalities.

Run the app in a simulator/emulator

Now let us run our app in a virtual device. You can select the device from the dropdown as shown in *Figure 3.4* from the list of available Android emulators and iOS simulators. Upon running the app, the resulting screen will resemble the *Figure 3.12:*

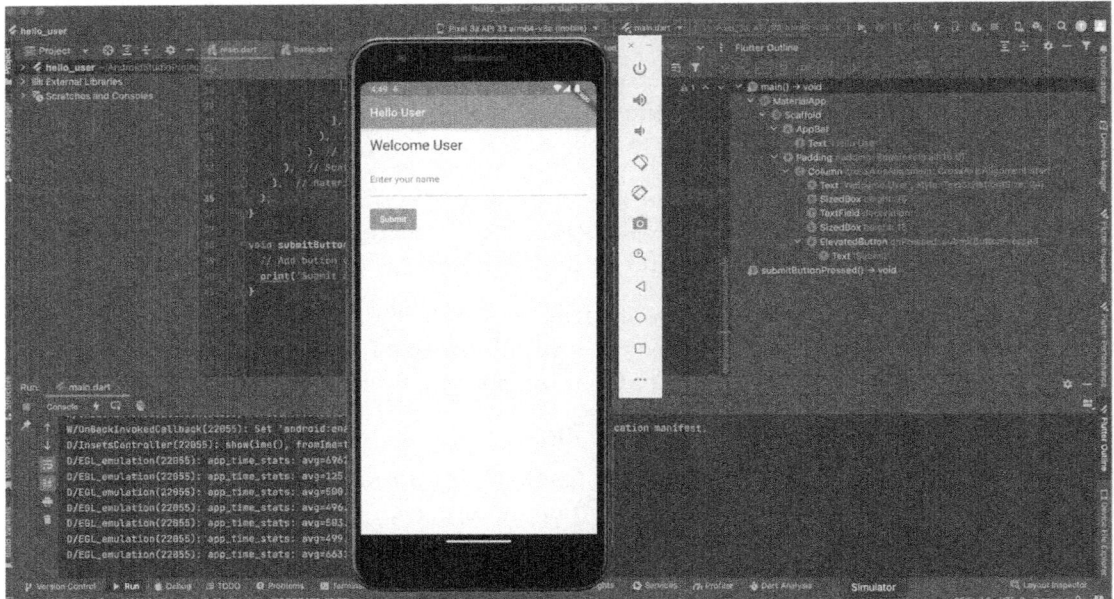

Figure 3.12: *Running our first Flutter app*

Run the app in a physical device

To run your app on a physical device, follow these steps discussed in the upcoming sections.

Running on Android device

So far, you have run the app in an emulator or simulator; now it is time to run your first app on a physical device. This process requires a few steps. Let us start with a physical

Android device. To run the app on a physical Android device that first you need to enable developer options. By default, these options are hidden on most devices. Please follow the below steps to enable it:

1. Go to **Settings** | **About Phone** | **Software Information** | **Build Number**

   When you tap on the build number, you will get a message about how many steps away you are from enabling the developer option, so tap until it is enabled. You usually need to tap it seven times consecutively. After the seventh tap, you will see a message indicating that Developer Options have been enabled.

2. Once '**Developer Options**' is enabled, tap and enable USB Debugging. After that, you can use a USB cable to connect your device to the laptop. While using it for the first time, you will get an alert to allow USB debugging, and then you can see your own device in the list of devices available to run.

   Here is the step-by-step, explained using figures to enable the Developer Option and USB debugging:

3. Navigate to Settings, as shown in the following figure:

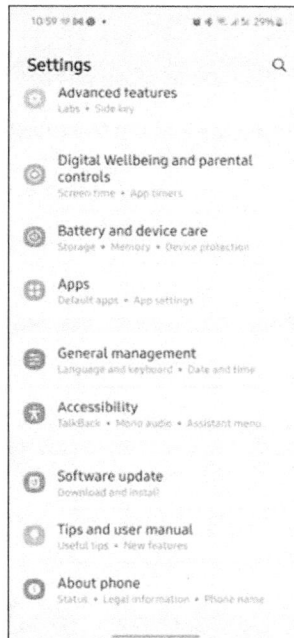

Figure 3.13: Navigating to settings

4. Tap on **About Phone**, as shown in the following figure:

Figure 3.14: *Tap on About Phone*

5.   Select the software information, as shown in *Figure 3.15:*

Figure 3.15: *Selecting software information*

Please note: On certain phones, accessing the build number may vary. It might be located directly within the '**About Phone**' section. If you're unable to find the Build number in the specified path, please utilize the search function within the settings menu to locate it.

6.   Keep on tapping the build number, as can be seen in *Figure 3.16:*

Figure 3.16: Tapping build number

7.   Enable the developer mode, as shown in the following figure:

Figure 3.17: Enabling developer mode

8. Please return to the settings menu to check if the developer options are now accessible (refer to *Figure 3.18*).

    This is again device specific. It could be in **System | Developer** options for other devices. Please utilize the search function within the settings menu to locate it.

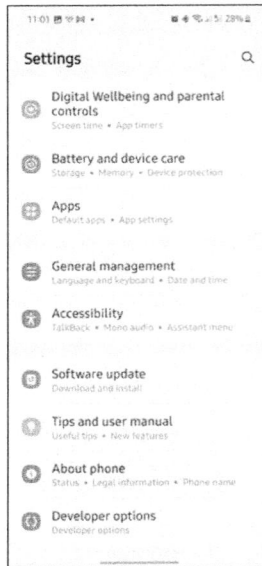

Figure 3.18: *Navigating back to Setting to reverify*

9. Tap on the **Developer options**, as can be seen in the following figure:

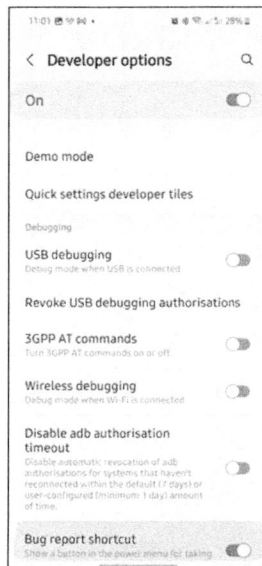

Figure 3.19: *Tap on developer option*

10. In the pop-up that appears, click on **OK**, thereby enabling the USB debugging. The same is demonstrated in the *Figure 3.20:*

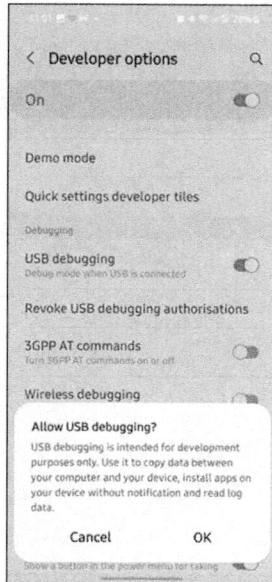

Figure 3.20: *Enable USB debugging*

11. Now, allow for the USB debugging, once the pop up appears, as can be seen in the following figure:

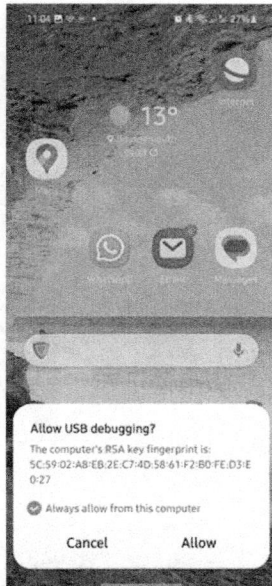

Figure 3.21: *Allow USB debugging*

12. If you do not have a USB cable and you still want to run the app in a physical device, you need to pair your device using WiFi. For that go to **Tools | Device Manager | Physical | Pair Using WiFi** as shown in *Figure 3.22*:

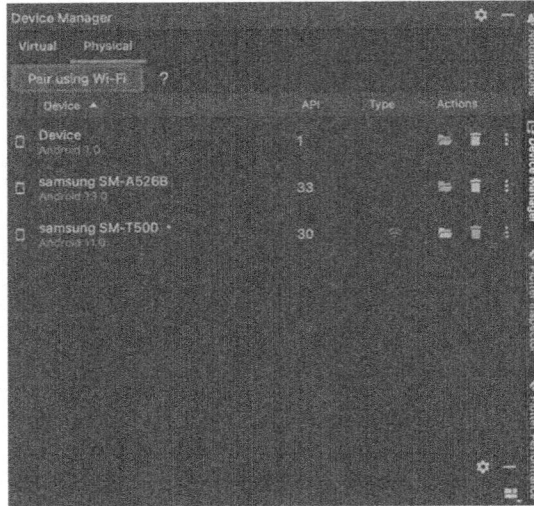

Figure 3.22: Open Device Manager and select Pair using wi-fi

Note: This feature is only available for devices running Android 11 or newer.

13. Now, you can either select Pair using QR code, as can be seen in the following figure or select Pair using a pairing code (*Figure 3.24):*

Figure 3.23: Select Pair using QR code

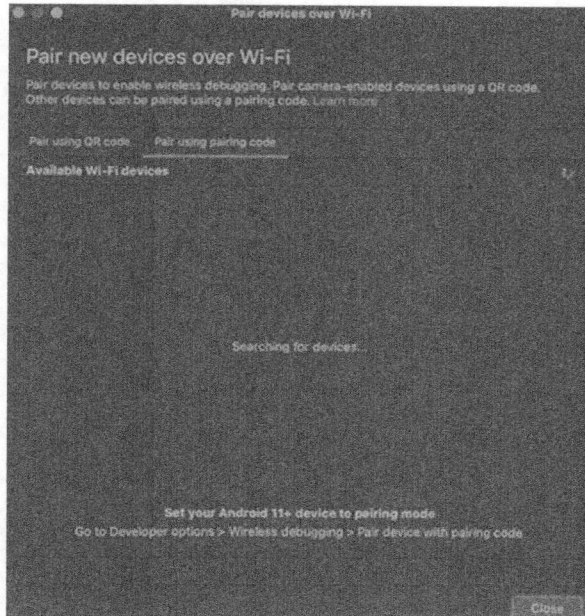

Figure 3.24: Select Pair using pairing code

14. Now after pairing, your device should be available in the list of devices to run, as can be seen in *Figure 3.25*:

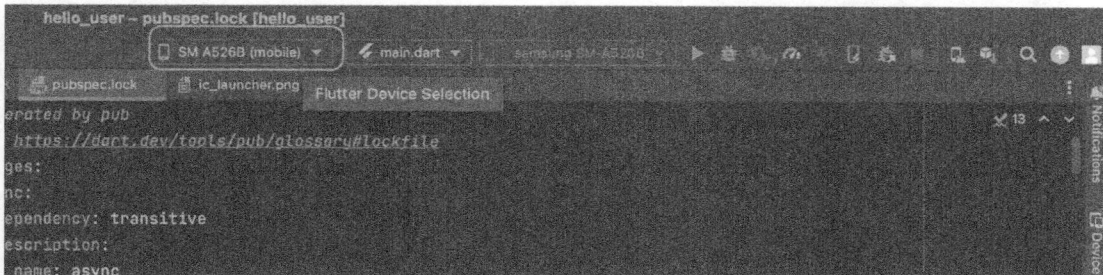

Figure 3.25: Android device added to the list

15. The screenshot provided below displays the app running on an Android device:

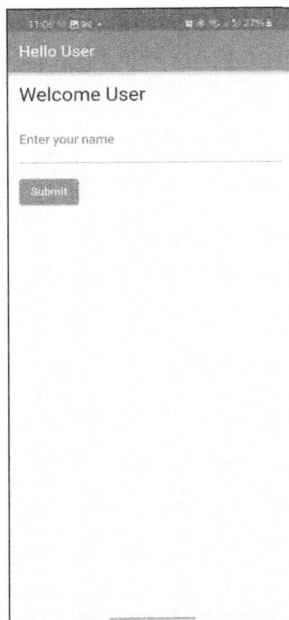

Figure 3.26: Running the app on Android device

Deploy app to iOS devices

Now, it is time to run the app on a physical iOS device like an iPhone or an iPad. Some pre-requisites are as follows:

- Apple Id
- Xcode
- iPhone/iPad

Let us go through the steps to install the app in a physical iPhone:

1. The device's **Operating System (OS)** version should be compatible with the Xcode version you are using. Typically, the Xcode version lags behind the iOS version by two versions. For instance, if your iPhone is running iOS version 16.3.1, a compatible Xcode version would be 14.3. Therefore, for compatibility reasons, your phone's iOS version should be two versions ahead of your Xcode version.

2. To take advantage of wireless debugging, make sure that both your device and computer are connected to the same network and that your device has a passcode set. While the device is attached, open **Xcode | Window | Devices and Simulators**. Select your phone, and check Connect via Network. Once the network icon appears next to the device name, you can unplug your device from USB.

3. When you connect a physical device for iOS development for the first time, there are a few steps you need to follow to establish trust between your Mac and the

device's Development Certificate. Additionally, on iOS 16 and higher, you must enable Developer Mode. Here is what you need to do:

a. When you connect the iOS device to your Mac, a dialog prompt will appear. Select "Trust" to establish trust between the device and your Mac.

b. On the iOS device, open the Settings app. Then, navigate to **General | Device Management**. Trust the Development Certificate by selecting it. In some cases, for first-time users, you might need to go to **General | Profiles | Device Management** instead.

c. If you are using iOS 16 or higher, go back to the top level of the Settings app. Then, select **Privacy & Security | Developer Mode** and toggle **Developer Mode** on.

By following these steps, you will ensure that both your Mac and the iOS device are trusted and properly set up for iOS development, including enabling Developer Mode on iOS 16 and higher.

4. To provision your project in Xcode, follow these steps:

a. From your Flutter project directory, where your project is saved, open or double tap '**ios/Runner.xcworkspace**' to open the project in Xcode.

b. From the device drop-down menu next to the run button, select the iPhone/iPad device you intend to deploy your project to.

c. In the left navigation panel, select the Runner project. On the Runner target settings page, navigate to **Signing & Capabilities | Team** and ensure that your Development Team is selected. Please refer to the following *Figure* for the exact location you need to set the team.

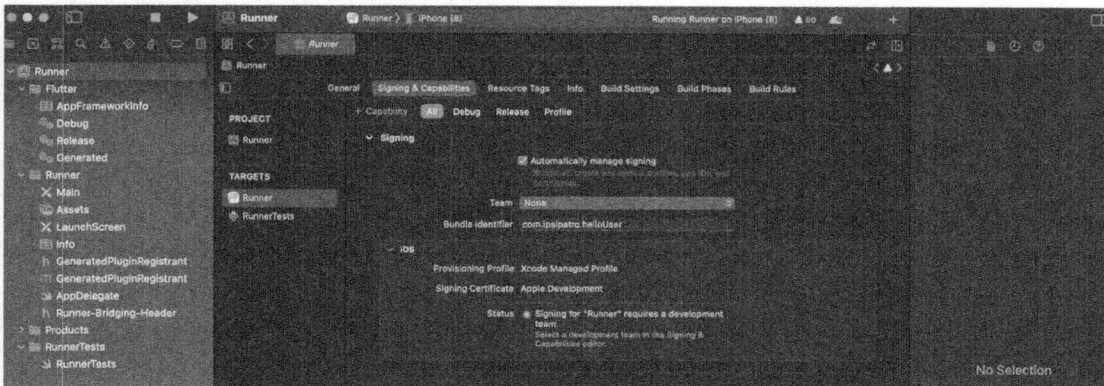

Figure 3.27: Xcode team setup

d. When you choose a team, Xcode will generate and download a Development Certificate, register your device with your account, and create and download a provisioning profile if necessary.

e. If this is your first iOS development project, you may need to sign in to Xcode using your Apple ID. Development and testing is supported for any Apple ID. Enrolling in the Apple Developer Program is required to distribute your app to the App Store.

The "**General | Identity | Bundle Identifier**" section in Xcode provides a field where developers specify a unique identifier for their app. The instruction advises verifying this identifier to ensure its uniqueness. The uniqueness of the Bundle Identifier is essential to avoid conflicts and ensure that the app can be properly identified and provisioned:

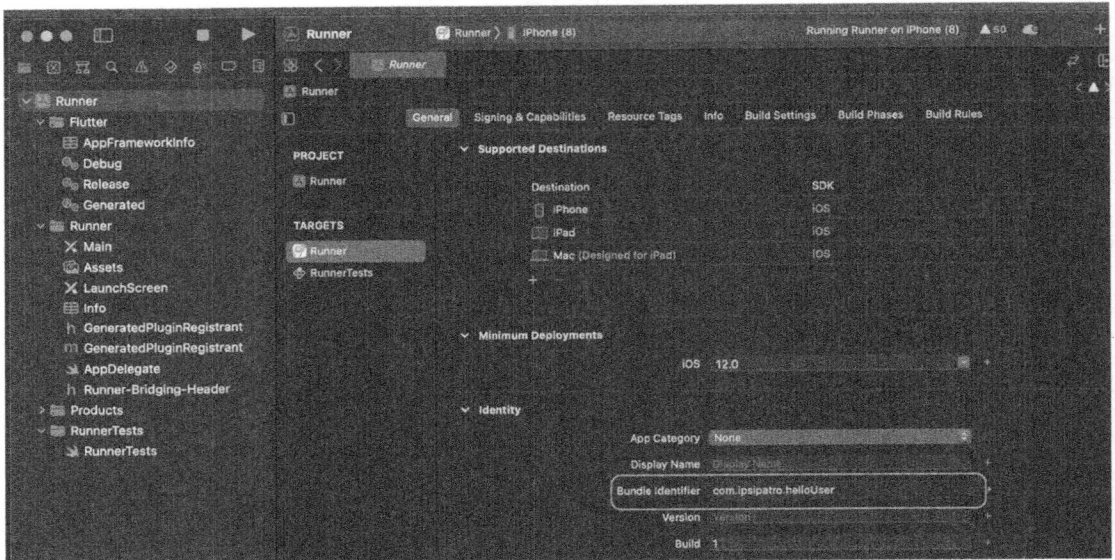

Figure 3.28: Unique bundle identifier

5. Click the **Run** button in Xcode or use flutter run command in terminal, while physical device is selected, this should launch the app on your physical device.

If you find any issue, please refer to the links given below for help.

*   Running on an Android Device (Windows): **https://docs.flutter.dev/get-started/install/windows# set-up-your-android-device**

*   Running on an Android Device (macOS): **https://docs.flutter.dev/get-started/install/macos# set-up-your-android-device**

*   Running on an Android Device (Linux): **https://docs.flutter.dev/get-started/install/linux# set-up-your-android-device**

*   Running on an iOS Device (macOS only): **https://docs.flutter.dev/get-started/install/macos# deploy-to-ios-devices**

By visiting the respective links, you will find detailed instructions specific to your operating system, allowing you to run your Flutter apps on the desired Android or iOS devices.

App icon

If you now close your app and go to device home screen, you can notice the default app icon provided by Flutter has been set for your app. Unless you set your own app icon, Flutter sets this icon for all Flutter apps. Now let us see how we can set the app icon for our app, so that we can easily identify our app.

For this process, begin by obtaining an image intended for your app icon. Once you have your chosen image, navigate to the website **https://www.appicon.co** to streamline the generation of app icons across various platforms. In your browser, open the provided link, and then seamlessly upload your selected app icon image by dragging and dropping it into the designated space. On the website, meticulously choose all the necessary platforms for which you require app icons; for our current purpose, we specifically need icons tailored for both iPhone and Android. After selecting the desired platforms, proceed by clicking on the 'Generate' button, as exemplified in the figure below. Subsequently, a zipped folder named "**AppIcons**" will be initiated for download. Upon unzipping this downloaded file, you'll discover two distinct folders—one designated for Android and the other exclusively for iPhone. Each folder encapsulates the meticulously generated app icons ready for integration into your respective application platforms. This user-friendly process ensures a seamless and organized approach to acquiring app icons tailored to the specific requirements of both iPhone and Android platforms:

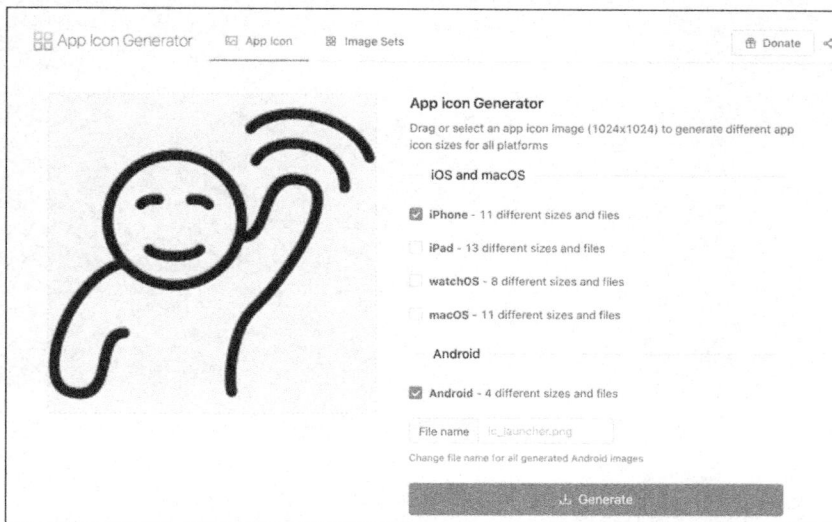

Figure 3.29: App icon generator

Upon clicking the "**Generate**" button, a zipped folder named "**AppIcons**" will be promptly downloaded to your system. This folder encompasses all the requested icons ready for use. Unzipping this file reveals two distinct folders - one tailored for Android and the other dedicated to iPhone. This streamlined process ensures that you receive a comprehensive set of icons conveniently packaged and labeled for your Android and iPhone application development needs.

Android folder contains multiple folders inside for different sized icons and similar is the case for iOS as well (**Assets.xcassats folder**). Now it is time for us to replace the default Flutter icon to the newly generated icon.

For that let us look at the folder structure of our app. The '**android**' folder holds all android code and the '**ios**' folder holds all the iOS code files. Let us replace Android icons first.

For that open the 'res' folder which is in this path, android - | **app** - | **src** - | **main**, there you can notice multiple folders starts with mipmap, which are the app icon folders. If you open them in finder by using option **open in** | **finder**, it will open the files in finder. Delete and replace the highlighted folders by the corresponding android app icon folders from the downloaded app icons as can be seen in the following figure.

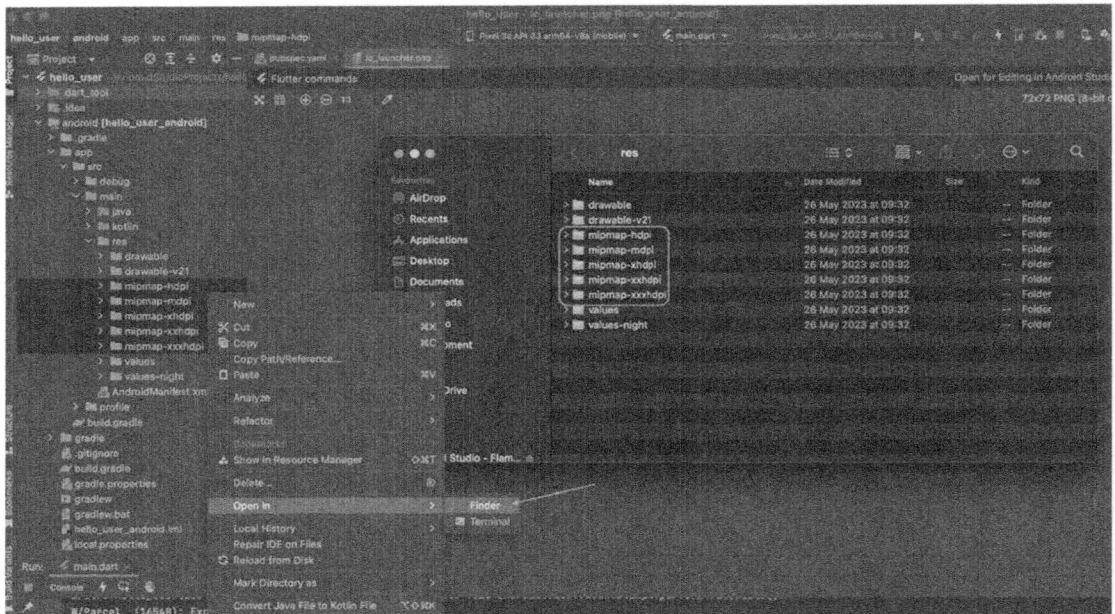

Figure 3.30: Android app icon

After this, close the app after running it and navigate to home page again, you must see the newly added app icon being set for your app, as it has been for the app shown in the following figure:

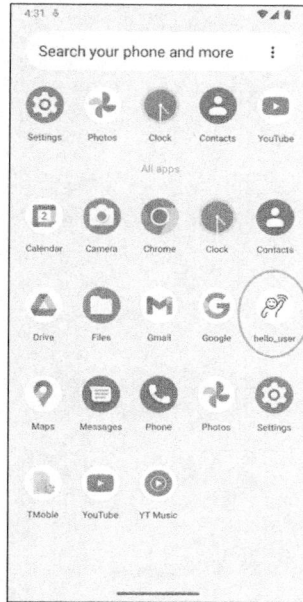

Figure 3.31: Updated Android app icon

Let us do the same for iPhone icons. For that navigate to **ios** | **Runner** folder and delete the **Assets.xcassets** folder. Then, replace it with the newly generated **Assets.xcassets** icons.

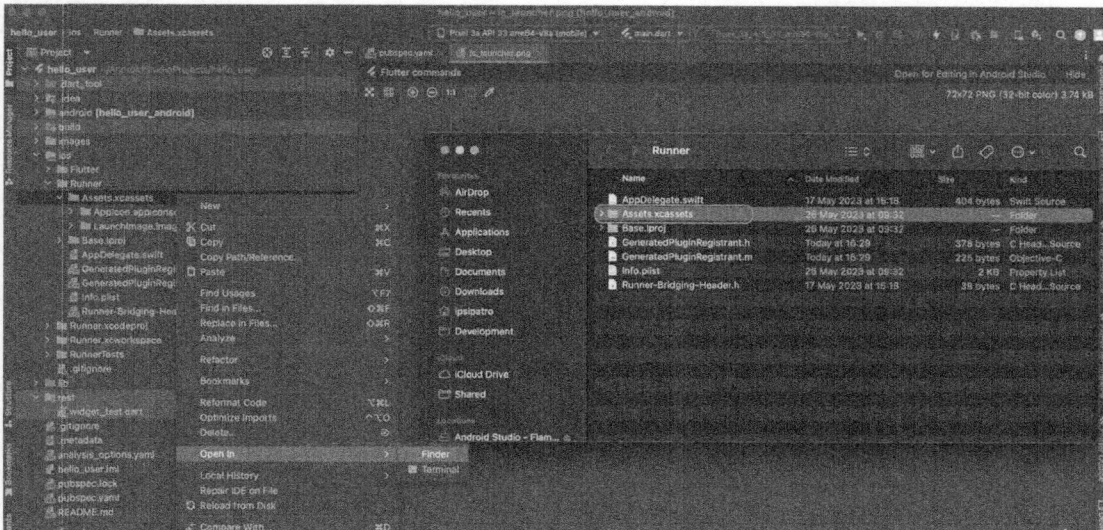

Figure 3.32: iOS app icon

After replacing the icon just run the app in an iPhone simulator/device and you can find the newly downloaded icon:

Figure 3.33: updated iOS app icon

Hot Reload

While discussing the advantages of using Flutter, hot reload is of great importance.

Let us understand what is Hot Reload. Hot reload is a feature in Flutter that allows you to quickly see the changes you make to your code without having to restart or rebuild the entire application. With hot reload, you can make code modifications, save the changes, and instantly see the updated results in the running app.

Here is how hot reload works:

- While your Flutter application is running, you can make changes to the Dart code files in your project.
- Instead of stopping the app and rebuilding it from scratch, you can simply save the changes you made.
- Flutter's hot reload mechanism will analyze the code differences, apply the modifications, and update the running application with the new code.
- The app's UI will reflect the changes immediately, allowing you to see the effects of your code modifications in real-time.

Hot reload is a powerful tool for developers as it significantly speeds up the development process and allows for rapid experimentation and iteration. It helps maintain the app's state, allowing you to continue from where you left off, and eliminates the need for lengthy rebuild cycles during development.

To test that feature let us go back to our main method and add this code:

```
1. void main() {
2.   runApp(
3.     const MaterialApp(
4.       debugShowCheckedModeBanner: false,
5.       home: Scaffold(
6.         backgroundColor: Colors.blue,
7.       )
8.     ),
9.   );
10. }
```

Code 3.6: Code for a blank screen with some background color

Now to test hot reload update the background color of Scaffold and press hot reload button. The button shown in the image below:

Figure 3.34: Hot Reload Button

You will notice that the console statement will show Performing hot reload... But nothing changes in the emulator. The reason is that to perform hot reload, Flutter needs a Stateless or a Stateful Widget. We will learn more about them in the next chapter. For now, let us just create a Stateless widget and move the MaterialApp code to that widget, as shown in code below. To try out yourself just start typing '**stless**' outside the main method, and select Flutter's suggestion. Flutter will, then, create a new Stateless Widget for you. Just name it as you prefer, and return its object from main method as shown in code below:

```
1.  import 'package:flutter/material.dart';
2.
3.  void main() {
4.    runApp(
5.        const HelloApp()
6.    );
7.  }
8.
9.  class HelloApp extends StatelessWidget {
10.   const HelloApp({super.key});
11.
```

```
12.    @override
13.    Widget build(BuildContext context) {
14.      return  const MaterialApp(
15.          debugShowCheckedModeBanner: false,
16.         home: Scaffold(
17.            backgroundColor: Colors.green,
18.          )
19.      );
20.    }
21. }
```

Code 3.7: Stateless widget sample code

Replace your **main.dart** file code with the code given above and relaunch the app. After that change the background color and press the hot reload button to reflect the changes without stopping and starting again.

Hot reload in Flutter requires either a stateless or a stateful widget because Flutter searches for recent changes and a build method nearby when it is executed. If a direct Material app is returned without a build method in the Flutter code, hot reload fails. However, stateless or stateful widgets include a build method. Therefore, after updating your code, pressing hot reload or saving the code (using command or control + S) triggers hot reload, saving developers valuable time, particularly when working on UI development. This feature is highly appreciated by Flutter developers.

Conclusion

Congratulations on skillfully building your first Flutter app and deploying it on both virtual and physical devices. In the process, you've gained valuable insights into code formatting techniques, a skill set that will undoubtedly prove instrumental in your continued journey through the upcoming chapters. As you dive deeper into Flutter development, this foundation will serve as a bedrock for mastering more advanced concepts and refining your abilities. Keep up the excellent work and remember that each step forward contributes to your growth as a proficient and confident Flutter developer. The journey ahead holds exciting opportunities for further exploration and accomplishment!

In the upcoming chapter on Flutter widgets, you will explore the fundamental building blocks that empower the creation of rich and interactive user interfaces. Widgets are the heart of any Flutter application, providing a diverse set of tools to design and structure your app's visual elements. From basic components like text and buttons to more complex structures such as lists and grids, understanding how to leverage Flutter widgets effectively is essential for crafting dynamic and engaging user experiences. As you delve into this chapter, you'll discover the versatility of widgets, learning how to compose them, customize their appearance, and manage their behavior. This knowledge will be pivotal as you advance in your Flutter development journey, unlocking the potential to design seamless and visually appealing applications. Get ready to dive into the exciting world of Flutter widgets and elevate your app-building skills!

Multiple Choice Questions

1. **What programming language is used for Flutter app development?**
    a. Java
    b. C++
    c. Swift
    d. Dart

2. **Which Flutter widget is used to create a button?**
    a. Scaffold
    b. AppBar
    c. Text
    d. RaisedButton

3. **What command is used to run a Flutter app on an Android device or emulator?**
    a. flutter run
    b. flutter start
    c. flutter build
    d. flutter launch

4. **What is the 'main ()' function in a Flutter app responsible for?**
    a. Defining the app's layout
    b. Handling user interactions
    c. Initializing the app and running the 'main ()' UI thread
    d. Fetching data from an API

Answers

1. d. Dart
2. d. RaisedButton
3. a. flutter run
4. c. Initializing the app and running the main UI thread

Join our book's Discord space

Join the book's Discord Workspace for Latest updates, Offers, Tech happenings around the world, New Release and Sessions with the Authors:

https://discord.bpbonline.com

CHAPTER 4
Flutter Widgets

Introduction

In the previous chapter, we successfully built and run our first ever Flutter Project. However, there are certain widgets that were used in that project, but we have yet to explore them fully, we are going to do so in this chapter. So, let us begin.

Structure

This chapter covers the following topics:

- Layout widgets
- Sliver widget
- Asset image and network image widget
- Card widget
- Inkwell widget
- Widget styling
- Stateless and stateful widgets
- Material and Cupertino widgets
- Divider
- Slider widget

- Dropdown button
- Bottom sheet
- ListTile widget
- Animations in Flutter

Layout widgets

Layout widgets are a collection of widgets that help to structure and arrange the user interface elements within a Flutter application. These widgets allow us to define the layout and positioning of other widgets on the screen, ensuring a visually appealing and organized UI.

Before start working on any new widgets it is a good practice to go through the official documentation of the widget. Flutter has arranged the documentation in a very user-friendly way. So, for any widget's documentation, you can look for the widget catalog section inside flutter.dev, and now we are going to focus on Layout widgets. You can go through this link **https://docs.flutter.dev/ui/widgets/layout** for a deeper understanding.

Single-child layout widgets

This widget can contain only a single child widget and is typically used to control the layout and positioning of a single element within a parent widget. Let us go through some commonly used single-child layout widgets:

Container widget

This widget is like a layout box, you can position and move it around the screen. It is a versatile widget that can contain a single child, like an image or a text, and allows us to customize its appearance and layout properties.

A container widget with no child will take as much space as possible on the screen. When a container has a child, it takes up as much space as the child needs.

Let us try that out with the code given below:

```
1. void main() {
2.   runApp(
3.       const HelloApp()
4.   );
5. }
6.
7. class HelloApp extends StatelessWidget {
```

```
8.    const HelloApp({super.key});
9.
10.   @override
11.   Widget build(BuildContext context) {
12.     return MaterialApp(
13.         debugShowCheckedModeBanner: false,
14.         home: Scaffold(
15.           backgroundColor: Colors.green,
16.           body: Container(
17.             color: Colors.red,
18.           ),
19.         )
20.     );
21.   }
22. }
```

Code 4.1: *Container widget without child*

Once you run this code, your screen must look like the *Figure 4.1*:

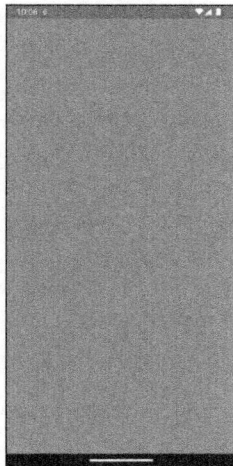

Figure 4.1: *Screen shot of container without child*

Now let us add a child to the container and see how the design changes:

```
1. void main() {
2.   runApp(
3.       const HelloApp()
```

```
4.    );
5. }
6.
7. class HelloApp extends StatelessWidget {
8.    const HelloApp({super.key});
9.
10.   @override
11.   Widget build(BuildContext context) {
12.     return MaterialApp(
13.         debugShowCheckedModeBanner: false,
14.         home: Scaffold(
15.           backgroundColor: Colors.green,
16.           body: Container(
17.             color: Colors.red,
18.             child: const Text("Hello User"),
19.           ),
20.         )
21.     );
22.   }
23. }
```

Code 4.2: *Container widget with a text widget child*

Figure 4.2 is the screenshot when this app is run in the emulator:

Figure 4.2: *Container widget with a text widget child*

Safe area

If you have observed, the text widget may not be clearly visible as it overlaps with the time displayed in the simulator. To resolve this problem, we can utilize a highly beneficial widget called SafeArea. By enclosing your container with SafeArea, the child widget will always remain within the safe and visible area of the device. Refer to the code snippet below, replace your existing build method with it, and you should see a screen as shown in *Figure 4.3*:

```
1.   @override
2.   Widget build(BuildContext context) {
3.     return MaterialApp(
4.         debugShowCheckedModeBanner: false,
5.         home: Scaffold(
6.           backgroundColor: Colors.green,
7.           body: SafeArea(
8.             child: Container(
9.               color: Colors.red,
10.              child: const Text("Hello User")
11.            ),
12.          ),
13.        )
14.    );
15.  }
```

Code 4.3: SafeArea example

Figure 4.3: SafeArea demo

Margin and padding

Now, we also need some spacing around the text, we can achieve it with margin and padding. After adding the same, the codes can be seen below:

```
1. void main() {
2.    runApp(
3.        const HelloApp()
4.    );
5. }
6.
7. class HelloApp extends StatelessWidget {
8.    const HelloApp({super.key});
9.
10.   @override
11.   Widget build(BuildContext context) {
12.     return MaterialApp(
13.         debugShowCheckedModeBanner: false,
14.         home: Scaffold(
15.           backgroundColor: Colors.green,
16.           body: Container(
17.             color: Colors.red,
18.             margin: const EdgeInsets.symmetric(vertical: 40,
                 horizontal: 20),
19.             padding: const EdgeInsets.all(40),
20.             child: const Text("Hello User")
21.           ),
22.         )
23.     );
24.   }
25. }
```

Code 4.4: Margin and padding

To get a better understanding of both padding and margin and how it works, we should use the overlay guideline feature of Flutter inspector as shown in *Figure 4.4:*

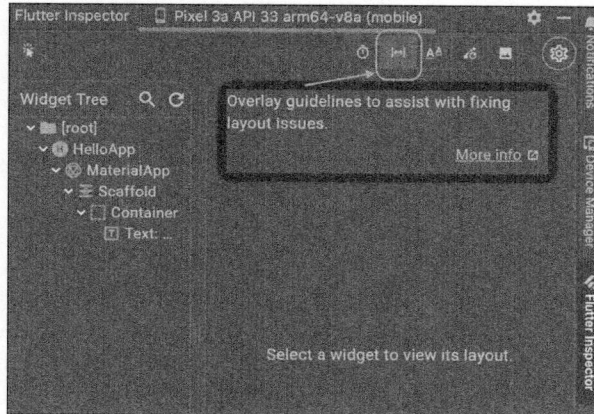

Figure 4.4: *Flutter Inspector overlay guidelines*

Figure 4.5 and *Figure 4.6* show how the screens will look with and without guidelines:

Figure 4.5: *With guideline*

Figure 4.6: Without guideline

As you can see in the above code, we have used margin and padding inside the container for the Text widget's layout. Margin is used by the container for spacing from the outer widget.

In this case, the outer widget is a Scaffold, and padding is used for inside container spacing or spacing of the child within the parent's space. In this case, the child is the text, and the parent is the Container.

We need EdgeInset for both margin and padding. There are different methods available to give different values in different directions. Here are some commonly used methods of the EdgeInsets class:

- **EdgeInsets.all(double value)**: Creates insets with the same distance on all sides. For example, **EdgeInsets.all(16.0)** creates insets with 16 pixels of padding on all sides.

- **EdgeInsets.only({left, top, right, bottom})**: Creates insets with different distances on specific sides. For example, **EdgeInsets.only(left: 16.0, right: 8.0)** creates insets with 16 pixels of padding on the left side and 8 pixels on the right side.

- **EdgeInsets.symmetric({vertical, horizontal})**: Creates insets with the same distance on the vertical or horizontal axis. For example, **EdgeInsets.symmetric(vertical: 16.0)** creates insets with 16 pixels of padding on the top and bottom.

- EdgeInsets.fromLTRB(double left, double top, double right, double bottom): Creates insets with specific distances for left, top, right, and bottom sides.

These methods provide a convenient way to define padding or margins for widgets, allowing you to easily control the spacing around a widget or its content. You can apply these insets by using the padding or margin properties of the respective widgets.

Padding widget

We have explored the 'padding' property of a 'Container' and its interaction with 'EdgeInsets.' Now, let's consider applying similar padding to a Text widget without relying on a Container. To achieve this, we can leverage the Padding widget. Explore the example below for a practical demonstration and refer to the attached screenshot labeled as *Figure 4.7*:

```
1.   @override
2.   Widget build(BuildContext context) {
3.     return const MaterialApp(
4.       debugShowCheckedModeBanner: false,
5.       home: Scaffold(
6.         backgroundColor: Colors.green,
7.         body: SafeArea(
8.           child: Padding(
9.             padding: EdgeInsets.all(20.0),
10.            child: Text("Hello User"),
11.          ),
12.        ),
13.      ),
14.    );
15.  }
```

Code 4.5: Padding widget

Figure 4.7: Padding widget

There are many other useful single child layout widgets, but it is difficult to go through all of them. So, for now if you are interested you can look at the official documentation for the full list. We will also be covering more widgets as we go ahead.

In summary, while the padding property directly applies padding to the content of a widget, the Padding widget wraps around a child widget and applies padding to it, especially when the widget cannot directly accept padding through its properties. The choice between using the property or the widget depends on the specific use case and the widget you are working with.

Centre widget

It is quite a useful widget as the name says, as it is a widget that centers its single child both horizontally and vertically within the available space. One important thing to remember is that this widget is, if the dimensions of this widget are restricted and both the **widthFactor** and **heightFactor** are null, it will attempt to occupy as much space as possible. However, if a dimension is not restricted and its corresponding size factor is null, the widget will adjust its size to match its child's size in that particular dimension.

In summary, the Center widget works with both restricted and unrestricted child widgets by aligning them at the center of the available space. The positioning is adjusted based on the specific constraints of the child widget and the available space provided by the parent widget or the overall layout constraints, as shown in the code blocks and *Figure 4.8*:

```
1.  @override
2.  Widget build(BuildContext context) {
3.    return MaterialApp(
```

```
4.        debugShowCheckedModeBanner: false,
5.      home: Scaffold(
6.        backgroundColor: Colors.green,
7.        body: Center(
8.          child: Container(
9.            color: Colors.red,
10.            child: const Text("Hello User"),
11.          ),
12.        ),
13.      ),
14.    );
15.  }
```

Code 4.6: Center widget with Container child

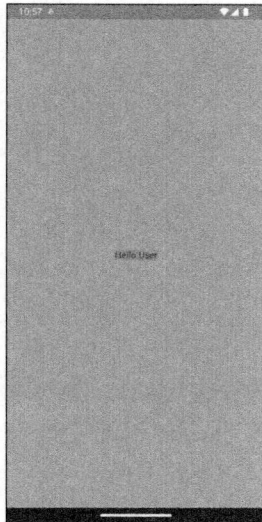

Figure 4.8: Centered container

```
1.    @override
2.    Widget build(BuildContext context) {
3.      return MaterialApp(
4.        debugShowCheckedModeBanner: false,
5.        home: Scaffold(
6.          backgroundColor: Colors.green,
7.          body: Container(
```

```
8.              color: Colors.red,
9.              child: const Center(
10.                child: Text("Hello User"),
11.              ),
12.            ),
13.          ),
14.      );
15.  }
```

Code 4.7: *Center widget with Text child*

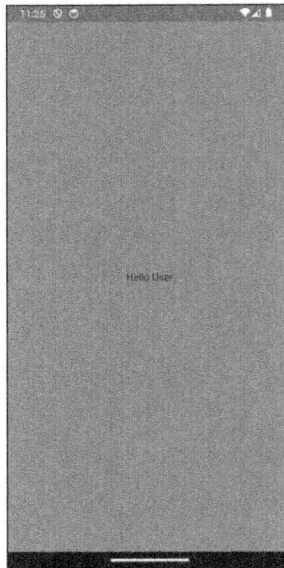

Figure 4.9: *Centered text*

By examining the code and screenshot in the two examples above, you can easily grasp the contrasting behavior of the Center widget with restricted and unrestricted child widgets. To gain a deeper understanding, you are encouraged to experiment with various combinations of widgets and properties. This hands-on approach will provide you with a clearer picture of how the Center widget behaves in different scenarios.

Align widget

To specify how a child will be layout or positioned inside its parent we use Align widget. For example, if you would like to align the text widget ('**Hello User**') inside the container on bottom left position, we can take help of Align widget's alignment property as shown by the below code:

```
1.  @override
2.    Widget build(BuildContext context) {
3.      return MaterialApp(
4.        debugShowCheckedModeBanner: false,
5.        home: Scaffold(
6.          backgroundColor: Colors.green,
7.          body: Center(
8.            child: Container(
9.              color: Colors.red,
10.             width: 120,
11.             height: 120,
12.             child: const Align(
13.               alignment: Alignment.bottomLeft,
14.               child: Text("Hello User"),
15.             ),
16.           ),
17.         ),
18.       ),
19.     );
20.  }
```

Code 4.8: Align widget

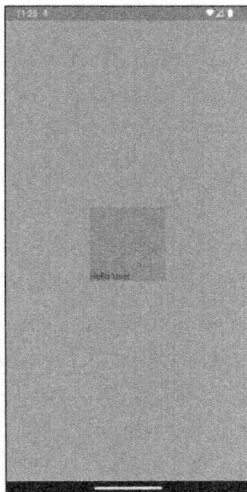

Figure 4.10: Align widget

You can also specify the alignment values (x, y) ranges from -1 to 1 for both left to right and top to bottom, as shown below:

```
1. const Align(
2.                 alignment: Alignment(1,1),
3.                 child: Text("Hello User"),
4.               ),
```

Code 4.9: Alignment value

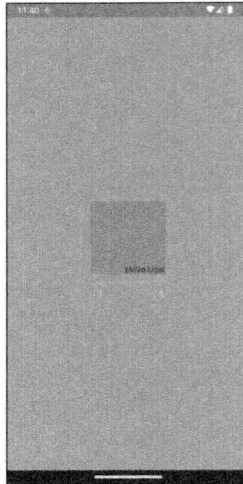

Figure 4.11: Alignment value (1,1)

Play with different values for better understanding. Here is the summary of how the Align widget works:

- **Alignment property**: The alignment property of the Align widget specifies the desired alignment of the child widget within the available space. It uses an Alignment object to define the alignment.

- **Available space**: The available space for the Align widget is determined by its parent widget or the overall layout constraints.

- **Child widget size**: The size of the child widget can be either restricted or unrestricted, depending on the constraints applied to it.

- **Positioning**: The Align widget positions the child widget within the available space based on the specified alignment. The child widget will be aligned according to the alignment property, relative to the available space.

- **Scaling**: If the child widget is smaller than the available space, the Align widget can also apply scaling to the child widget. The Align widget has a `widthFactor` and `heightFactor` property that can be used to scale the child widget within the available space.

Multi-child layout widgets

Multi-child layout widgets in Flutter are a category of widgets that can contain multiple child widgets and define their layout and positioning within a parent widget. These widgets allow you to create complex and dynamic UI structures by arranging multiple widgets in various ways.

Here are some commonly used multi-child layout widgets in Flutter:

Column

Column widget is responsible for arranging its children in a vertical column. We have already utilized it in our initial Flutter application, but now let us explore it more extensively. As we mentioned earlier, the Column widget can contain multiple child widgets. To enhance its functionality, we can leverage other widgets such as `SizedBox` widget to allocate specific sizes or spacing between the children and Expanded widget to allow a child to expand and occupy the available vertical space. Below is the structure of a column widget:

```
Column(
    mainAxisAlignment: mainAxisAlignment,
    crossAxisAlignment: crossAxisAlignment,
    children: children,
)
```

- **mainAxisAlignment**: Determines how the children are aligned vertically (along the main axis). It defaults to **MainAxisAlignment.start**.
- **crossAxisAlignment**: Determines how the children are aligned horizontally (along the cross axis). It defaults to **CrossAxisAlignment.center**
- **children**: A list of widgets that you want to display vertically in the column.

Let us examine an example that demonstrates these concepts:

```
1.  @override
2.    Widget build(BuildContext context) {
3.      return MaterialApp(
4.        debugShowCheckedModeBanner: false,
5.        home: Scaffold(
6.          backgroundColor: Colors.green,
7.          body: SafeArea(
```

```
8.              child: Column(
9.                verticalDirection: VerticalDirection.up,
10.               mainAxisAlignment: MainAxisAlignment.spaceAround,
11.               crossAxisAlignment: CrossAxisAlignment.end,
12.           children: [
13.             Container(
14.               color: Colors.orange,
15.               height: 100,
16.               width: 100
17.             ),
18.             const SizedBox(
19.               height: 20.0,
20.             ),
21.             Container(
22.                 color: Colors.blue,
23.                 height: 100,
24.                 width: 100
25.             ),
26.             const SizedBox(
27.               height: 20.0,
28.             ),
29.             Expanded(
30.               child: Container(
31.                   color: Colors.pink,
32.                   height: 100,
33.                   width: 100
34.               ),
35.             ),
36.             Container(
37.               width: double.infinity,
38.             )
39.           ],
40.         )),
41.       ),
```

```
42.      );
43.   }
```

Code 4.10: Column widget

Figure 4.12: Column widget

Let us discuss some important concepts in the code and how it works:

At *line number 8*, a column has been included as a child of the SafeArea. Line 12 represents the array of children for the column, arranging them vertically.

- At *line number* 9 of the code, we are specifying the **verticalDirection** for the Column widget. By default, the **verticalDirection** for a Column is set to "down", which means that it arranges its children from top to bottom in the same order as they are defined. However, in the given code snippet, we have explicitly set the **verticalDirection** to "up".

  As a result, the sequence of widgets is reversed. The last item in the array of widgets, which is the pink container, will appear as the first item on the screen. This reversal of the widget order is why the pink container is displayed at the top.

- At *line number 10* of the code, we are setting the **mainAxisAlignment** property for the Column widget. In a Column, the main axis represents the vertical space on the screen. By default, if we do not specify a **mainAxisAlignment**, the children widgets will be stacked vertically, one after the other.

  However, in the given code snippet, we have used **MainAxisAlignment. spaceAround**. This property ensures that the available space is evenly distributed around the widgets within the Column. As a result, the space between the widgets will be distributed evenly, creating equal spacing around each child widget. Try updating the **spaceAround** value to other available values and see how it affects the layout.

- At *line number 11* of the code, we are setting the **crossAxisAlignment** property for the Column widget. In a Column, the cross axis represents the horizontal space on the screen.

  To observe the effect of the **crossAxisAlignment**, we have added a Container with an Infinity width. This causes the Column to stretch and occupy the full available width on the screen. If we remove this widget, the width of the entire Column will be determined by the width of the widest child widget within it, typically set to 100.

- At the provided code, we have set the **crossAxisAlignment** to end. As a result, all the containers within the Column will be aligned to the right-hand side or the end of the horizontal direction. By default, the **crossAxisAlignment** is set to start, which aligns the children to the beginning or left-hand side of the horizontal direction.

- On *line number 18*, a **SizedBox** has been incorporated, commonly utilized for spacing between widgets. When employed inside a column, a height is assigned. For rows, a width value can be added to create space between children.

- At *line number 29*, we have surrounded our container inside an Expanded widget so that the container can get maximum available space. This is very useful when you add a listview to a column. As columns do not scroll, we must fix the height; otherwise, we may get an unbounded height error.

Now let us look at Row Widget.

Row

Row widget is very similar to column, the main difference is that row arranges its children in a horizontal column. So, for a row, x direction is the **mainAxis** and y is the cross axis. Keeping that in mind, let us take a challenge, and try to design the layout shown in the *Figure 4.13*:

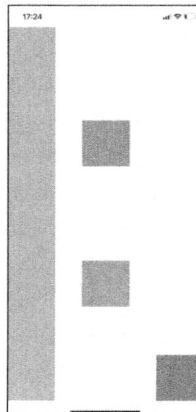

Figure 4.13: Assignment

Give the task a try and aim for success. If you haven't attempted it yet, it is recommended that you take a moment to try it on your own before referring to the provided solution code. This approach can enhance your learning speed. Once your code is ready, you can compare it with the provided solution:

```dart
1.  import 'package:flutter/material.dart';
2.
3.  void main() {
4.    runApp(const HelloApp());
5.  }
6.
7.  class HelloApp extends StatelessWidget {
8.    const HelloApp({super.key});
9.
10.   @override
11.   Widget build(BuildContext context) {
12.     return MaterialApp(
13.       debugShowCheckedModeBanner: false,
14.       home: Scaffold(
15.         backgroundColor: Colors.white,
16.         body: SafeArea(
17.           child: Row(
18.             crossAxisAlignment: CrossAxisAlignment.end,
19.             children: [
20.               Container(
21.                 color: Colors.orange,
22.                 height: double.infinity,
23.                 width: 100
24.               ),
25.               Expanded(
26.                 child: Column(
27.                   mainAxisAlignment: MainAxisAlignment.spaceEvenly,
28.                   children: [
29.                     Container(
30.                       color: Colors.blue,
31.                       height: 100,
```

```
32.                        width: 100
33.                     ),
34.                  Container(
35.                     color: Colors.green,
36.                     height: 100,
37.                     width: 100
38.                  ),
39.               ],
40.            ),
41.         ),
42.         Container(
43.            color: Colors.pink,
44.            height: 100,
45.            width: 100
46.         ),
47.       ],
48.    ),
49.   ),
50.  ),
51. );
52. }
53. }
```

Code 4.11: Solution for the assignment

Stack

The Stack widget in Flutter allows you to stack multiple child widgets on top of each other, giving you the flexibility to create complex and layered UI compositions. It positions its children relative to the edges of the stack or according to specific alignment and positioning parameters.

Here are some key points about the Stack widget:

- **Child stacking order**: The order in which you add the child widgets to the Stack determines their stacking order. The first child widget will be at the bottom, followed by the next child on top of it, and so on.

- **Alignment and positioning**: You can use properties like alignment, positioned, and fit to control the alignment and positioning of the child widgets within the stack. The alignment property allows you to align the children in the stack using Alignment values. The positioned property lets you explicitly position a child widget using Positioned widgets. The fit property controls how the child widgets are sized within the stack.

- **Overlapping widgets**: Child widgets in a Stack can overlap each other, allowing you to create visually interesting compositions. By adjusting the order of child widgets or using the positioned property, you can control which widget appears on top.

- **Size determination**: By default, the Stack sizes itself to accommodate its largest child. However, you can control the size of the Stack using constraints or by wrapping it in parent widgets like Container or SizedBox.

To understand better, go through this sample code and notice the resulting screen in below example:

```
1.  import 'package:flutter/material.dart';
2.
3.  void main() {
4.    runApp(const HelloApp());
5.  }
6.
7.  class HelloApp extends StatelessWidget {
8.    const HelloApp({super.key});
9.
10.   @override
11.   Widget build(BuildContext context) {
12.     return MaterialApp(
13.       debugShowCheckedModeBanner: false,
14.       home: Scaffold(
15.         backgroundColor: Colors.white,
16.         body: SafeArea(
17.           child: Center(
18.             child: Stack(
19.               alignment: AlignmentDirectional.bottomCenter,
20.               children: [
21.                 Container(color: Colors.orange, height: 140, width:
                      140),
22.                 Positioned(
```

```
23.                    top: 50,
24.                    left: 50,
25.                    child: Container(
26.                      width: 100,
27.                      height: 100,
28.                      color: Colors.blue,
29.                    ),
30.                  ),
31.                Container(color: Colors.pink, height: 60, width: 80),
32.              ],
33.            ),
34.          ),
35.        ),
36.      ),
37.    );
38.  }
39. }
```

Code 4.12: Stack widget example

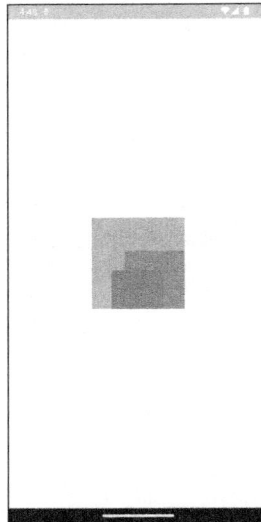

Figure 4.14: Stack widget

List View

So far, we have covered the multi child layout widgets where we are not expecting the contents to scroll, but in case we need a scrollable list of widgets, we should use list view. List view can scroll vertically or horizontally. Just replace your scaffold body with the below code and get the result as shown in *Figure 4.15*:

```
1.  SafeArea(
2.          child: Center(
3.            child: ListView(
4.              padding: const EdgeInsets.all(8),
5.              scrollDirection: Axis.horizontal,
6.              children: <Widget>[
7.                Container(
8.                  width: 230,
9.                  color: Colors.teal[600],
10.                  child: const Center(child: Text('Item 1')),
11.                ),
12.                Container(
13.                  width: 230,
14.                  color: Colors.yellow[200],
15.                  child: const Center(child: Text('Item 2')),
16.                ),
17.                Container(
18.                  width: 230,
19.                  color: Colors.blue[400],
20.                  child: const Center(child: Text('Item 3')),
21.                ),
22.              ],
23.            )
24.          ),
25.        ),
```

Code 4.13: ListView example

This list will scroll horizontally. You can play with code with the small modifications in scroll direction, change the colors and height and more:

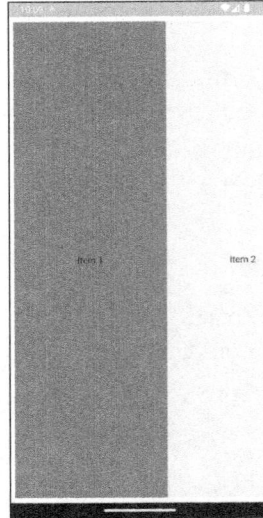

Figure 4.15: ListView Widget

The **ListView.builder** widget in Flutter allows you to create a scrollable list of items efficiently, especially when dealing with a large number of items. It creates and lazily builds the list items as they become visible on the screen, which helps optimize performance and memory usage.

The **ListView.builder** widget efficiently handles the creation and recycling of list items as they scroll off the screen, allowing you to build dynamic and efficient lists without having to create all the items upfront.

You can customize the appearance and behavior of each list item by modifying the widget returned inside the **itemBuilder** function.

Or you can use the **ListView.separated** widget in Flutter which is similar to **ListView.builder**, but it provides a built-in way to add separators between items in the list. This widget is useful when you want to display a list with distinct separators, such as dividing lines or custom widgets, between each item.

Here is an example of how to use **ListView.separated**:

```
1. ListView.separated(
2.            padding: const EdgeInsets.all(8),
3.           itemCount: 100, // The total number of items in the list
4.           itemBuilder: (BuildContext context, int index) {
5.              // itemBuilder is a callback function that builds
                 each item in the list
6.              // based on its index
```

```
7.
8.             // Return a widget for each item in the list
9.             return  Container(
10.               height: 50,
11.               color: Colors.teal[100],
12.               child: Center(child: Text('Entry $index')),
13.             );
14.           },
15.           separatorBuilder: (BuildContext context, int index) =>
               const Divider(),
16.         )
```

Code 4.14: *ListView.separted example*

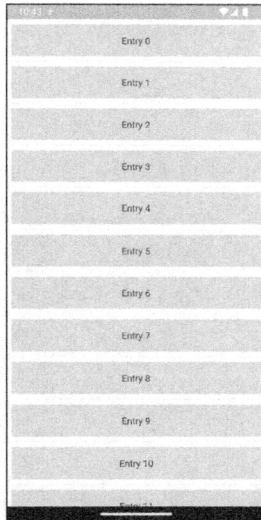

Figure 4.16: *ListView.separated*

GridView

GridView widget allows you to create a scrollable grid of items, similar to a table or a collection of cards. It provides a flexible way to display a collection of widgets in a grid layout, where items can be arranged in rows and columns.

Here is an example of how to use GridView:

```
1. GridView.count(
2.         crossAxisCount: 2, // Number of columns in the grid
```

```
3.          padding: const EdgeInsets.all(8),
4.          crossAxisSpacing: 10,
5.          mainAxisSpacing: 10,
6.          children: List.generate(
7.            10, // Total number of items in the grid
8.              (index) {
9.            return Container(
10.             color: Colors.blueGrey, // Example widget, replace
                with your own
11.             child: Center(
12.               child: Text('Item $index'),
13.             ),
14.           );
15.         },
16.       ),
17.     )
```

Code 4.15: GridView example

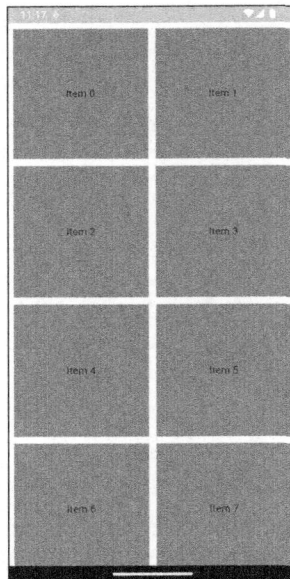

Figure 4.17: GridView example

There are a few other multi-child layout widgets; please go through the official documentation for the whole list.

Tab Bar

TabBar is a widget that displays a horizontal row of tabs. It is commonly used in combination with a **TabBarView** to create a tabbed interface, where each tab corresponds to a different content or view.

Here is an example of how to use **TabBar** and **TabBarView** together:

```
1.  DefaultTabController(
2.              length: 3, // Number of tabs
3.            child: Column(
4.             children: [
5.              TabBar(
6.                 indicatorColor: Colors.teal,
7.                 labelColor: Colors.blueGrey,
8.                 tabs: [
9.                  Tab(text: 'Tab 1'),
10.                 Tab(text: 'Tab 2'),
11.                 Tab(text: 'Tab 3'),
12.                ],
13.              ),
14.             Expanded(
15.               child: TabBarView(
16.                children: [
17.                  // Content for Tab 1
18.                  Center(
19.                    child: Text('Tab 1 Content'),
20.                  ),
21.                  // Content for Tab 2
22.                  Center(
23.                    child: Text('Tab 2 Content'),
24.                  ),
25.                  // Content for Tab 3
26.                  Center(
27.                    child: Text('Tab 3 Content'),
28.                  ),
29.                ],
```

```
30.                    ),
31.                  ),
32.              ],
33.            ),
34.          )
```

Code 4.16: TabBar example

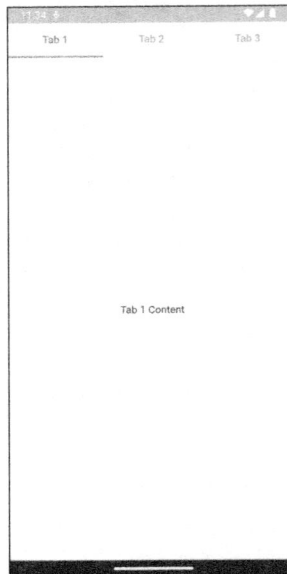

Figure 4.18: TabBar example

Sliver Widget

In Flutter, a *Sliver* refers to a portion of a scrollable area. Sliver widgets are specifically designed to work with scrollable views, such as **CustomScrollView**, **NestedScrollView**, or **SliverAppBar**. They provide flexible and powerful ways to build dynamic and efficient scrollable layouts.

Here are a few commonly used Sliver widgets in Flutter:

- **SliverAppBar**: This widget creates a flexible app bar that can expand and collapse as the user scrolls. It typically appears at the top of the scrollable area and can include titles, icons, and other interactive elements.

- **SliverList**: This widget creates a scrollable list of items. It lazily builds and displays only the items that are visible on the screen, which helps optimize performance and memory usage. You can use it to create a vertically scrollable list.

- **SliverGrid**: Similar to **SliverList**, this widget creates a scrollable grid of items. It lazily builds and displays only the items that are visible on the screen, allowing for efficient handling of large grids.

- **SliverFixedExtentList**: This widget creates a scrollable list of items with a fixed extent, meaning all items have the same height. It is useful when you have a list of items with consistent heights and want to optimize performance.

- **SliverPadding**: This widget adds padding around other sliver widgets. It's handy when you need to add spacing or insets to the content within a scrollable area.

These are just a few examples of Sliver widgets available in Flutter. Sliver widgets offer great flexibility in creating complex and efficient scrollable layouts. They allow you to build custom scrollable views tailored to your specific needs.

Here is an example that demonstrates the usage of **SliverAppBar**, **SliverList**, and **CustomScrollView**:

```
1.  CustomScrollView(
2.          slivers: [
3.            const SliverAppBar(
4.              title: Text('Sliver Example'),
5.              expandedHeight: 200,
6.              backgroundColor: Colors.teal,
7.            ),
8.            SliverList(
9.              delegate: SliverChildBuilderDelegate(
10.                (BuildContext context, int index) {
11.                  return Container(
12.                    height: 50,
13.                    color: Colors.teal[100],
14.                    child: Padding(
15.                      padding: const EdgeInsets.all(8.0),
16.                      child: Text('Entry $index'),
17.                    ),
18.                  );
19.                },
20.                childCount: 20,
21.              ),
22.            ),
```

```
23.                    ],
24.                ),
```

Code 4.17: *Slivers example*

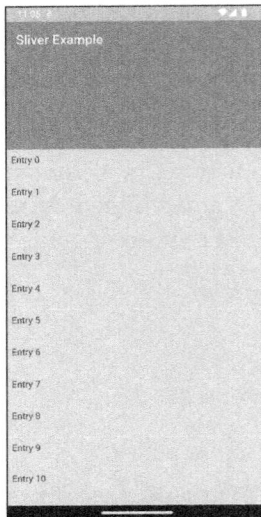

Figure 4.19: *Slivers example*

There are a few other widgets that are going to be useful in almost all apps. Let us go through them:

Asset image and network image widget

Images are a very important part of any mobile app; they make the app look better and more user-friendly. Let us see now how we can add an image widget to our app.

The terms *Asset Image* and *Network Image* are commonly used in the context of mobile and web application development when working with images.

Asset image

An asset image refers to an image file that is bundled and packaged with the application during the build process. These images are typically stored locally within the application's resources and can be accessed directly. Asset images are commonly used for static images, icons, logos, or any other visual elements that are part of the application's user interface.

To display an asset image in a user interface, you would typically use an appropriate widget provided by the framework or library you are using. For example, in Flutter (a popular UI framework), you can use the **Image.asset** widget to load and display an asset image. Here is an example of how you might use it:

```
1. Image.asset('assets/images/mastercard-logo.png')
```

Code 4.18: Image asset widget

In this example, **mastercard-logo.png** is the asset image file located in the assets/images directory of the project as shown below:

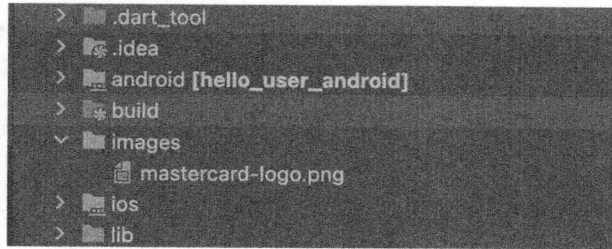

Figure 4.20: images folder

Along with this, there is one more additional important step, which is updating the **pubspec.yaml** file with the path for the image. There are two ways to do that. One is specifying the full path of the image as shown below:

```
1.    assets:
2.        - images/mastercard-logo.png
```

Code 4.19: Full image path

The above approach requires adding the full path for each image that is going to be used in the app, may not be practical when dealing with many images in a production-ready app. Instead, a more convenient alternative is to utilize an "images" folder, as demonstrated in the following code snippet:

```
1.    assets:
2.        - images/
```

Code 4.20: images path

Network image

A network image refers to an image that is loaded from a remote server or network location. Unlike asset images, network images are not bundled with the application and are fetched dynamically at runtime. They are commonly used to display images that are stored on a remote server, such as user-uploaded images or images fetched from an API.

To display a network image in a user interface, you would typically use a widget that supports loading images from a URL. Again, using Flutter as an example, you can use the **Image.network** widget to load and display a network image. Here is an example:

```
1.  Image.network('https://example.com/images/image.jpg')
```

Code 4.21: Network image widget

In this example, **https://example.com/images/image.jpg** is the URL of the network image you want to display.

Both asset images and network images are essential for displaying visual content in applications, but they differ in how the images are sourced and accessed.

Card Widget

A card widget is a user interface element commonly found in mobile and web applications. It displays information or content in a compact and visually appealing manner, resembling a physical card. Card widgets are often used to showcase snippets of information, such as a summary of an article, a product listing, or a contact card.

Key features of a card widget include:

- **Visual representation**: A card widget typically has a defined shape, such as a rectangle with rounded corners, resembling a physical card. It may include a background color or image to enhance its visual appeal.

- **Content display**: The card widget contains various elements to display relevant information, such as text, images, icons, buttons, and other interactive components. These elements are arranged within the card's boundaries to present a coherent and concise view.

- **Concise information**: Card widgets aim to provide a snapshot or summary of information, presenting only essential details at a glance. They often include a title, a brief description, and additional relevant data, depending on the context.

- **Interactivity**: Card widgets can be interactive, allowing users to perform actions like tapping, swiping, or clicking on different parts of the card to access further details or initiate specific actions.

- **Flexibility**: Card widgets can be used in various contexts and layouts, allowing them to adapt to different screen sizes and orientations. They can be displayed individually or grouped together in grids or lists.

Card widgets have become popular due to their versatility, usability, and visually appealing nature. They provide a convenient way to present information in a structured format, enabling users to quickly scan and interact with content on mobile devices and websites. For sample code please refer to the *Code 4.23*: Solution for the exercise, in line number 10 you can see we have added a card widget.

Inkwell widget

In *Code 4.23*, on *line 14* we have added an Inkwell widget. **InkWell** is a widget that provides a visual touch response to user input. It is commonly used to wrap other widgets to make them interactive and respond to taps, long presses, and other gestures. When a user interacts with the **InkWell**, it displays ink splash effects and triggers the specified callbacks.

In the solution, the **InkWell** is wrapping a **SizeBox** widget. The **onTap** property specifies the callback function to execute when the **InkWell** is tapped. In this case, it prints a message "card tapped." to the console.

You can customize the appearance of the **InkWell** and its ink effects using various properties such as **highlightColor**, **splashColor**, radius, and more . These properties allow you to define how the **InkWell** responds visually to different user gestures.

In *Code 4.23*, at line 30, certain text styling has been implemented, called widget styling. Let us now discuss the concept.

Widget styling

In Flutter, widget styling can be achieved using various properties and techniques. Here are some common approaches to styling widgets:

- **Text styling:**
  - **style property**: It allows you to define the text style for widgets like Text and TextField.
  - **TextStyle class**: You can create a **TextStyle** object with properties like **fontSize**, **color**, **fontWeight**, and more, and apply it to the desired widgets, as shown in code 4.23, at line 30.
- **Container styling:**
  - **decoration property**: It allows you to apply background colors, borders, gradients, and more, to the Container widget.
  - **padding property**: It specifies the padding around the container's content.
  - **margin property**: It sets the margin around the container.
- **Button styling:**
  - **FlatButton, RaisedButton, ElevatedButton, and so on**: These button widgets have properties like **color**, **textColor**, **disabledColor**, and so on, to customize their appearance.
  - **ButtonStyle class**: It provides more advanced customization options for buttons, such as defining custom button themes and states.

- **Box styling:**
  - o **SizedBox widget**: It allows you to set fixed dimensions (width and height) for spacing purposes.
  - o **AspectRatio widget**: It maintains a specific aspect ratio for its child widget.
  - o **Expanded widget**: It expands its child to fill the available space within a Row, Column, or Flex.
- **Theme styling:**
  - o **Theme widget**: It enables you to define a theme for your app, specifying properties like colors, fonts, and styles, which are automatically applied to the relevant widgets.
  - o **ThemeData class**: It represents the visual styling for a theme and allows you to define properties like `primaryColor`, `textTheme`, and more. For better understanding and practical example, please refer to the *Code 4.31*: Bottom Sheet widget, line number 12.
- **Custom styling:**
  - o You can create custom styles by defining your own classes that extend existing widgets or by using composition.
  - o Container, Row, Column, and Stack are commonly used for composing custom layouts.

Remember to explore the available properties and options for each widget you want to style, as they may vary depending on the widget's purpose and functionality. Flutter provides extensive documentation and examples to guide you in styling your widgets effectively.

Stateless and stateful widgets

In Flutter, there are two types of widgets: stateless widgets and stateful widgets. Understanding the differences between these two widget types is important for building Flutter applications.

Stateless Widgets:
- A stateless widget is immutable, meaning its properties cannot change once it's built.
- The `build()` method of a stateless widget defines the widget's UI based on the provided properties.
- Stateless widgets are used when the UI does not need to change dynamically based on user interactions or external data.

In our previous chapter we started our very own app let us look at it again:

```dart
1.  import 'package:flutter/material.dart';
2.
3.  void main() {
4.    runApp(const HelloApp());
5.  }
6.
7.  class HelloApp extends StatelessWidget {
8.    const HelloApp({Key? key}) : super(key: key);
9.
10.   @override
11.   Widget build(BuildContext context) {
12.     void submitButtonPressed() {
13.       // Add button click logic here
14.       print('Submit button pressed!');
15.     }
16.
17.     return MaterialApp(
18.       home: Scaffold(
19.         appBar: AppBar(
20.           title: const Text('Hello User'),
21.         ),
22.         body: Padding(
23.           padding: const EdgeInsets.all(16.0),
24.           child: Column(
25.             crossAxisAlignment: CrossAxisAlignment.start,
26.             children: [
27.               const Text(
28.                 'Welcome User',
29.                 style: TextStyle(fontSize: 24),
30.               ),
31.               const SizedBox(height: 16),
32.               const TextField(
33.                 decoration: InputDecoration(
```

```
34.                    labelText: 'Enter your name',
35.                  ),
36.                ),
37.              const SizedBox(height: 16),
38.              ElevatedButton(
39.                onPressed: submitButtonPressed,
40.                child: const Text('Submit'),
41.              ),
42.            ],
43.          ),
44.        ),
45.      ),
46.    );
47.  }
48. }
```

Code 4.24: Stateless widget

It is the same code, we have just moved the Material app to a separate widget into a new stateless widget HelloApp and returning it from **runApp**. In this case, we have used a **StatelessWidget** as we are not updating anything on user action or we can say the state of the widget does not change. But if we would like to update the text with the submitted button tapped then we need a stateful widget.

Stateful Widgets:

- A stateful widget is mutable, meaning it can change its internal state during its lifetime.
- The **StatefulWidget** class is paired with a separate **State** class that holds the mutable state data.
- The **build()** method of the **StatefulWidget** is responsible for building the widget based on the current state.
- Stateful widgets are used when the UI needs to update dynamically based on user interactions or external data.

```
1.  import 'package:flutter/material.dart';
2.
3.  void main() {
4.    runApp(const HelloApp());
5.  }
```

```
6.
7.   // Define a stateful widget called HelloApp
8.   class HelloApp extends StatefulWidget {
9.     const HelloApp({Key? key}) : super(key: key);
10.
11.    // Create a corresponding state for HelloApp
12.    @override
13.    State<HelloApp> createState() => _HelloAppState();
14.  }
15.
16.  // State class for HelloApp
17.  class _HelloAppState extends State<HelloApp> {
18.    // Define a variable to store the username
19.    String userName = 'User';
20.
21.    // Create a TextEditingController to control the text input field
22.    final TextEditingController _textEditingController =
         TextEditingController();
23.
24.    // Dispose method to clean up resources
25.    @override
26.    void dispose() {
27.      _textEditingController.dispose();
28.      super.dispose();
29.    }
30.
31.    // Method to update the username when the submit button is pressed
32.    void submitButtonPressed() {
33.      setState(() {
34.        userName = _textEditingController.text;
35.      });
36.    }
37.
38.    // Build method to construct the UI
```

```
39.   @override
40.   Widget build(BuildContext context) {
41.     return MaterialApp(
42.       home: Scaffold(
43.         appBar: AppBar(
44.           title: const Text('Hello User'),
45.         ),
46.         body: Padding(
47.           padding: const EdgeInsets.all(16.0),
48.           child: Column(
49.             crossAxisAlignment: CrossAxisAlignment.start,
50.             children: [
51.               // Display a welcome message with the username
52.               Text(
53.                 'Welcome $userName',
54.                 style: const TextStyle(fontSize: 24),
55.               ),
56.               const SizedBox(height: 16),
57.               // Text input field for entering the username
58.               TextField(
59.                 controller: _textEditingController,
60.                 decoration: const InputDecoration(
61.                   labelText: 'Enter your name',
62.                 ),
63.               ),
64.               const SizedBox(height: 16),
65.               // Submit button to update the username
66.               ElevatedButton(
67.                 onPressed: submitButtonPressed,
68.                 child: const Text('Submit'),
69.               ),
70.             ],
71.           ),
72.         ),
```

```
73.        ),
74.     );
75.  }
76. }
```

Code 4.25: Stateful widget

In the code above, we have transformed our previous stateless widget into a stateful widget. The build method remains mostly the same, but now we have a new State class declared on line number 14, which allows us to manage the application's state. When a value needs to be dynamically updated, we use the **setState** method. In line number 25, we have used **setState** to update the value of 'username'. Whenever **setState** is called, it triggers the build method, causing the compiler to rebuild the widgets that rely on the 'username' value. In our case the text widget is using username value, so that will be rebuilt on update of 'username'. There is a small update on the **Textfield** widget as we need the value entered on **textfield** we have declared a **TextEditingController** outside of build method, which we can access **fromsubmitButtonPressed** method.

TextEditingController class is used to manage the text entered by the user in a text field or text input widget. It allows us to control and manipulate the text programmatically.

To use the **TextEditingController** in Flutter, follow these steps:

- Declare a **TextEditingController** variable in your widget's state class:

  TextEditingController _textEditingController = TextEditingController();

- Assign the TextEditingController to the text field or text input widget:

  TextField(controller: _textEditingController, // other properties)

- Access the text value entered by the user:

  String text = _textEditingController.text;

- Modify the text programmatically:

  _textEditingController.text = 'New text value';

- Dispose of the TextEditingController to avoid memory leaks:

  @override void dispose() {

      _textEditingController.dispose();

  super.dispose();

  }

By using the **TextEditingController**, you can easily retrieve and manipulate the text entered by the user in real-time, allowing for dynamic interactions and validations within your Flutter app.

Material and Cupertino widgets

In Flutter, the Material and Cupertino widgets are two different design systems that we can use to create user interfaces with different visual styles. Here is an overview of each:

Material widgets

Material widgets follow the Material Design guidelines created by Google, providing a modern and visually appealing UI. To use Material widgets, we need to import the **material.dart** package.

Some commonly used Material widgets include **AppBar**, **Button**, **Card**, **TextField**, **SnackBar**, and more. Material widgets are typically used for Android-like UIs but can also be used for cross-platform apps.

Example usage of Material widgets:

```
1.  import 'package:flutter/material.dart';
2.
3.  void main() {
4.    runApp(const HelloApp());
5.  }
6.  class HelloApp extends StatelessWidget {
7.    const HelloApp({super.key});
8.    @override
9.    Widget build(BuildContext context) {
10.    return MaterialApp(
11.      home: Scaffold(
12.        appBar: AppBar(
13.          title: Text('Material App'),
14.        ),
15.        body: Center(
16.          child: ElevatedButton(
17.            child: Text('Button'),
18.            onPressed: () {
19.              // Button press logic
20.            },
21.          ),
22.        ),
```

```
23.        ),
24.      );
25.    }
26. }
```

Code 4.26: Material widget

Cupertino widgets

Cupertino widgets provide the iOS-specific visual style inspired by Apple's Human Interface Guidelines. To use Cupertino widgets, you need to import the **cupertino.dart** package. Some commonly used Cupertino widgets include **CupertinoNavigationBar**, **CupertinoButton**, **CupertinoTextField**, **CupertinoActivityIndicator**, and more. Cupertino widgets are typically used for iOS-like UIs but can also be used for cross-platform apps.

Example usage of Cupertino widgets:

```
1. import 'package:flutter/cupertino.dart';
2. void main() {
3.   runApp(const HelloApp());
4. }
5. class HelloApp extends StatelessWidget {
6.   const HelloApp({super.key});
7.   @override
8.   Widget build(BuildContext context) {
9.     return CupertinoApp(
10.      home: CupertinoPageScaffold(
11.        navigationBar: const CupertinoNavigationBar(
12.          middle: Text('Cupertino App'),
13.        ),
14.        child: Center(
15.          child: CupertinoButton(
16.            child: const Text('Button'),
17.            onPressed: () {
18.              // Button press logic
19.            },
20.          ),
```

```
21.          ),
22.        ),
23.      );
24.  }
25. }
```

Code 4.27: Cupertino widget

Divider widget

The Divider widget in Flutter is used to create a horizontal line that visually separates content. It is commonly used to add visual distinction between different sections of a user interface.

Here is an example of using the Divider widget in Flutter:

```
1.  import 'package:flutter/material.dart';
2.
3.  void main() {
4.    runApp(const MyWidget());
5.  }
6.
7.  class MyWidget extends StatelessWidget {
8.    const MyWidget({super.key});
9.
10.   @override
11.   Widget build(BuildContext context) {
12.     return MaterialApp(
13.       home: Directionality(
14.         textDirection: TextDirection.ltr, // Set the desired text
                direction
15.         child: Scaffold(
16.           appBar: AppBar(
17.             title: const Text('My App'),
18.           ),
19.           body: const Column(
20.             children: [
21.               Text('Section 1'),
```

```
22.              Divider(),
23.              Text('Section 2'),
24.           ],
25.         ),
26.       ),
27.     ),
28.   );
29. }
30.}
```

Code 4.28: Divider widget

Slider widget

The Slider widget in Flutter is used to create a horizontal slider control that allows users to select a value from a continuous range. It is commonly used for scenarios where you need to capture a numeric input or allow users to adjust a setting within a specific range.

Here is an example of using the Slider widget in Flutter:

```
1.   @override
2.   Widget build(BuildContext context) {
3.     return MaterialApp(
4.       home: Scaffold(
5.         appBar: AppBar(
6.           title: const Text('Slider Example'),
7.         ),
8.         body: Center(
9.           child: Material(
10.            child: Slider(
11.              value: _sliderValue,
12.              onChanged: (newValue) {
13.                setState(() {
14.                  _sliderValue = newValue;
15.                });
16.              },
17.            ),
18.          ),
```

```
19.            ),
20.          ),
21.        );
22.      }
```

Code 4.29: Slider widget

To make the above code work, you need to implement a Stateful widget and define the **_sliderValue** variable within its state. **_sliderValue** is used to hold the current value of the slider. This variable is updated whenever the slider value changes.

DropdownButton widget

To create a dropdown button in Flutter, you can use the **DropdownButton** widget provided by the Flutter framework. To do so, follow these steps:

1. Define a list of items for the dropdown menu
2. Declare a variable to keep track of the currently selected item
3. Use the **DropdownButton** widget in your Flutter widget tree

Here is an example of using the **DropdownButton** widget:

```
1.  class MyDropdownButtonWidget extends StatefulWidget {
2.    const MyDropdownButtonWidget({super.key});
3.
4.    @override
5.    State<MyDropdownButtonWidget> createState() => _
      MyDropdownButtonWidgetState();
6.  }
7.
8.  class _MyDropdownButtonWidgetState extends
    State<MyDropdownButtonWidget> {
9.    List<String> items = ['Item 1', 'Item 2', 'Item 3'];
10.   String? selectedItem;
11.
12.   @override
13.   Widget build(BuildContext context) {
14.     return MaterialApp(
15.       home: Scaffold(
16.         appBar: AppBar(
```

```
17.          title: const Text('Dropdown Button Example'),
18.        ),
19.      body: Directionality(
20.        textDirection: TextDirection.ltr,
21.        child: Center(
22.          child: DropdownButton<String>(
23.            value: selectedItem,
24.            onChanged: (String? newValue) {
25.              setState(() {
26.                selectedItem = newValue;
27.              });
28.            },
29.            items: items.map((String item) {
30.              return DropdownMenuItem<String>(
31.                value: item,
32.                child: Text(item),
33.              );
34.            }).toList(),
35.          ),
36.        ),
37.      ),
38.      ),
39.    );
40.  }
41. }
```

Code 4.30: DropdownButton widget

In this example, the **DropdownButton** widget takes several parameters:

- value represents the currently selected item.
- **onChanged** is a callback function that will be triggered when the selected item changes.
- items is a list of dropdown menu items. Here, we are using the map function to convert each item in the items list to a **DropdownMenuItem** widget.

When the user selects an item from the dropdown menu, the **onChanged** callback will be called, and the selected item will be updated in the **selectedItem** variable. By wrapping the **DropdownButton** widget in a **StatefulWidget**, you can use **setState** to trigger a rebuild of the widget when the selected item changes.

This is a basic example, and you can customize the appearance and behavior of the dropdown button further based on your requirements.

Bottom sheet Widget

To create a bottom sheet in Flutter, you can use the **showModalBottomSheet** function provided by the Flutter framework. Here is an example of how you can use it:

```
1. import 'package:flutter/material.dart';
2.
3. void main() => runApp(const MyApp());
4.
5. class MyApp extends StatelessWidget {
6.   const MyApp({Key? key}) : super(key: key);
7.
8.   @override
9.   Widget build(BuildContext context) {
10.    return MaterialApp(
11.      title: 'Bottom Sheet Demo',
12.      theme: ThemeData(
13.        primarySwatch: Colors.blue,
14.      ),
15.      home: BottomSheetPage(title: 'Flutter Bottom sheet', key:
         UniqueKey()),
16.    );
17.  }
18. }
19.
20. class BottomSheetPage extends StatelessWidget {
21.   const BottomSheetPage({required Key key, required this.title}) :
      super(key: key);
22.   final String title;
23.
24.   void _settingModalBottomSheet(context) {
25.     showModalBottomSheet(
```

```
26.        context: context,
27.        builder: (BuildContext bc) {
28.          return Wrap(
29.            children: <Widget>[
30.              ListTile(
31.                 leading: const Icon(Icons.male),
32.                 title: const Text('Male'),
33.                 onTap: () {
34.                   // Handle male tile tap here
35.                 },
36.              ),
37.              ListTile(
38.                 leading: const Icon(Icons.female),
39.                 title: const Text('Female'),
40.                 onTap: () {
41.                   // Handle female tile tap here
42.                 },
43.              ),
44.            ],
45.          );
46.        },
47.      );
48.  }
49.
50.  @override
51.  Widget build(BuildContext context) {
52.    return Scaffold(
53.      appBar: AppBar(
54.        title: Text(title),
55.      ),
56.      body: Center(
57.        child: ElevatedButton(
58.          onPressed: () {
59.            _settingModalBottomSheet(context);
```

```
60.            },
61.            child: const Text('Open Bottom Sheet'),
62.          ),
63.        ),
64.      );
65.    }
66. }
```

Code 4.31: Bottom Sheet widget

The **showModalBottomSheet** function handles the presentation of the bottom sheet with animation and allows users to dismiss it by tapping outside the sheet or swiping it down.

Please note that the **showModalBottomSheet** function should be called within a **BuildContext** that has a material ancestor. In the example above, we wrap the Scaffold widget with the **MaterialApp** widget to provide the material ancestor context.

ListTile Widget

The ListTile widget in Flutter is a convenient way to create a single row or item in a list. It typically includes an optional leading or trailing icon, as well as a title and subtitle. Here is an example of how we can use the ListTile widget:

```
1.  import 'package:flutter/material.dart';
2.
3.  class MyListTileExample extends StatelessWidget {
4.    const MyListTileExample({super.key});
5.
6.    @override
7.    Widget build(BuildContext context) {
8.      return Scaffold(
9.        appBar: AppBar(
10.         title: const Text('ListTile Example'),
11.       ),
12.       body: ListView(
13.         children: <Widget>[
14.           ListTile(
15.             leading: const Icon(Icons.person),
16.             title: const Text('John Doe'),
```

```
17.              subtitle: const Text('johndoe@example.com'),
18.              trailing: const Icon(Icons.arrow_forward),
19.              onTap: () {
20.                 // Handle tile tap here
21.                },
22.            ),
23.          ListTile(
24.            leading: const Icon(Icons.person),
25.            title: const Text('Jane Smith'),
26.            subtitle: const Text('janesmith@example.com'),
27.            trailing: const Icon(Icons.arrow_forward),
28.            onTap: () {
29.                // Handle tile tap here
30.                },
31.            ),
32.          // Add more ListTile widgets as needed
33.        ],
34.      ),
35.    );
36.  }
37. }
38.
39. void main() {
40.   runApp(const MyApp());
41. }
42.
43. class MyApp extends StatelessWidget {
44.   const MyApp({super.key});
45.
46.   @override
47.   Widget build(BuildContext context) {
48.     return const MaterialApp(
49.       title: 'ListTile Example',
50.       home: MyListTileExample(),
```

```
51.    );
52.  }
53.}
```

Code 4.32: ListTile widget

In this example, we create a **ListView** to display a list of **ListTile** widgets. Each **ListTile** represents an item in the list and includes properties such as leading, title, subtitle, trailing, and **onTap**.

The leading property allows you to specify an icon or widget to display on the left side of the **ListTile**. The title and subtitle properties define the main text and optional secondary text of the **ListTile**, respectively. The trailing property can be used to display an icon or widget on the right side of the **ListTile**.

You can handle the tap event on a **ListTile** by providing an **onTap** callback. In the example, the onTap callback is empty, but you can add your own logic to handle the tile tap.

Try to customize the example by adding more **ListTile** widgets or modifying the properties according to your requirements.

Animations in Flutter

Flutter provides a variety of options for adding animations to your applications. Here are some commonly used animation techniques in Flutter:

- **Implicit animations with AnimatedContainer**: The **AnimatedContainer** widget allows you to animate changes to its properties automatically. For example, you can animate the size, color, or position of a container. When you modify the properties, the widget will automatically animate the transition between the old and new values.

- **Explicit animations with AnimationController**: The **AnimationController** class allows you to create explicit animations by controlling the animation's progress manually. You can define the animation duration, set up animation listeners, and interpolate values between animation states. By calling **controller.forward()** or **controller.reverse()**, you can start or reverse the animation.

- **Tween animations**: Flutter provides Tween classes (for example, **Tween<double>**, **Tween<Color>**) that interpolate values between two endpoints. By using a Tween along with an **AnimationController**, you can create custom animations for properties like opacity, position, or scale.

- **Hero animations**: Hero animations create smooth transitions between two widgets across different screens. It is commonly used to animate a widget from one screen to another, such as a thumbnail image expanding to fill the entire screen. By wrapping the widgets in Hero widgets and providing matching tag values, Flutter will automatically animate the transition.

- **AnimatedBuilder**: The `AnimatedBuilder` widget is useful when you want to create complex animations or animate multiple properties simultaneously. It allows you to define custom animations using a builder function that runs on each frame update. The `AnimatedBuilder` widget reduces the boilerplate code required for animations by separating the animation logic from the UI.
- **Flare animations**: Flutter integrates with Flare, a powerful vector animation tool. Flare animations are created in external design tools and imported into Flutter. They can be used to create complex and interactive animations, including character animations, particle effects, and more.

These are just a few examples of the animation capabilities in Flutter. Flutter provides a rich set of APIs and widgets for creating smooth and engaging animations in your applications. You can explore the Flutter documentation and packages like **flutter_animation_builder** and rive (Flare) for more advanced animation techniques and examples.

Remember to import the necessary packages and use **setState()** or a **StatefulWidget** to trigger the rebuild of UI elements when animating properties.

Here is an example of how you can use an **AnimatedContainer** widget to animate the color and size of a container:

```
1.  import 'package:flutter/material.dart';
2.
3.  class AnimatedContainerExample extends StatefulWidget {
4.     const AnimatedContainerExample({super.key});
5.
6.     @override
7.     State<AnimatedContainerExample> createState() =>
8.         _AnimatedContainerExampleState();
9.  }
10.
11. class _AnimatedContainerExampleState extends
       State<AnimatedContainerExample> {
12.   bool isToggled = false;
13.
14.   void toggleContainer() {
15.     setState(() {
16.       isToggled = !isToggled;
17.     });
18.   }
```

```
19.
20.    @override
21.    Widget build(BuildContext context) {
22.      return Scaffold(
23.        appBar: AppBar(
24.          title: const Text('AnimatedContainer Example'),
25.        ),
26.        body: Center(
27.          child: GestureDetector(
28.            onTap: toggleContainer,
29.            child: AnimatedContainer(
30.              duration: const Duration(seconds: 1),
31.              width: isToggled ? 200.0 : 100.0,
32.              height: isToggled ? 200.0 : 100.0,
33.              color: isToggled ? Colors.blue : Colors.red,
34.              curve: Curves.easeInOut,
35.            ),
36.          ),
37.        ),
38.      );
39.    }
40. }
41.
42. void main() {
43.   runApp(const MyApp());
44. }
45.
46. class MyApp extends StatelessWidget {
47.   const MyApp({super.key});
48.
49.   @override
50.   Widget build(BuildContext context) {
51.     return const MaterialApp(
52.       title: 'AnimatedContainer Example',
```

```
53.      home: AnimatedContainerExample(),
54.    );
55.  }
56. }
```

Code 4.33: Flutter animation using AnimatedContainer

In this example, we have a simple **AnimatedContainer** that toggles its width, height, and color when tapped. The **isToggled boolean** variable is used to keep track of the container state.

When the container is tapped, the **toggleContainer** function is called, which triggers a call to **setState** and updates the value of **isToggled**. The **setState** call triggers a rebuild, and since the properties of the **AnimatedContainer** are tied to **isToggled**, the container animates smoothly between the old and new values.

The duration property specifies the duration of the animation, while the curve property defines the easing curve for the animation.

To use the Tween class for animations in Flutter, you will typically need to use it in conjunction with an **AnimationController**. Here is an example of how you can use Tween to animate the opacity of a widget:

```
1.  import 'package:flutter/material.dart';
2.
3.  class TweenAnimationExample extends StatefulWidget {
4.    const TweenAnimationExample({super.key});
5.
6.    @override
7.    State<TweenAnimationExample> createState() => _
       TweenAnimationExampleState();
8.  }
9.
10. class _TweenAnimationExampleState extends State<TweenAnimationExample>
11.     with SingleTickerProviderStateMixin {
12.   AnimationController? _animationController;
13.   Animation<double>? _animation;
14.
15.   @override
16.   void initState() {
17.     super.initState();
```

```
18.     _animationController = AnimationController(
19.       vsync: this,
20.       duration: const Duration(seconds: 2),
21.     );
22.
23.     final tween = Tween<double>(begin: 0.0, end: 1.0);
24.     _animation = tween.animate(_animationController!);
25.
26.     _animationController!.forward();
27.   }
28.
29.   @override
30.   void dispose() {
31.     _animationController!.dispose();
32.     super.dispose();
33.   }
34.
35.   @override
36.   Widget build(BuildContext context) {
37.     return Scaffold(
38.       appBar: AppBar(
39.         title: const Text('Tween Animation Example'),
40.       ),
41.       body: Center(
42.         child: FadeTransition(
43.           opacity: _animation!,
44.           child: Container(
45.             width: 200,
46.             height: 200,
47.             color: Colors.blue,
48.           ),
49.         ),
50.       ),
51.     );
```

```
52.   }
53. }
54.
55. void main() {
56.   runApp(const MyApp());
57. }
58.
59. class MyApp extends StatelessWidget {
60.   const MyApp({super.key});
61.
62.   @override
63.   Widget build(BuildContext context) {
64.     return const MaterialApp(
65.       title: 'Tween Animation Example',
66.       home: TweenAnimationExample(),
67.     );
68.   }
69. }
```

Code 4.34: Flutter animation using Tween

In this example, we use a **Tween<double>** to interpolate values between the initial and final states of the animation. We define the Tween with a starting value (begin) of 0.0 and an ending value (end) of 1.0, representing the range of opacity we want to animate.

Inside the **initState** method, we create an **AnimationController** with a specified duration. We then create an animation instance using the Tween and the animate method of the **AnimationController**. Finally, we start the animation by calling forward() on the **AnimationController**.

In the build method, we use the **FadeTransition** widget, which takes an Animation<double> and applies the animation to the opacity of its child. The Container is wrapped with **FadeTransition**, and its opacity will be animated according to the Tween and the current animation value.

Remember to dispose of the **AnimationController** in the dispose method to prevent memory leaks.

This example demonstrates a simple opacity animation using Tween. You can apply the same concept to other properties such as position, scale, or color by using different Tween types (**Tween<Color>**, **Tween<Offset>**, and more) and updating the respective properties of the animated widget.

Conclusion

This chapter has provided an in-depth exploration of various Flutter widgets, covering both single-child and multi-child layout widgets. Notable topics include the versatile Container and SafeArea widgets, the flexibility offered by Margin and Padding, and the alignment options using Main Axis and Cross Axis Alignment. The discussion extends to multi-child layout widgets such as Column, Row, Stack, List View, Grid View, and Tab Bar, offering a comprehensive understanding of their functionalities.

Additionally, the chapter delves into the Sliver widget, Asset Image, and Network Image widgets, as well as the Card and InkWell widgets. Widget styling has been introduced, shedding light on text styling techniques. The distinction between Stateless and Stateful widgets is clarified, and both Material and Cupertino widgets are explored. The chapter rounds off with a look at Divider, Slider, Dropdown Button, Bottom Sheet, ListTile, and the incorporation of animations in Flutter. This comprehensive coverage serves as a solid foundation for mastering widget usage in Flutter app development.

Multiple choice questions

1. **Which widget is commonly used to display a large number of items efficiently in a scrollable list?**

   a. Card

   b. ListView

   c. Container

   d. Text

2. **What is the purpose of the AppBar widget in a Flutter app?**

   a. Display text on the screen

   b. Allow users to input text

   c. Provide a basic layout structure

   d. Represent the top app bar

3. **Which widget allows users to select one option from a list or dropdown menu?**

   a. TextField

   b. RaisedButton

   c. DropdownButton

   d. ListTile

4. **What is the role of the ElevatedButton widget in Flutter?**

   a. Display a raised button with an elevation effect

   b. Show an icon with an elevated appearance

   c. Create a drop-down menu

   d. Provide a text input field

5. **Which widget is used to customize the visual appearance and layout properties of its child widget?**

   a. Container

   b. Scaffold

   c. ListTile

   d. ListView

6. What does the Text widget in Flutter do?

   a. Display an image on the screen

   b. Allow users to input text

   c. Create a button with text

   d. Display text on the screen

7. **Which widget is used to load images from local assets or network URLs in Flutter?**

   a. Card

   b. TextField

   c. Image

   d. ListTile

8. **What is the purpose of the FloatingActionButton widget in Flutter?**

   a. Create a floating action button with an icon

   b. Display a list of options when pressed

   c. Allow users to input text

   d. Show a floating container with custom content

9. **Which widget is used to create a dropdown or selection menu in Flutter?**

   a. Card

   b. TextField

   c. DropdownButton

   d. ListTile

10. **What is the purpose of the ListTile widget in Flutter?**

    a. Display an image on the screen

    b. Create a button with text

    c. Represent a single row or item in a list.

    d. Allow users to select multiple options

Answer

1. b. ListView
2. d. Represent the top app bar
3. c. DropdownButton
4. a. Display a raised button with an elevation effect
5. a. Container
6. d. Display text on the screen
7. c. Image
8. a. Create a floating action button with an icon
9. c. DropdownButton
10. c. Represent a single row or item in a list

Exercises

With the knowledge you have gained so far, try to achieve this resulting screen.

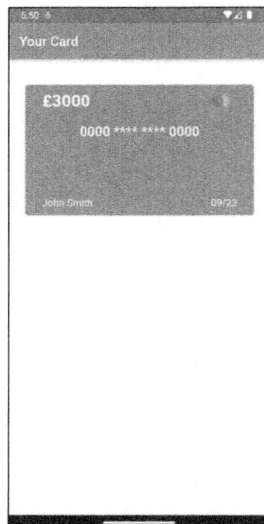

Figure 4.21: exercise screen

The most effective learning approach involves initially trying to create the layout, encountering challenges, and learning from the experience.

Now, let us proceed to review the solution:

```
1.    Widget build(BuildContext context) {
2.      return MaterialApp(
3.        debugShowCheckedModeBanner: false,
4.        home: Scaffold(
5.          backgroundColor: Colors.white,
6.          appBar: AppBar(
7.            title: const Text('Your Card'),
8.          ),
9.          body: SafeArea(
10.           child: Card(
11.             margin: const EdgeInsets.symmetric(vertical: 40,
                  horizontal: 25),
12.             clipBehavior: Clip.hardEdge,
13.             color: Colors.teal,
14.             child: InkWell(
15.               splashColor: Colors.blue.withAlpha(30),
16.               onTap: () {
17.                 debugPrint('Card tapped.');
18.               },
19.               child: SizedBox(
20.                 width: double.infinity,
21.                 height: 200,
22.                 child: Padding(
23.                   padding: const EdgeInsets.symmetric(vertical: 10,
                      horizontal: 25),
24.                   child: Column(
25.                     children: [
26.                       Row(
27.                         children: [
28.                           const Text(
29.                             '£3000',
```

```
30.              style: TextStyle(
31.                fontSize: 25,
32.                color: Colors.white,
33.                fontWeight: FontWeight.bold,
34.              ),
35.            ),
36.            const Expanded(
37.              child: SizedBox(height: 10),
38.            ),
39.            Image.asset('images/mastercard-logo.png',
                 height: 30, width: 50,),
40.          ],
41.        ),
42.        const SizedBox(height: 20),
43.        const Text(
44.          '0000 **** **** 0000',
45.          style: TextStyle(
46.            fontSize: 20,
47.            color: Colors.white,
48.            fontWeight: FontWeight.bold,
49.          ),
50.        ),
51.        const Expanded(
52.          child: SizedBox(width: 10),
53.        ),
54.        const Row(
55.          children: [
56.            Text(
57.              'John Smith',
58.              style: TextStyle(
59.                fontSize: 15,
60.                color: Colors.white,
61.              ),
62.            ),
```

```
63.                     Expanded(
64.                       child: SizedBox(height: 10),
65.                     ),
66.                     Text(
67.                       '09/23',
68.                       style: TextStyle(
69.                         fontSize: 15,
70.                         color: Colors.white,
71.                       ),
72.                     ),
73.                   ],
74.                 ),
75.               ],
76.             ),
77.           ),
78.         ),
79.       ),
80.     ),
81.   ),
82.   ),
83.   );
84. }
```

Code 4.23: Solution for the exercise

Now, let us delve into the topics that we haven't covered yet. On, line number 10, we have added a Card widget. You may have considered using a container instead, but the design necessitates rounded corners and a shadow effect, both of which can be easily achieved with a Card widget.

Join our book's Discord space

Join the book's Discord Workspace for Latest updates, Offers, Tech happenings around the world, New Release and Sessions with the Authors:

https://discord.bpbonline.com

CHAPTER 5
Prep Up with Advanced Flutter

Introduction

Welcome to the *Prep Up with Advanced Flutter* chapter! In this exciting section of our comprehensive training program, we will take your Flutter development journey to new heights. If you have already grasped the fundamentals of Flutter and are eager to unlock the potential of this versatile framework, you are in the right place.

As you embark on this chapter, get ready to dive into the world of advanced Flutter app development. We will equip you with the skills, techniques, and insights needed to tackle complex challenges, create polished user interfaces, and build robust applications that stand out in today's competitive digital landscape.

Structure

The chapter covers the following topics:

- Flutter themes
- .of and .copyWith operator
- Custom widgets
- Flutter packages
- Gesture detection

- Passing functions as parameters
- Routing and navigation
- Mixin
- Selecting platform-specific widgets
- Data persistence in Flutter Apps

Flutter themes

To keep consistent styling throughout our app across different screen, we should provide a **ThemeData** widget to our **materialApp**. When we do not apply any theme, then Flutter uses a default theme to style our app.

In this chapter, we will create a brand-new app called '**EMICalculator**.' Throughout this chapter, we will integrate various concepts by applying them to our **EMICalculator** app, as demonstrated below:

```
1.  import 'package:flutter/material.dart';
2.
3.  void main() => runApp(const EMICalculator());
4.
5.  class EMICalculator extends StatelessWidget {
6.    const EMICalculator({super.key});
7.
8.    // This widget is the root of your application.
9.    @override
10.   Widget build(BuildContext context) {
11.     return const MaterialApp(
12.       debugShowCheckedModeBanner: false,
13.       home: UserInputPage(),
14.     );
15.   }
16. }
17.
18. class UserInputPage extends StatefulWidget {
19.   const UserInputPage({super.key});
20.
21.   @override
```

```
22.    State<UserInputPage> createState() => _UserInputPageState();
23. }
24.
25. class _UserInputPageState extends State<UserInputPage> {
26.    @override
27.    Widget build(BuildContext context) {
28.      return Scaffold(
29.        appBar: AppBar(title: const Text('EMI Calculator')),
30.        body: const Center(child: Text('body text')),
31.        floatingActionButton: FloatingActionButton(
32.          onPressed: () {},
33.          child: const Icon(Icons.add),
34.        ),
35.      );
36.    }
37. }
```

Code 5.1: *Default styling for app*

Executing this code should yield a screen with the appearance illustrated in the figure below.

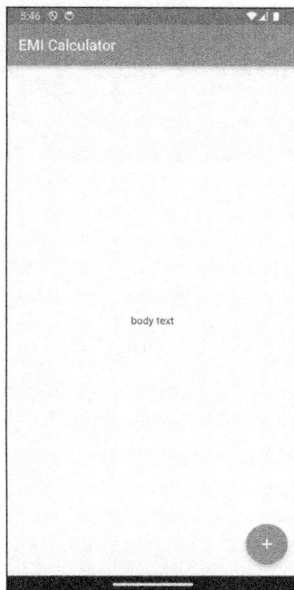

Figure 5.1: *Default styling for app*

In this scenario, no specific theme has been employed. Therefore, Flutter has utilized its default theme, resulting in a blue appbar, a blue floating action button, and black body text within the app.

Now, let us customize the theme for our application. To do so, if you review the available properties for the material app, you will come across an attribute named "theme," as illustrated in the following *Figure 5.2*:

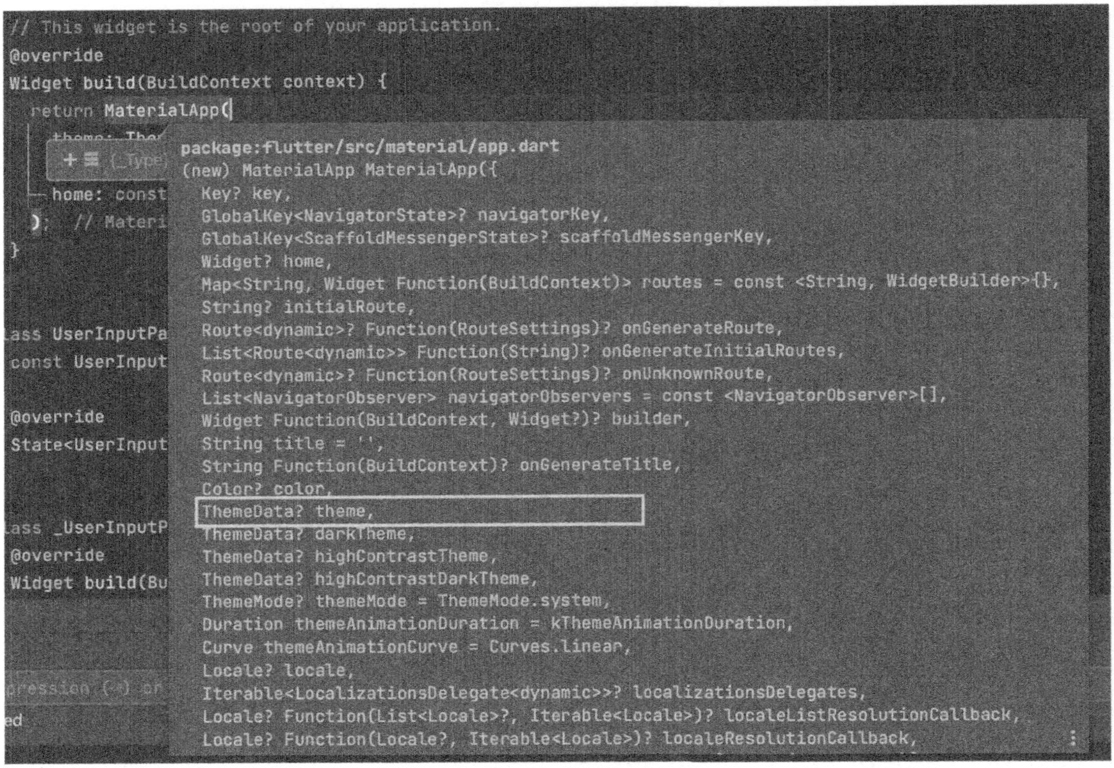

Figure 5.2: MaterialApp properties

As you can see, it expects a widget, which is a **ThemeData** widget. **ThemeData** will be able to define visual properties such as colors, fonts, and shapes for everything inside the app.

So, let us add a theme. Now, if you start typing 'Theme', you can see a couple of default ones that come prepackaged and one of them is **ThemeData.light()**. It is the default one, now let us pick **ThemeData.dark()** and save it. Let us see how it looks.

```
1. import 'package:flutter/material.dart';
2.
3. void main() => runApp(const EMICalculator());
4.
5. class EMICalculator extends StatelessWidget {
```

```
6.    const EMICalculator({super.key});
7.
8.    // This widget is the root of your application.
9.    @override
10.   Widget build(BuildContext context) {
11.     return MaterialApp(
12.       theme: ThemeData.dark(),
13.       debugShowCheckedModeBanner: false,
14.       home: const UserInputPage(),
15.     );
16.   }
17. }
18.
19. class UserInputPage extends StatefulWidget {
20.   const UserInputPage({super.key});
21.
22.   @override
23.   State<UserInputPage> createState() => _UserInputPageState();
24. }
25.
26. class _UserInputPageState extends State<UserInputPage> {
27.   @override
28.   Widget build(BuildContext context) {
29.     return Scaffold(
30.       appBar: AppBar(title: const Text('EMI Calculator')),
31.       body: const Center(child: Text('body text')),
32.       floatingActionButton: FloatingActionButton(
33.         onPressed: () {},
34.         child: const Icon(Icons.add),
35.       ),
36.     );
37.   }
38. }
```

Code 5.2: Testing dark theme

Run the code, and you should see a screen as shown in the image below:

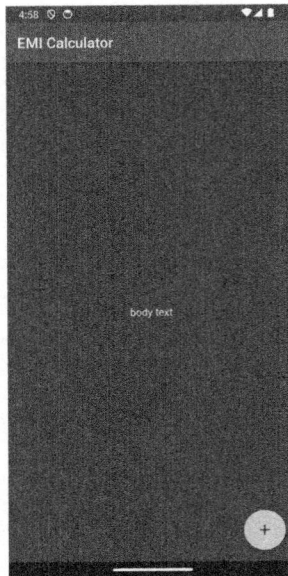

Figure 5.3: Dark theme

The background and app bar turn dark, and the floating action button, now, has a turquoise color. If you like the dark theme more than the light one, you can use this as it is. But if you need more customization, like control over app bar color, font color, and other stylings, then it is time for you to create your own **ThemeData** widget. Theme data has loads of properties in it that you can change, so it is a good idea to go through official documentation for the **ThemeData** widget to see what you can change and what these properties can do.

For instance, as illustrated in *Figure 5.4*, the **actionIconTheme** allows customization of icons for the back or close button, while an **appBarTheme** can be utilized to tailor the appearance of your app's app bar. As you can see, it expects an **appBarTheme** widget as a parameter. Now you need to look at what properties you can set for an **AppbarTheme** to specify its background color, foreground color, shadow color and much more.

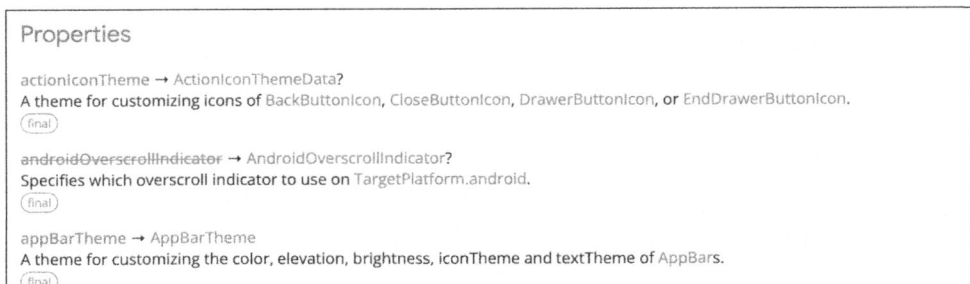

Figure 5.4: ThemeData properties

Now, let us change some properties in our theme data. If you just update the **appBarTheme**, then Flutter will apply the new app bar theme on top of the default light theme. Let us start with an update on **appbar** color. There are two ways we can do it:

- By updating the **appBarTheme** property of **ThemeData**:

```
1.  Widget build(BuildContext context) {
2.     return MaterialApp(
3.       theme: ThemeData(appBarTheme: const
         AppBarTheme(backgroundColor: Colors.blueGrey,
         foregroundColor: Colors.white)),
4.       debugShowCheckedModeBanner: false,
5.       home: const UserInputPage(),
6.     );
7.  }
```

Code 5.3: Updating AppBar style by using AppBarTheme

The resulting screen will look like *Figure 5.5:*

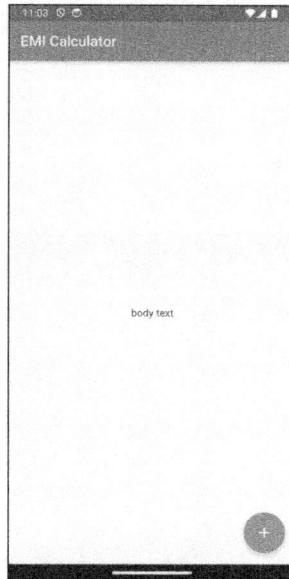

Figure 5.5: Customised appBar styling

- By updating **colorScheme** property of **ThemeData**:

```
1.  @override
2.  Widget build(BuildContext context) {
3.     return MaterialApp(
```

```
4.          theme: ThemeData(
5.            colorScheme: ColorScheme.fromSwatch().copyWith(
6.              primary: Colors.blueGrey,
7.              secondary: Colors.teal,
8.            ),
9.          ),
10.         debugShowCheckedModeBanner: false,
11.         home: const UserInputPage(),
12.       );
13.     }
```

Code 5.4: Updating Theme by using colorScheme

The primary and secondary colors defined in the **ThemeData** affect various UI elements throughout the app. Here is a breakdown of where these colors typically apply:

- **Primary Color:** The primary color is often used for major UI elements like app bars, buttons, selected tabs, and more. It serves as the main color theme for the application.
- **Secondary Color:** The secondary color typically complements the primary color and is used for accents, such as floating action buttons, sliders, progress indicators, and selection controls.

The resulting screen will look like *Figure 5.6*:

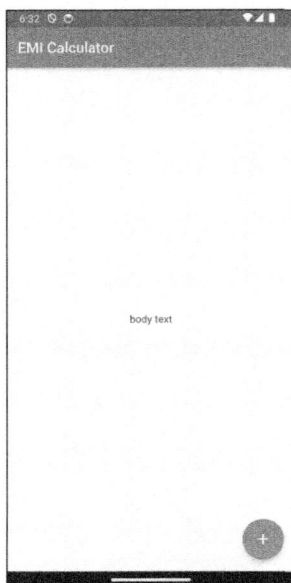

Figure 5.6: Customised styling with colorScheme

There are more properties inside colorScheme, go through the official documentation **https://api.flutter.dev/flutter/material/ColorScheme-class.html** and try them out to see the changes impacting your screen design. So far, we have not discussed the text color. Let us see how we can do that:

```
1.    Widget build(BuildContext context) {
2.      return MaterialApp(
3.        theme: ThemeData(
4.          colorScheme: ColorScheme.fromSwatch().copyWith(
5.            primary: Colors.blueGrey,
6.            secondary: Colors.teal,
7.          ),
8.          textTheme: const TextTheme(
9.            bodyMedium: TextStyle(
10.             color: Color(0XFFab3d00),
11.           ),
12.         )),
13.       debugShowCheckedModeBanner: false,
14.       home: const UserInputPage(),
15.     );
16.   }
```

Code 5.5: *Adding TextTheme*

The resulting screen will look like *Figure 5.7:*

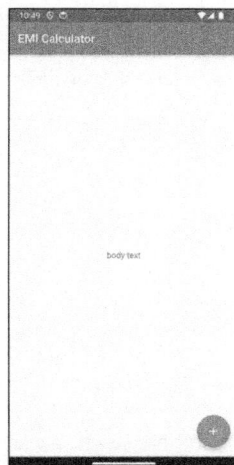

Figure 5.7: *Added TextTheme*

In the above code, there are two new things for you. One is how to set the body text color, and the second thing is how to use hex code for a color. In the code above, we have entered **0XFFab3d00** as the hex value. Here is a breakdown of each component in the above value:

- **0XFF - Alpha (A):** Represents the level of transparency or opacity of a color. A higher alpha value means greater opacity, and a lower value means greater transparency. An alpha value of 255 is fully opaque, and an alpha value of 0 is fully transparent.
- **Ab - Red (R):** Represents the intensity of the red color component, ranging from 0 (no red) to 255 (full red).
- **3d - Green (G):** Represents the intensity of the green color component, ranging from 0 (no green) to 255 (full green).
- **00 - Blue (B):** Represents the intensity of the blue color component, ranging from 0 (no blue) to 255 (full blue).

.of and .copyWith operator:

In Flutter, the .of and **.copyWith** operators are often used with the concept of data immutability to manage and update the properties of widgets or objects without directly modifying them. These operators are commonly associated with classes that support them, such as **BuildContext** and certain widget classes.

.of operator

The .of operator is used to obtain a reference to a particular inherited widget from the nearest ancestor in the widget tree. An inherited widget can be accessed by its descendants without explicitly passing it down through the constructor.

To access the theme using the .of operator, you typically use the **Theme.of** method, which is a convenience method provided by Flutter to access the current theme data from the nearest ancestor Theme widget in the widget tree. Here is how you can use it:

```
1.  import 'package:flutter/material.dart';
2.
3.  void main() {
4.    runApp(
5.      MaterialApp(
6.        theme: ThemeData(
7.          primaryColor: Colors.blue,
8.        ),
9.        home: const MyWidget(),
10.     ),
```

```
11.   );
12. }
13.
14. class MyWidget extends StatelessWidget {
15.   const MyWidget({super.key});
16.
17.   @override
18.   Widget build(BuildContext context) {
19.     // Access the theme using Theme.of(context)
20.     final ThemeData theme = Theme.of(context);
21.
22.     return Container(
23.       color: theme.primaryColor,
24.     );
25.   }
26. }
```

Code 5.6: Using .of operator for theme data

The resulting screen will look as shown in *Figure 5.8:*

Figure 5.8: theme data using copy of

In this example, the MaterialApp widget's theme property is set to define the theme data that will be accessible using **Theme.of(context)** throughout the app.

.copyWith operator

In Flutter, the **.copyWith** method is commonly used to create a new instance of an object with specific properties changed while keeping the rest of the properties the same as the original object. The **ThemeData** class also provides a **.copyWith** method that allows us to create a new instance of the theme with specific properties modified while keeping the rest of the theme's properties the same. Here is an example of using **.copyWith** to modify the primary color of a theme:

```
1.  @override
2.  Widget build(BuildContext context) {
3.    return MaterialApp(
4.      theme: ThemeData.dark().copyWith(
5.          appBarTheme: const AppBarTheme(color: Colors.black38),
6.          scaffoldBackgroundColor: Colors.blueGrey),
7.      debugShowCheckedModeBanner: false,
8.      home: const UserInputPage(),
9.    );
10.  }
11. }
```

Code 5.7: Using copyWith for theme data

Now let us look at the resulting screen:

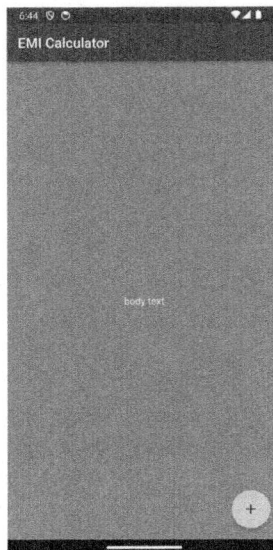

Figure 5.9: Theme data using copy of

As observed, the newly created theme retains all the default properties from the dark theme, like body text color, accent color and incorporates the specific theme property adjustments we have specified.

The **copyWith** method is a common pattern used in Dart and Flutter to create a copy of an object with some properties modified. Let us say you have a class with multiple properties, and you want to create a new instance of that class with some changes while keeping the other properties unchanged. You can define a **copyWith** method in your class to make this process easier.

Here is an example of how you might implement **copyWith** in a Dart class:

```
1.  void main() {
2.    final person1 = Person(name: "Alice", age: 30);
3.    final person2 = person1.copyWith(name: "Bob");
4.
5.    print(person1.name); // Output: Alice
6.    print(person2.name); // Output: Bob
7.    print(person2.age); // Output: 30 (age is not changed)
8.  }
9.
10. class Person {
11.   final String name;
12.   final int age;
13.
14.   Person({required this.name, required this.age});
15.
16.   Person copyWith({String? name, int? age}) {
17.     return Person(
18.       name: name ?? this.name,
19.       age: age ?? this.age,
20.     );
21.   }
22. }
```

Code 5.8: Using .copyWith operator for object

Console output will be:

```
1. I/flutter (14274): Alice
2. I/flutter (14274): Bob
3. I/flutter (14274): 30
```

Custom widgets

Creating a custom widget in Flutter allows us to build reusable components for the app. Custom widgets are created by extending existing widgets or creating a new widget from scratch. Look at the below code and see how we can improve it by using the custom widget and achieve the dry principle aimed at reducing redundancy in code. The DRY principle encourages developers to write code in such a way that each piece of knowledge or logic is stored in a single, well-defined place in the codebase.

```
1.  Widget build(BuildContext context) {
2.    return Scaffold(
3.      appBar: AppBar(title: const Text('EMI Calculator')),
4.      body: Column(
5.        mainAxisAlignment: MainAxisAlignment.center,
6.        children: [
7.          Container(
8.            margin: const EdgeInsets.all(15),
9.            decoration: BoxDecoration(
10.             color: const Color(0XFF00e7f8),
11.             borderRadius: BorderRadius.circular(5.0),
12.           ),
13.           height: 100,
14.           width: double.infinity,
15.           child: const Center(
16.             child: Text(
17.               "Home Loan",
18.               style: TextStyle(
19.                   color: Colors.black,
20.                   fontWeight: FontWeight.bold,
21.                   fontSize: 18),
22.             ),
```

```
23.              ),
24.            ),
25.          Container(
26.            margin: const EdgeInsets.all(15),
27.            decoration: BoxDecoration(
28.              color: const Color(0XFF00e7f8),
29.              borderRadius: BorderRadius.circular(5.0),
30.            ),
31.            height: 100,
32.            width: double.infinity,
33.            child: const Center(
34.              child: Text(
35.                "Personal Loan",
36.                style: TextStyle(
37.                    color: Colors.black,
38.                    fontWeight: FontWeight.bold,
39.                    fontSize: 18),
40.              ),
41.            ),
42.          ),
43.          Container(
44.            margin: const EdgeInsets.all(15),
45.            decoration: BoxDecoration(
46.              color: const Color(0XFF00e7f8),
47.              borderRadius: BorderRadius.circular(5.0),
48.            ),
49.            height: 100,
50.            width: double.infinity,
51.            child: const Center(
52.              child: Text(
53.                "Car Loan",
54.                style: TextStyle(
55.                    color: Colors.black,
```

```
56.                          fontWeight: FontWeight.bold,
57.                          fontSize: 18),
58.                   ),
59.                 ),
60.               )
61.             ],
62.           ),
63.       );
64.    }
```

Code 5.9: Code without using custom widget

When you run the app, the screen will look as in *Figure 5.10*:

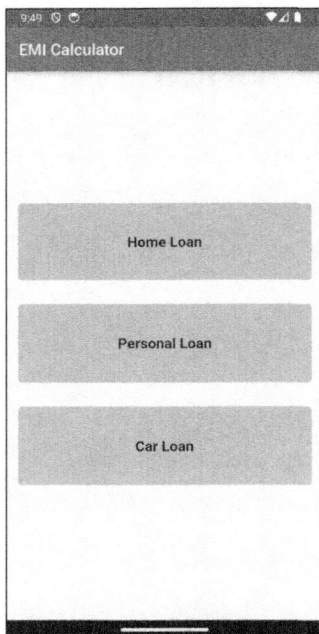

Figure 5.10: Without using a custom widget.

The screen looks great, but if you observe, we are repeating almost similar container code three times. Let us try to move it to a new custom widget. Now, just open Flutter outline, right click on the container and select '**Extract widget**' as shown in *Figure 5.11*:

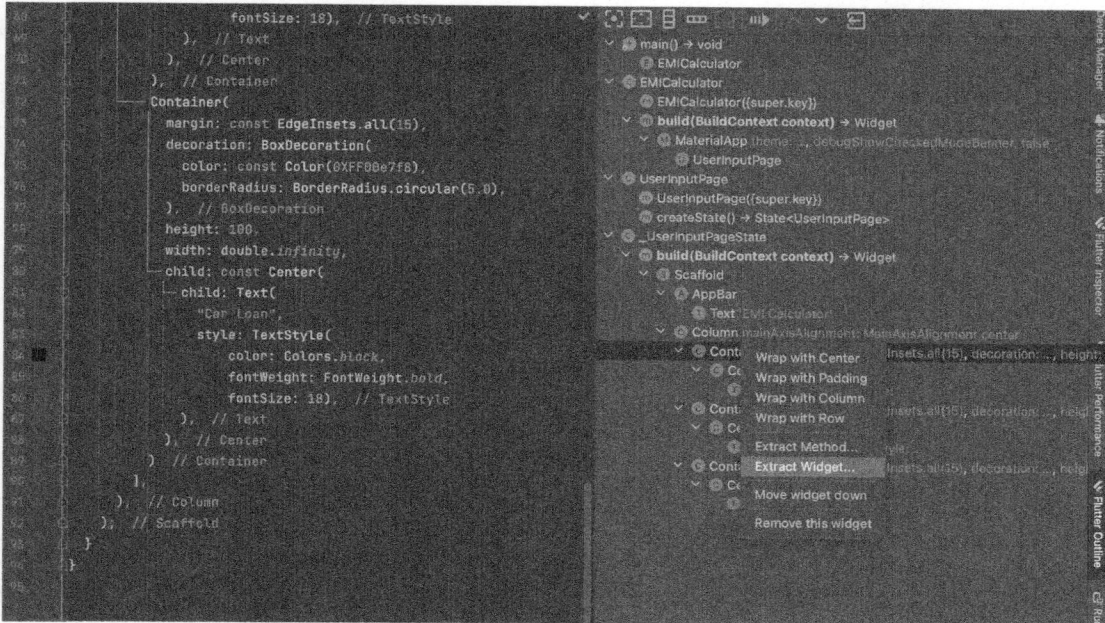

Figure 5.11: *Flutter outline for extracting widget*

Now, give a meaningful name then Flutter will create a new stateless widget with the same main file. Now, you can create a new dart file inside lib and move the code there, as shown in the following code:

```
1.  class ReusableCard extends StatelessWidget {
2.      final String label;
3.
4.      const ReusableCard({super.key, required this.label});
5.
6.      @override
7.      Widget build(BuildContext context) {
8.        return Container(
9.          margin: const EdgeInsets.all(15),
10.         decoration: BoxDecoration(
11.           color: const Color(0XFF00e7f8),
12.           borderRadius: BorderRadius.circular(5.0),
13.         ),
14.         height: 100,
```

```
15.        width: double.infinity,
16.        child: Center(
17.          child: Text(
18.            label,
19.            style: const TextStyle(
20.              color: Colors.black,
21.              fontWeight: FontWeight.bold,
22.              fontSize: 18,
23.            ),
24.          ),
25.        ),
26.      );
27.  }
28. }
```

Code 5.10: Custom widget ReusableCard

Now observe how much the main file code is reduced.

```
1.   Widget build(BuildContext context) {
2.     return Scaffold(
3.       appBar: AppBar(title: const Text('EMI Calculator')),
4.       body: const Column(
5.         mainAxisAlignment: MainAxisAlignment.center,
6.         children: [
7.           ReusableCard(
8.             label: 'Home loan',
9.           ),
10.          ReusableCard(
11.            label: 'car loan',
12.          ),
13.          ReusableCard(
14.            label: 'Personal loan',
15.          ),
16.        ],
17.      ),
```

```
18.    );
19.  }
```

Code 5.11: Main file with ReusableCard

When you run the app, you can find the exact same result with a much improved code.

Flutter packages

In Flutter, packages are pre-built libraries or collections of code that can be easily added to a Flutter project to extend its functionality or simplify common tasks. Flutter packages can include UI components, network utilities, state management solutions, and more. These packages can be found on the official Flutter package repository called "**pub.dev.**"

Here is how you can work with Flutter packages:

- **Adding a package:** To add a package to your Flutter project, you need to specify it in your project's **pubspec.yaml** file. Open this file in your project directory and add the package name under the dependencies section. For example, there is a package in Flutter that is helpful for adding icon images to your screen called '**font_awesome_flutter**'.

    Let us add it to our **pubspec.yaml**'s dependencies section and use it our project as shown below:

```
1.  name: emi_calculator
2.  description: A new Flutter project.
3.  publish_to:
4.  version: 1.0.0+1
5.
6.  environment:
7.    sdk: '>=3.0.5 <4.0.0'
8.  dependencies:
9.    flutter:
10.     sdk: flutter
11.    cupertino_icons: ^1.0.2
12.    font_awesome_flutter: ^10.5.0
13.
14. dev_dependencies:
15.    flutter_test:
16.      sdk: flutter
```

```
17.   flutter_lints: ^2.0.0
18. flutter:
19.   uses-material-design: true
```

Code 5.12: pubspec.yaml file

Now let us update our code for Reusable card and **main** files to add a suitable icon using **font_awesome_flutter** package.

```
1.  import 'package:flutter/material.dart';
2.  import 'package:font_awesome_flutter/font_awesome_flutter.dart';
3.
4.  class ReusableCard extends StatelessWidget {
5.    final String label;
6.    final IconData icon;
7.
8.    const ReusableCard({super.key, required this.label, required this.
      icon});
9.
10.   @override
11.   Widget build(BuildContext context) {
12.     return Container(
13.       margin: const EdgeInsets.all(15),
14.       decoration: BoxDecoration(
15.         color: const Color(0XFF00e7f8),
16.         borderRadius: BorderRadius.circular(5.0),
17.       ),
18.       height: 100,
19.       width: double.infinity,
20.       child: Center(
21.         child: Padding(
22.           padding: const EdgeInsets.all(8),
23.           child: Row(
24.             mainAxisAlignment: MainAxisAlignment.center,
25.             children: [
26.               //FaIcon is a widget provided by the flutter_font_
                  awesome package.
```

```
27.              // It allows you to display Font Awesome icons in your
                 Flutter app
28.              FaIcon(icon),
29.              const SizedBox(width: 16),
30.              Text(
31.                label,
32.                style: const TextStyle(
33.                  color: Colors.black,
34.                  fontWeight: FontWeight.bold,
35.                  fontSize: 18,
36.                ),
37.              ),
38.            ],
39.          ),
40.        ),
41.      ),
42.    );
43.  }
44. }
```

Code 5.13: Reusable card code with using Font Awesome package

```
1.  Widget build(BuildContext context) {
2.    return Scaffold(
3.      appBar: AppBar(title: const Text('EMI Calculator')),
4.      body: const Column(
5.        mainAxisAlignment: MainAxisAlignment.center,
6.        children: [
7.          ReusableCard(
8.            label: 'Home loan',
9.            icon: FontAwesomeIcons.house,
10.          ),
11.          ReusableCard(
12.            label: 'car loan',
13.            icon: FontAwesomeIcons.car,
14.          ),
```

```
15.              ReusableCard(
16.                label: 'Personal loan',
17.                icon: FontAwesomeIcons.handHoldingDollar,
18.              ),
19.            ],
20.          ),
21.        );
22.      }
```

Code 5.14: Main.dart file code with using Font Awesome package

The resulting screen will look like *Figure 5.12:*

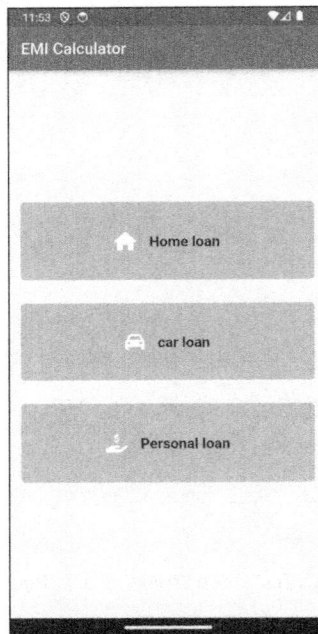

Figure 5.12: Screen using Font Awesome icons

Gesture detection

It's now the moment to identify the user's taps on one of the options or containers within the screen. There are two possible ways, one of which is wrapping our container inside a **MaterialButton** and get access to **onPressed** method. The only problem is that **MaterialButton** comes with its own styling, so you may have to update your container stylings. If you do not want to go through that route the second option is that you can detect gestures using the **GestureDetector** widget, which allows you to recognize various touch gestures and respond to them with specific actions. Here is an overview of how to use the **GestureDetector** widget to detect common gestures in Flutter.

Gesture detection in Flutter involves recognizing user interactions like taps, swipes, pinches, and more. Flutter provides a rich set of widgets and gestures detectors to make it easy to handle various touch gestures. Here are some common gestures and how you can detect them in Flutter:

1. **Tap gesture**: To detect a simple tap on a widget, you can use the **GestureDetector** widget. Here is an example of how to use it:

```
2.  GestureDetector(
3.    onTap: () {
4.      // Handle the tap gesture here
5.    },
6.    child: YourWidget(),
7.  )
```

Code 5.15: GestureDetector onTap

2. **Long press gesture**: To detect a long press, you can use the **onLongPress** property of the **GestureDetector**:

```
1.  GestureDetector(
2.    onLongPress: () {
3.      // Handle the long press gesture here
4.    },
5.    child: YourWidget(),
6.  )
```

Code 5.16: GestureDetector onLongPress

3. **Double tap gesture**: You can use the **onDoubleTap** property of **GestureDetector** to detect a double tap:

```
1.  GestureDetector(
2.    onDoubleTap: () {
3.      // Handle the double tap gesture here
4.    },
5.    child: YourWidget(),
6.  )
```

Code 5.17: GestureDetector onDoubleTap

4. **Swipe or drag gesture**: To detect swipe or drag gestures, you can use the Draggable widget or a combination of **GestureDetector** and **GestureDetector. onPanUpdate**:

```
1. GestureDetector(
2.   onPanUpdate: (details) {
3.     // Handle swipe/drag gestures here
4.     // details.delta gives you the change in position
5.   },
6.   child: YourWidget(),
7. )
```

Code 5.17: GestureDetector onPanUpdate

5. **Pinch gesture**: To detect a pinch gesture (for example, zoom in/out), you can use the onScaleUpdate property of GestureDetector:

```
1. GestureDetector(
2.   onScaleUpdate: (details) {
3.     // Handle pinch gestures here
4.     // details.scale gives you the scale factor
5.   },
6.   child: YourWidget(),
7. )
```

Code 5.18: GestureDetector onScaleUpdate

6. **Custom gestures**: You can create custom gestures by combining the touch input and logic in the **onPanUpdate** or **onScaleUpdate** callbacks.

Remember to wrap your widgets with **GestureDetector** when you want to detect specific gestures. You can customize these gestures based on your app's requirements and perform actions accordingly within the callback functions.

Additionally, Flutter provides other widgets like *InkWell* for handling taps with ink splash effects and Dismissible for swipe-to-dismiss behavior in lists. Explore these options based on your specific needs.

Now let us update our code for the **EMICalculator** to detect tap on the options or cards:

```
1. Widget build(BuildContext context) {
2.   return Scaffold(
3.     appBar: AppBar(title: const Text('EMI Calculator')),
4.     body: Column(
```

```
5.            mainAxisAlignment: MainAxisAlignment.center,
6.            children: [
7.              GestureDetector(
8.                onTap: () {
9.                  print("Home loan tapped");
10.               },
11.               child: const ReusableCard(
12.                 label: 'Home loan',
13.                 icon: FontAwesomeIcons.house,
14.               ),
15.             ),
16.             GestureDetector(
17.               onTap: () {
18.                 print("Car loan tapped");
19.               },
20.               child: const ReusableCard(
21.                 label: 'Car loan',
22.                 icon: FontAwesomeIcons.car,
23.               ),
24.             ),
25.             GestureDetector(
26.               onTap: () {
27.                 print("Personal loan tapped");
28.               },
29.               child: const ReusableCard(
30.                 label: 'Personal loan',
31.                 icon: FontAwesomeIcons.handHoldingDollar,
32.               ),
33.             ),
34.           ],
35.         ),
36.     );
37.   }
```

Code 5.19: ReusableCard with tap detection

Now when you tap any card, you can view the print statement inside your Logcat.

Pass function as parameter

In Flutter, functions are first-class citizens in the Dart programming language, which means they can be treated as first-class objects, including being passed as arguments to other functions, returned from functions, and assigned to variables. This capability allows for the use of higher-order functions in Flutter.

A higher-order function is a function that takes one or more functions as arguments and/or returns a function as its result. It is a concept from functional programming that enables more flexible and expressive coding patterns.

Here is an example of how you can use higher-order functions in Flutter:

```
1.  // A higher-order function that takes a function as an argument
2.  int operate(int a, int b, int Function(int, int) operation) {
3.    return operation(a, b);
4.  }
5.
6.  // Functions that can be passed as arguments
7.  int add(int a, int b) => a + b;
8.  int subtract(int a, int b) => a - b;
9.  int multiply(int a, int b) => a * b;
10.
11. void main() {
12.   // Using the higher-order function with different operations
13.   print(operate(5, 3, add));        // Output: 8
14.   print(operate(10, 4, subtract));  // Output: 6
15.   print(operate(7, 6, multiply));   // Output: 42
16. }
```

Code 5.20: Flutter functions

Now let us see how we can utilize the method as a parameter in our app, '**EMICalculator**'. If you observe the *Code 5.19*, we are repeating the wrapping of **GestureDetector** to **ReusableCard** three times. This code could be optimized by wrapping **ReusableCard** with Gesture detector just once and passing **onPressed** method as a parameter to the widget, as shown below:

```
1.  import 'package:flutter/material.dart';
2.  import 'package:font_awesome_flutter/font_awesome_flutter.dart';
```

```
3.
4.  class ReusableCard extends StatelessWidget {
5.    final String label;
6.    final IconData icon;
7.    final void Function()? onPress;
8.
9.    const ReusableCard({
10.     required this.label,
11.     required this.icon,
12.     this.onPress,
13.     Key? key,
14.   }) : super(key: key);
15.
16.   @override
17.   Widget build(BuildContext context) {
18.     return Container(
19.       margin: const EdgeInsets.all(15),
20.       decoration: BoxDecoration(
21.         color: const Color(0XFF00e7f8),
22.         borderRadius: BorderRadius.circular(5.0),
23.       ),
24.       height: 100,
25.       width: double.infinity,
26.       child: GestureDetector(
27.         onTap: onPress,
28.         child: Center(
29.           child: Padding(
30.             padding: const EdgeInsets.all(8),
31.             child: Row(
32.               mainAxisAlignment: MainAxisAlignment.center,
33.               children: [
34.                 FaIcon(icon),
35.                 const SizedBox(width: 16),
36.                 Text(
```

```
37.              label,
38.              style: const TextStyle(
39.                color: Colors.black,
40.                fontWeight: FontWeight.bold,
41.                fontSize: 18,
42.              ),
43.            ),
44.          ],
45.        ),
46.      ),
47.    ),
48.  ),
49. );
50. }
51. }
```

Code 5.21: ReusableCard with gesture detection

```
1.  Widget build(BuildContext context) {
2.    return Scaffold(
3.      appBar: AppBar(title: const Text('EMI Calculator')),
4.      body: Column(
5.        mainAxisAlignment: MainAxisAlignment.center,
6.        children: [
7.          ReusableCard(
8.            label: 'Home loan',
9.            icon: FontAwesomeIcons.house,
10.           onPress: () {
11.             print("Home loan tapped");
12.           },
13.         ),
14.         ReusableCard(
15.           label: 'Car loan',
16.           icon: FontAwesomeIcons.car,
17.           onPress: () {
18.             print("Car loan tapped");
```

```
19.              },
20.            ),
21.          ReusableCard(
22.            label: 'Personal loan',
23.            icon: FontAwesomeIcons.handHoldingDollar,
24.            onPress: () {
25.              print("Personal loan tapped");
26.            },
27.          ),
28.        ],
29.      ),
30.    );
31.  }
```

Code 5.22: ReusableCard with gesture detection

In the above code, we are passing the '**onPress**' function as a parameter to the **ReusableCard** widget. Now test the functionality by tapping the button and verifying the console log print statement.

Routing and navigation

So far, we have created single page apps, but for making any real time app, we need multiple pages. Routing and navigation are essential aspects of building apps in Flutter. They allow us to navigate between different screens or pages within your app. Flutter provides a flexible and powerful routing system. Here is a step-by-step guide on how to set up routing and navigation in Flutter:

1. **Use MaterialPageRoute:** For simple navigation without named routes, you can use **MaterialPageRoute**:

```
2. Navigator.push(
3.   context,
4.   MaterialPageRoute(builder: (context) => const InputScreen()),
5. );
```

Code 5.23: Navigation without routing

2. **Create multiple screens (pages):** Start by creating different screens or pages for your app. Each screen should be represented by a separate widget. For example, you might have a "**Home**" screen, a "**Settings**" screen, and so on.

3. **Define named routes:** In your `main.dart` or the root of your app, define named routes for each screen using the routes property of `MaterialApp`. A named route is a unique identifier for a screen. Here is an example:

```
1. MaterialApp(
2.    routes: {
3.       '/home': (context) => HomeScreen(),
4.       '/settings': (context) => SettingsScreen(),
5.    },
6.    // ...
7. )
```

Code 5.24: Flutter routing

4. **Navigate to a screen:** To navigate from one screen to another, you can use the Navigator class. For example, to navigate to the "**Settings**" screen, you can use:

```
1. Navigator.pushNamed(context, '/settings');
```

Code 5.25: Navigation using pushNamed

This code pushes the ***Settings*** screen onto the navigation stack, allowing the user to go back to the previous screen.

5. **Navigate back**: To navigate back to the previous screen, you can use:

```
1. Navigator.pop(context);
```

Code 5.26: Navigating back to previous screen

This code pops the current screen from the navigation stack and returns to the previous screen.

6. **Pass data between screens:** You can pass data between screens by providing arguments when navigating to a screen. For example:

```
1. Navigator.pushNamed(context, '/details', arguments: {
2.    'title': 'Detail Page',
3.    'description': 'This is a detailed view.',
4. });
```

Code 5.27: Passing data between screens using navigator

In the receiving screen, you can retrieve the arguments using `ModalRoute.of(context).settings.arguments`.

7. **Handle routing with MaterialApp**: You can use `MaterialApp` to define the initial route and theme for your app. It also provides a Navigator that manages the navigation stack. You can access the Navigator using `Navigator.of(context)`.

8. **Handle unknown routes:** You can define a function to handle unknown routes by setting the **onGenerateRoute** property of **MaterialApp**. This is useful for error handling or handling dynamic routes.

```
1. onGenerateRoute: (settings) {
2.    return MaterialPageRoute(
3.      builder: (context) => NotFoundScreen(),
4.    );
5. },
```

Code 5.28: Error handling for route not found

Now, let's put our routing theory into practice by implementing routing in our BMI Calculator app. Let's start with main.dart file by adding routing to MaterialApp

```
1. import 'package:flutter/material.dart';
2.
3. import 'input_screen.dart';
4. import 'loan_selection_page.dart';
5.
6. void main() => runApp(const EMICalculator());
7.
8. class EMICalculator extends StatelessWidget {
9.    const EMICalculator({Key? key}) : super(key: key);
10.
11.   @override
12.   Widget build(BuildContext context) {
13.     return MaterialApp(
14.       theme: ThemeData.dark().copyWith(
15.         appBarTheme: const AppBarTheme(color: Color(0XFF0564EB)),
16.         scaffoldBackgroundColor: const Color(0XFFF2F6FA),
17.       ),
18.       debugShowCheckedModeBanner: false,
19.       initialRoute: </>, // Set the initial route
20.       routes: {
21.         '/': (context) => const LoanSelectionPage(), // Loan
              Selection Screen
22.         </input>: (context) => const InputScreen(), // Input Screen
```

```
23.        },
24.        );
25.    }
26. }
```

Code 5.29: *main.dart with routes*

Up to this point, we've incorporated the Loan Options screen. It's now the opportune moment to introduce a user input screen featuring a slider:

```
1.  import 'package:flutter/material.dart';
2.
3.  class CustomSlider extends StatefulWidget {
4.    final String title;
5.    final String? preText;
6.    final double minValue;
7.    final double maxValue;
8.    final double initialValue;
9.    final ValueChanged<double>? onValueChanged; // Callback function
10.
11.    const CustomSlider({
12.      required this.title,
13.      required this.minValue,
14.      required this.maxValue,
15.      required this.initialValue,
16.      Key? key,
17.      this.preText,
18.      this.onValueChanged, // Callback function parameter
19.    }) : super(key: key);
20.
21.    @override
22.    State<CustomSlider> createState() => _CustomSliderState();
23. }
24.
25. class _CustomSliderState extends State<CustomSlider> {
26.    double _value = 50;
27.
```

```
28.  @override
29.  void initState() {
30.    super.initState();
31.    _value = widget.initialValue;
32.    if (widget.onValueChanged != null) {
33.      widget
34.          .onValueChanged!(_value); // Call the callback with the
             initial value
35.    }
36.  }
37.
38.  @override
39.  Widget build(BuildContext context) {
40.    return Container(
41.      margin: const EdgeInsets.all(15),
42.      decoration: BoxDecoration(
43.        color: const Color(0XFFD6EAF8),
44.        borderRadius: BorderRadius.circular(5.0),
45.      ),
46.      child: SliderTheme(
47.        data: SliderTheme.of(context).copyWith(
48.          activeTrackColor: const Color(0XFF99B7D1),
49.          inactiveTrackColor: const Color(0XFF99B7D1),
50.          thumbColor: const Color(0XFF004C8E),
51.          valueIndicatorTextStyle: const TextStyle(
52.            color: Colors.black,
53.          ),
54.        ),
55.        child: Padding(
56.          padding: const EdgeInsets.all(8),
57.          child: Column(
58.            mainAxisAlignment: MainAxisAlignment.center,
59.            children: [
60.              Text(
```

```
61.              widget.title,
62.              style: const TextStyle(
63.                  color: Colors.black,
64.                  fontWeight: FontWeight.w900,
65.                  fontSize: 15),
66.            ),
67.          Slider(
68.            value: _value,
69.            min: widget.minValue,
70.            max: widget.maxValue,
71.            divisions: (widget.maxValue - widget.minValue) ~/ 1,
72.            label: widget.preText != null
73.                ? '${widget.preText} ${_value.toStringAsFixed(0)}'
74.                : _value.toStringAsFixed(0),
75.            onChanged: (newValue) {
76.              setState(() {
77.                _value = newValue;
78.              });
79.              if (widget.onValueChanged != null) {
80.                widget.onValueChanged!(
81.                    _value); // Call the callback with the
                            updated value
82.              }
83.            },
84.          ),
85.          Row(
86.            mainAxisAlignment: MainAxisAlignment.spaceBetween,
87.            children: [
88.              Text(
89.                (widget.preText != null
90.                    ? '${widget.preText} ${widget.minValue.
                        toStringAsFixed(0)}'
91.                    : widget.minValue.toStringAsFixed(0)),
92.                style: const TextStyle(
93.                  color: Colors.black,
```

```
94.                    fontWeight: FontWeight.w500,
95.                    fontSize: 15,
96.                  ),
97.                ),
98.              Text(
99.                widget.preText != null
100.                    ? '${widget.preText} ${_value.
                       toStringAsFixed(0)}'
101.                    : _value.toStringAsFixed(0),
102.                style: const TextStyle(
103.                    color: Colors.black,
104.                    fontWeight: FontWeight.w500,
105.                    fontSize: 15),
106.              ),
107.              Text(
108.                (widget.preText != null
109.                    ? '${widget.preText} ${widget.minValue.
                       toStringAsFixed(0)}'
110.                    : widget.maxValue.toStringAsFixed(0)),
111.                style: const TextStyle(
112.                  color: Colors.black,
113.                  fontWeight: FontWeight.w500,
114.                  fontSize: 15,
115.                ),
116.              ),
117.            ],
118.          ),
119.        ],
120.      ),
121.    ),
122.   ),
123.   );
124.  }
125. }
```

Code 5.30: Custom slider for user input

Now let us create a new screen for user input and calculate EMI for home loan option.

```
1.  import 'dart:math';
2.  import 'package:flutter/material.dart';
3.  import 'custom_slider.dart';
4.
5.  class InputScreen extends StatefulWidget {
6.    const InputScreen({super.key});
7.
8.    @override
9.    State<InputScreen> createState() => _InputScreenState();
10. }
11.
12. class _InputScreenState extends State<InputScreen> {
13.   double loanAmount = 2500000;
14.   double tenureInYears = 30;
15.   double interestRate = 8.8;
16.   double emi = 0;
17.
18.   // Function to calculate EMI
19.   double calculateEMI() {
20.     double principal = loanAmount;
21.     double monthlyInterestRate = (interestRate / 12) / 100;
22.     int totalMonths = (tenureInYears * 12).toInt();
23.
24.     if (monthlyInterestRate == 0) {
25.       return principal / totalMonths;
26.     } else {
27.       double emi = principal *
28.           monthlyInterestRate *
29.           (pow(1 + monthlyInterestRate, totalMonths)) /
30.           (pow(1 + monthlyInterestRate, totalMonths) - 1);
31.       return emi;
32.     }
33.   }
```

```
34.
35.    @override
36.    Widget build(BuildContext context) {
37.      return Scaffold(
38.        appBar: AppBar(
39.          title: const Text("EMI Calculator"),
40.        ),
41.        body: Column(
42.          mainAxisAlignment: MainAxisAlignment.center,
43.          children: [
44.            CustomSlider(
45.              title: "Loan Amount",
46.              minValue: 100000,
47.              maxValue: 100000000,
48.              initialValue: 2500000,
49.              preText: "₹",
50.              onValueChanged: (newValue) {
51.                Future.delayed(Duration.zero, () {
52.                  setState(() {
53.                    loanAmount = newValue;
54.                  });
55.                });
56.              },
57.            ),
58.            CustomSlider(
59.              title: "Tenure (Years)",
60.              minValue: 1,
61.              maxValue: 30,
62.              initialValue: 30,
63.              onValueChanged: (newValue) {
64.                Future.delayed(Duration.zero, () {
65.                  setState(() {
66.                    tenureInYears = newValue;
67.                  });
```

```
68.                    });
69.                 },
70.             ),
71.         CustomSlider(
72.            title: "Interest Rate (% P.A.)",
73.            minValue: 0.5,
74.            maxValue: 15,
75.            initialValue: 8.8,
76.            onValueChanged: (newValue) {
77.               Future.delayed(Duration.zero, () {
78.                  setState(() {
79.                     interestRate = newValue;
80.                  });
81.               });
82.            },
83.         ),
84.         ElevatedButton(
85.            onPressed: () {
86.               double calculatedEMI = calculateEMI();
87.               setState(() {
88.                  emi = calculatedEMI;
89.               });
90.               print('EMI: $emi');
91.            },
92.            child: const Text('Calculate'),
93.         ),
94.         const SizedBox(height: 20),
95.         Text(
96.            'EMI: ₹${emi.toStringAsFixed(2)}',
97.            // Display the calculated EMI
98.             style: const TextStyle(color: Colors.black, fontSize: 18),
99.         ),
100.        ],
101.     ),
```

```
102.        );
103.     }
104.   }
```

Code 5.31: User input screen

Observing how navigation occurs between screens and the introduction of a new widget type, the 'slider', has been highlighted. Now if you run the app and tap on home loan, you should be able to navigate to the user input screen as shown below:

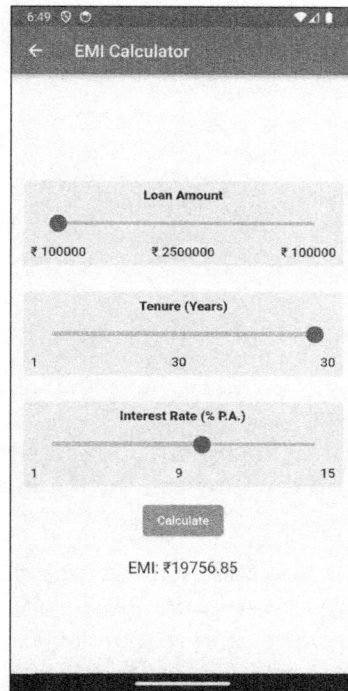

Figure 5.13: User input screen with slider

Mixin

Mixin is a commonly used programming concept in Flutter to reuse and share code across different classes. A mixin is a way to add functionalities to a class without inheriting from that class. In Flutter, mixins are often used with the with keyword.

Here is an example of how to use a mixin in Flutter:

```
1. // Define a mixin
2. mixin LoggingMixin {
3.    void log(String message) {
```

```
4.      print(message);
5.    }
6.  }
7.
8.  // Create a class that uses the mixin
9.  class MyClass with LoggingMixin {
10.   void doSomething() {
11.     log("Doing something...");
12.   }
13. }
14.
15. void main() {
16.   var myObject = MyClass();
17.   myObject.doSomething(); // This will log "Doing something..." to
       the console.
18. }
```

Code 5.14: Flutter Mixin

In this example, **LoggingMixin** is defined with a log method. The **MyClass** class uses the mixin with the with keyword and can now call the log method as if it were a part of the class.

Mixins are helpful for code organization and reusability, especially when you have common functionality that you want to share among multiple classes without creating a deep inheritance hierarchy. Keep in mind that mixins can not be used with classes that have their own constructors, but you can use them with Object or classes that have a default constructor.

Mixins are a powerful tool in Flutter and Dart, allowing you to compose classes with reusable functionality and promote code modularity. But Mixins have some restrictions compared to regular classes. Here are the main restrictions:

- **No constructors**: Mixins cannot have constructors. This means you cannot instantiate a mixin directly, nor can you pass arguments to it during its initialization. However, mixins can define methods that can be called from the classes that use them.

- **No super calls**: Mixins cannot use super to call constructors or methods from the superclass. Since mixins do not have constructors, they cannot call the superclass constructor.

- **No superclass**: A mixin cannot be a superclass of another class. In other words, you cannot extend a mixin to create a subclass.

- **Cannot** Declare Instance Variables: Mixins cannot declare instance variables unless they are final and are initialized at declaration or by a constructor. This is because mixins do not have constructors, so instance variables cannot be initialized in the constructor.

- **Cannot be instantiated**: Mixins cannot be instantiated directly. They can only be used by mixing them into a class using the with keyword.

- **Order matters**: The order in which mixins are applied can affect the behavior of the class. Mixins are applied from left to right, and if multiple mixins have conflicting members (e.g., methods or properties with the same name), the member from the rightmost mixin takes precedence.

Selecting platform specific widget

In Flutter, you can use platform-specific widgets or customize the appearance of your widgets based on the platform (iOS or Android) by using the Platform class and conditional statements. This allows you to create a consistent user experience across different platforms.

Utilize platform-specific widgets or tailor widgets to suit various platforms using the following approach:

1. **Import the dart:io library to access the Platform class.**

    Use conditional statements (such as if, else if, or switch) to determine the current platform and choose the appropriate widget or customization:

```
1.  Widget myPlatformSpecificWidget() {
2.    if (Platform.isIOS) {
3.      // Use an iOS-specific widget or customization
4.      return CupertinoButton(
5.        child: Text('iOS Button'),
6.        onPressed: () {
7.          // iOS-specific action
8.        },
9.      );
10.   } else if (Platform.isAndroid) {
11.     // Use an Android-specific widget or customization
12.     return ElevatedButton(
13.       child: Text('Android Button'),
14.       onPressed: () {
```

```
15.          // Android-specific action
16.       },
17.     );
18.   } else {
19.     // Use a default widget for other platforms (e.g., web, desktop)
20.     return ElevatedButton(
21.       child: Text('Default Button'),
22.       onPressed: () {
23.         // Default action
24.       },
25.     );
26.   }
27. }
```

Code 5.15: Platform specific widget

In this example, we use Platform.isIOS and Platform.isAndroid to conditionally render different buttons depending on the current platform.

2. **Use the Cupertino and material widgets for platform-specific styling:**

Flutter provides Cupertino and Material widgets that are designed to match the iOS and Android design guidelines, respectively. You can wrap your widgets with these widgets to ensure a consistent look and feel on each platform:

```
1.  Widget myPlatformSpecificWidget() {
2.    if (Platform.isIOS) {
3.      return CupertinoPageScaffold(
4.        navigationBar: CupertinoNavigationBar(
5.          middle: Text('iOS Page'),
6.        ),
7.        child: Center(
8.          child: Text('Hello, iOS!'),
9.        ),
10.     );
11.   } else if (Platform.isAndroid) {
12.     return Scaffold(
13.       appBar: AppBar(
14.         title: Text('Android Page'),
```

```
15.        ),
16.        body: Center(
17.          child: Text('Hello, Android!'),
18.        ),
19.      );
20.    } else {
21.      return Center(
22.        child: Text('Hello, Default!'),
23.      );
24.    }
25. }
```

Code 5.16: Platform specific Scaffold

Similarly, while designing a screen with dropdown, we can choose iOS style Cupertino picker for iOS and Android style DropdownButton for Android.

Data persistence in Flutter apps

Data persistence in Flutter apps is essential for storing and retrieving data across app launches or sessions. There are several methods and libraries available in Flutter to achieve data persistence, and the choice depends on the type of data and the requirements of your app. Here are some common methods for data persistence in Flutter:

- **SharedPreferences**: **SharedPreferences** is a simple key-value store that is useful for storing small amounts of data, such as user preferences or settings.

```
1.  // Import the package
2.  import 'package:shared_preferences/shared_preferences.dart';
3.
4.  // Saving data
5.  Future<void> saveData(String key, String value) async {
6.    final prefs = await SharedPreferences.getInstance();
7.    prefs.setString(key, value);
8.  }
9.
10. // Retrieving data
11. Future<String?> loadData(String key) async {
12.   final prefs = await SharedPreferences.getInstance();
```

```
13.  return prefs.getString(key);
14. }
```

Code 5.17: Data persistence using SharedPreferences

- **File storage:** For more extensive data storage, you can read and write data to files on the device's file system using the **dart:io** package:

```
1.  // Writing to a file
2.  Future<void> writeToFile(String fileName, String data) async {
3.    final file = File(fileName);
4.    await file.writeAsString(data);
5.  }
6.
7.  // Reading from a file
8.  Future<String> readFromFile(String fileName) async {
9.    final file = File(fileName);
10.   return await file.readAsString();
11. }
```

Figure 5.18: Data persistence using file storage

- **SQLite database:** SQLite is a popular relational database that you can use for structured data storage. You can use the sqflite package to interact with SQLite databases in Flutter.

```
1.  // Import the package
2.  import 'package:sqflite/sqflite.dart';
3.
4.  // Creating a database and table
5.  final database = await openDatabase('my_database.db', version: 1,
6.     onCreate: (Database db, int version) async {
7.     await db.execute(
8.        'CREATE TABLE my_table(id INTEGER PRIMARY KEY, name TEXT,
          value INTEGER)');
9.  });
10.
11. // Inserting data
12. Future<void> insertData(Map<String, dynamic> data) async {
```

```
13.  final db = await database;
14.  await db.insert('my_table', data);
15. }
16.
17. // Querying data
18. Future<List<Map<String, dynamic>>> fetchData() async {
19.  final db = await database;
20.  return await db.query('my_table');
21. }
```

Figure 5.19: *Data persistence using sqlite*

- **NoSQL databases:** If you prefer a NoSQL approach, you can use libraries like Firebase Firestore or Hive, which provide data persistence with NoSQL databases.

  o **Firebase Firestore:** Firebase provides Firestore as a NoSQL cloud database, and you can use the **firebase_core** and **cloud_firestore** packages for Flutter Firebase integration.

  o **Hive**: Hive is a lightweight and fast NoSQL database for Flutter. It is particularly useful for storing data locally.

- **State management:** If you need to persist and manage the app's state, you can use state management solutions like Provider or Riverpod. These libraries allow you to create and manage app-wide state that persists across different parts of your app.

- **Caching:** For temporary data storage and caching, you can use packages like **flutter_cache_manager** or the caching mechanisms provided by network request libraries like Dio or http.

- **Secure storage:** For sensitive data like authentication tokens or API keys, consider using packages like **flutter_secure_storage** for secure storage.

When selecting a data persistence method for your Flutter app, consider the type of data you need to store, the data's size, and how long it should persist. Different scenarios may require different approaches, and you can even combine multiple methods to meet your app's needs.

Conclusion

We delved into the significance of Flutter themes, understanding how they contribute to the consistent and appealing visual design of applications. The exploration of the .copyWith operator showcased its utility in efficiently modifying theme attributes.

Custom widgets emerged as a fundamental aspect, empowering developers to encapsulate and reuse UI components. We also examined the role of Flutter packages, emphasizing their importance in extending functionality and enhancing the overall development process.

Gesture detection mechanisms were explored, highlighting their role in creating interactive and responsive user interfaces. The ability to pass functions as parameters and the implementation of routing and navigation strategies were crucial aspects in building dynamic and navigable applications.

The discussion on mixins shed light on the flexibility and code reuse achieved through this powerful composition mechanism. We also touched upon the concept of multiple inheritance in Flutter, emphasizing its role in crafting well-structured and modular code.

In the upcoming chapter, we will explore the exciting world of fetching data over the internet in Flutter. We will discuss techniques and best practices for integrating data from various sources, enhancing the functionality and dynamism of our applications. So buckle up, as we take the next step in our Flutter journey!

Multiple choice questions

1. **In Flutter, which method is used to access the theme data of the nearest ancestor Theme widget?**

    a. .accessTheme()

    b. .retrieveTheme()

    c. .of()

    d. .copyWith()

2. **What is the primary use of the `.copyWith()` method when working with Flutter themes?**

    a. To create a new theme from an existing one with some modifications.

    b. To copy all the widgets in the current theme

    c. To change the theme's name

    d. To delete the current theme

3. **What is the primary purpose of using packages in a Flutter project?**

    a. To increase the app's size

    b. To reduce the app's performance

    c. To reuse code and add functionality to the app

    d. To make the app's code more complex

4. **Which Flutter widget is commonly used to detect gestures like taps and swipes?**

   a. GestureDetector

   b. Text

   c. Container

   d. ListView

5. **In Flutter, what is the benefit of passing a function as a parameter to another function or widget?**

   a. It reduces the app's size

   b. It improves the app's performance

   c. It allows for callback behavior and interactivity

   d. It simplifies the app's code structure

6. **How can you navigate to a new screen in Flutter?**

   a. Using the Navigator widget

   b. By changing the app's theme

   c. By using the GestureDetector widget

   d. By modifying the device's system settings

7. **What is a mixin in Flutter?**

   a. A type of dessert

   b. A way to achieve multiple inheritance in Dart

   c. A built-in Flutter widget

   d. A tool for managing data persistence

Answers

1. c. .of()
2. a. To create a new theme from an existing one with some modifications
3. c. To reuse code and add functionality to the app
4. a. GestureDetector
5. c. It allows for callback behavior and interactivity
6. a. Using the Navigator widget
7. b. A way to achieve multiple inheritance in Dart

Join our book's Discord space

Join the book's Discord Workspace for Latest updates, Offers, Tech happenings around the world, New Release and Sessions with the Authors:

https://discord.bpbonline.com

CHAPTER 6

Fetch Data from Internet

Introduction

In today's digital age, mobile applications often rely on data from the internet to provide real-time information, updates, and enhanced user experiences. Flutter, a versatile and powerful framework for building cross-platform mobile applications, offers a range of tools and techniques to fetch and handle data from the internet seamlessly.

Structure

This chapter covers the following key topics:

- Network call with http library in Flutter
- Futures in Flutter
- Parsing JSON
- Spinner widget
- Passing data backwards through navigator
- Location service.
- Sample app with networking call

Objectives

By the end of this chapter, you will have a strong understanding of how to fetch and handle data from the internet in Flutter applications. You will be able to make network calls using the http library, efficiently manage asynchronous operations using futures, parse JSON data, implement loading indicators using the Spinner widget, pass data backward through the navigator, and integrate location services for location-based functionalities. Additionally, you will have built a sample Flutter app that showcases these concepts, equipping you with practical knowledge to enhance your Flutter projects with internet data fetching capabilities.

Network call with http library in Flutter

To make network calls in Flutter, you can use the http package, which provides a simple and flexible way to send HTTP requests and handle responses. Here is how you can make network calls with the http library in Flutter:

1. Add the http package to your **pubspec.yaml** file.

   a. Open your project's **pubspec.yaml** file and add the http package as a dependency:

   ```
   1. dependencies:
   2.   flutter:
   3.     sdk: flutter
   4.   http: ^0.13.3  # Replace with the latest version
   ```

   Code 6.1: Adding http package

   b. Run **flutter pub get** to fetch the package.

2. **Import the http package**: In your Dart code, import the http package:

   ```
   1. import 'package:http/http.dart' as http;
   ```

   Code 6.2: Import http package

3. Make a **GET** request:

   To make a **GET** request to a remote server, use the **http.get()** function. Here is an example:

   ```
   1. Future<void> fetchData() async {
   2.   final url = Uri.parse('https://jsonplaceholder.typicode.com/
        posts/1 '); // Replace with your API endpoint
   3.   final response = await http.get(url);
   4.
   ```

```
5.    if (response.statusCode == 200) {
6.      // Request was successful
7.      print('Response data: ${response.body}');
8.    } else {
9.      // Request failed
10.     print('Failed to fetch data. Status code: ${response.
        statusCode}');
11.   }
12. }
```

Code 6.3: Making a get request

Replace the URL with the API endpoint you want to access. The **http.get()** function returns a Response object, and you can check its **statusCode** to determine if the request was successful. If you're unfamiliar with the '**async**' and '**await**' keywords and unsure of their usage, do not worry. We will delve into them later in this chapter.

4. Make other types of requests like you can use **http.post()**, **http.put()**, and **http.delete()** functions to make **POST**, **PUT**, and **DELETE** requests, respectively.

Example of a POST request:

```
1.  Future<void> postData() async {
2.    final url = Uri.parse('https://api.example.com/add_data'); //
      Replace with your API endpoint
3.    final response = await http.post(url, body: {'key': 'value'});
4.
5.    if (response.statusCode == 200) {
6.      // Request was successful
7.      print('Response data: ${response.body}');
8.    } else {
9.      // Request failed
10.    print('Failed to add data. Status code: ${response.statusCode}');
11.   }
12. }
```

Code 6.4: Making a post request

a. Replace the URL (**https://api.example.com/post-data**) with the URL of the API where you want to send data.

b. Modify the headers and request body as needed for your API.

5. Be sure to handle errors by checking the HTTP response's status code. You can customize the error-handling logic to suit your application's needs.

6. If the response from the server is in JSON format, you can use the **json.decode** method to parse it into Dart objects.

7. Network calls are asynchronous, so it's common to use the async and await keywords to work with them. Make sure to call these methods within async functions.

8. If your app requires internet access, ensure that you've added the necessary permissions in your app's **AndroidManifest.xml** and **Info.plist** files for Android and iOS, respectively. To add necessary permissions for internet access in your app's **AndroidManifest.xml** and **Info.plist** files for Android and iOS respectively, follow these steps:

    For Android (**AndroidManifest.xml**):

    a. Open your Android project in Android Studio.

    b. Navigate to the '**app**' folder and open the **AndroidManifest.xml** file.

    c. Inside the **<manifest>** tag, add the following line if it's not already present:

    <uses-permission android:name="android.permission.INTERNET" />

    This permission allows the app to access the internet.

    For iOS (**Info.plist**):

    a. Open your iOS project in Xcode.

    b. Navigate to the '**Runner**' folder and open the **Info.plist** file.

    c. Add the following key-value pair if it is not already present:

    - **Key**: **NSAppTransportSecurity**
    - **Type**: Dictionary
    - Inside **NSAppTransportSecurity**, add another key-value pair:
      o Key: **NSAllowsArbitraryLoads**
      o Type: Boolean
      o Value: YES

    This configuration allows the app to access arbitrary URLs without needing specific permissions.

    After making these changes, your app should have the necessary permissions to access the internet on both Android and iOS platforms.

9. Use tools like Postman or Insomnia to test your API endpoints before integrating them into your Flutter app.

This is a basic example of how to perform network calls in Flutter using the **http** package.

Futures in Flutter

In Flutter, **Future** and `FutureBuilder` are essential concepts for handling asynchronous operations. Here is an overview of how they work:

Future

A Future represents a potential value or error that will be available at some point in the future. It is used to work with asynchronous operations like network requests, file I/O, or any task that does not block the main thread:

```
1.  Future<int> fetchSomeData() {
2.    return Future.delayed(Duration(seconds: 2), () => 42); //
      Simulating a delay
3.  }
4.
5.  void main() {
6.    fetchSomeData().then((value) {
7.      print("Received data: $value");
8.    }).catchError((error) {
9.      print("Error: $error");
10.   });
11. }
```

Code 6.5: Usage of Future

In this example, **fetchSomeData** returns a Future that simulates a delay of two seconds and then provides the value 42. We use **.then()** to handle the successful result and **.catchError()** for error handling.

FutureBuilder

`FutureBuilder` is a widget that helps you build UI components based on the result of a Future. It is especially useful in Flutter for handling asynchronous operations within your UI:

```
1.  Future<int> fetchSomeData() {
2.    return Future.delayed(Duration(seconds: 2), () => 42); //
      Simulating a delay
3.  }
4.
```

```
5. void main() {
6.    runApp(
7.      MaterialApp(
8.        home: Scaffold(
9.          appBar: AppBar(title: Text("FutureBuilder Example")),
10.         body: FutureBuilder<int>(
11.           future: fetchSomeData(),
12.           builder: (context, snapshot) {
13.             if (snapshot.connectionState == ConnectionState.waiting)
                 {
14.               return CircularProgressIndicator();
15.             } else if (snapshot.hasError) {
16.               return Text("Error: ${snapshot.error}");
17.             } else {
18.               return Text("Received data: ${snapshot.data}");
19.             }
20.           },
21.         ),
22.       ),
23.     ),
24.   );
25. }
```

Code 6.6: How to use FutureBuilder

In this example, we use **FutureBuilder** to handle the **fetchSomeData** future. Depending on the **snapshot.connectionState**, we return different widgets. This allows you to display loading spinners, error messages, or the fetched data as needed.

Async/Await

You can simplify working with Future by using async and await. The async keyword is used to mark a function as asynchronous and await is used to wait for the completion of a Future:

```
1. Future<int> fetchSomeData() async {
2.    await Future.delayed(Duration(seconds: 2)); // Simulating a delay
3.    return 42;
```

```
4. }
5.
6. void main() {
7.   print('Start of main function');
8.   fetchData().then((value) {
9.     print("Received data: $value");
10.  }).catchError((error) {
11.    print("Error: $error");
12.  });
13.  print('End of main function');
14. }
```

Code 6.7: How to use fetchSomeData

In this example, async and await make the code more readable and similar to synchronous code.

Understanding and effectively using **Future** and **FutureBuilder** is crucial for handling asynchronous tasks in Flutter, such as network requests and database operations. They allow you to create responsive and efficient apps.

Parsing JSON

Parsing JSON in Flutter is a common task when working with APIs and retrieving data. Here is an overview of how to parse JSON data in Flutter:

1. **Create a model class.**

   You should define a model class that represents the structure of the JSON data. This class should have fields that match the keys in the JSON data.

   For example, if you have JSON data like this:

```
1. {
2.   "name": "John",
3.   "age": 30
4. }
```

Code 6.8: Sample JSON

2. **Create a Dart class:**

```
1. class Person {
2.   final String name;
```

```
3.    final int age;
4.
5.    Person(this.name, this.age);
6.
7.    factory Person.fromJson(Map<String, dynamic> json) {
8.       return Person(json['name'], json['age']);
9.    }
10. }
```

Code 6.8: Model class

3. **Parsing JSON:**

   Once you have your model class, you can use the **json.decode** function to convert JSON data into Dart objects:

```
1.  import 'dart:convert';
2.
3.  void main() {
4.    String jsonText = '{"name": "John", "age": 30}';
5.    Map<String, dynamic> jsonMap = json.decode(jsonText);
6.
7.    Person person = Person.fromJson(jsonMap);
8.
9.    print('Name: ${person.name}, Age: ${person.age}');
10. }
```

Code 6.9: JSON parsing example

In this example, we use the **json.decode** function to convert a JSON string into a Dart map (**jsonMap**). We then use the **Person.fromJson** factory constructor to create a Person object from the JSON data.

4. **Handling JSON Arrays:**

   If your JSON data is an array of objects, you can parse it into a list of model objects:

```
1.  [
2.    { "name": "John", "age": 30 },
3.    { "name": "Alice", "age": 25 }
4.  ]
```

Code 6.10: json array

In this case, you can modify your model class to handle the list:

```
1.  class Person {
2.    final String name;
3.    final int age;
4.
5.    Person(this.name, this.age);
6.
7.    factory Person.fromJson(Map<String, dynamic> json) {
8.      return Person(json['name'], json['age']);
9.    }
10. }
```

Code 6.11: Updated model

Parse the JSON array like this:

```
1.  import ‹dart:convert›;
2.
3.  void main() {
4.    String jsonText = ‹[{"name": "John", "age": 30}, {"name":
         "Alice", "age": 25}]';
5.    List<dynamic> jsonList = json.decode(jsonText);
6.
7.    List<Person> people = jsonList.map((json) => Person.
         fromJson(json)).toList();
8.
9.    for (Person person in people) {
10.     print('Name: ${person.name}, Age: ${person.age}');
11.   }
12. }
```

Code 6.12: Updated code for json parsing

5. **Error handling**:

When parsing JSON, it is important to handle errors, such as missing keys or incorrect data types. You can use try-catch blocks and conditional statements to handle different scenarios:

```
1.  import 'dart:convert';
2.
```

```
3.  void main() {
4.    String jsonText = '{"name": "John", "age": "30"}'; // Age is a
      string here
5.
6.    try {
7.      Map<String, dynamic> jsonMap = json.decode(jsonText);
8.      Person person = Person.fromJson(jsonMap);
9.
10.     print('Name: ${person.name}, Age: ${person.age}');
11.   } catch (e) {
12.     // Handle the exception
13.     print('Error while parsing JSON: $e');
14.   }
15. }
16.
17. class Person {
18.   final String name;
19.   final int age;
20.
21.   Person(this.name, this.age);
22.
23.   factory Person.fromJson(Map<String, dynamic> json) {
24.     // Check for missing or incorrect data types
25.     if (json['name'] is String && json['age'] is int) {
26.       return Person(json['name'], json['age']);
27.     } else {
28.       throw FormatException('Invalid JSON data format');
29.     }
30.   }
31. }
```

Code 6.13: Added try catch block for JSON parsing

By following these steps, you can effectively parse JSON data in Flutter and use it in your applications, whether it comes from an API response, local storage, or any other source.

As the JSON data structures become more extensive and complex, manually writing serialization and deserialization code can lead to errors and increase development time. To mitigate these challenges, it is generally recommended to use tools like the **json_serializable** package provided by the Dart Team. This package automates the process of generating serialization and deserialization code for Dart classes, improving code maintainability and reducing the risk of errors, especially as JSON data grows in complexity.

The **json_serializable** package, maintained by the Dart team, is a code generation library for Dart and Flutter that helps automate the process of serializing and deserializing JSON data. It generates the boilerplate code needed to convert JSON data into Dart objects (serialization) and vice versa (deserialization).

Here is how **json_serializable** works:

a. **Annotate your model classes**: You annotate your Dart model classes with **@ JsonSerializable()** to indicate that you want to generate serialization and deserialization code for them.

b. **Run code generation**: You then run the code generation tool provided by the **json_serializable** package, either through the command line or as part of your build process. This tool generates the serialization and deserialization code based on the annotations in your model classes.

c. **Use generated code**: Once the code generation is complete, you can use the generated code to easily serialize and deserialize JSON data in your application. This removes the need to manually write serialization and deserialization code, reducing the chance of errors and improving code maintainability.

By using **json_serializable**, you can streamline the process of working with JSON data in Dart and Flutter, especially for larger and more complex JSON structures. It helps to ensure that your serialization and deserialization logic is consistent, accurate, and efficient. Additionally, it integrates well with other Dart and Flutter libraries and tools, making it a popular choice for JSON serialization in the Dart ecosystem.

Here's an example demonstrating how to use the **json_serializable** package in Dart to serialize and deserialize JSON data:

First, add the **json_serializable** and **build_runner** dependencies to your **pubspec.yaml** file:

```
1. dependencies:
2.   json_annotation: ^4.0.1
3.
4. dev_dependencies:
5.   build_runner: ^2.1.4
```

```
6.    json_serializable: ^4.1.0
```

Code 6.14: Add dependencies

Then, create a Dart model class for the JSON data:

```
1.  import 'package:json_annotation/json_annotation.dart';
2.
3.  part 'person.g.dart'; // This is the generated file
4.
5.  @JsonSerializable() // Add this annotation to enable code generation
6.  class Person {
7.    final String name;
8.    final int age;
9.
10.   Person(this.name, this.age);
11.
12.   // This factory constructor is needed for deserialization
13.   factory Person.fromJson(Map<String, dynamic> json) =>
        _$PersonFromJson(json);
14.
15.   // This method is needed for serialization
16.   Map<String, dynamic> toJson() => _$PersonToJson(this);
17. }
```

Code 6.15: create a Dart model class

Next, run the code generation tool to generate serialization and deserialization code:

flutter pub run build_runner build

This generates a file named person.g.dart (assuming your class is named Person) containing the necessary serialization and deserialization code.

Now you can use the Person class to serialize and deserialize JSON data:

```
1.  import 'dart:convert';
2.  import 'person.dart'; // Import your model class
3.
4.  void main() {
5.    String jsonStr = '{"name": "John", "age": 30}'; // JSON string
```

```
6.    Map<String, dynamic> jsonMap = json.decode(jsonStr); // Decode
      JSON string
7.
8.    // Deserialize JSON data into a Person object
9.    Person person = Person.fromJson(jsonMap);
10.
11.   // Access the properties of the Person object
12.   print('Name: ${person.name}, Age: ${person.age}');
13.
14.   // Serialize the Person object back to JSON
15.   String serializedJson = json.encode(person.toJson());
16.   print('Serialized JSON: $serializedJson');
17. }
```

Code 6.16: serialize and deserialize JSON data

This example demonstrates how to use **json_serializable** to automatically generate serialization and deserialization code for a Dart class. It simplifies the process of working with JSON data in Dart and Flutter, making your code more maintainable and less error-prone.

Flutter applications are typically written in Dart, and Dart is a statically typed language. This means that Dart requires you to define the structure of your data explicitly, which includes defining classes to represent the structure of JSON data.

Comparatively, some dynamically typed languages, like JavaScript, allow for more flexibility when working with JSON data. JavaScript's loose typing allows you to work directly with JSON objects without defining corresponding classes.

Additionally, Dart's tree shaking feature, which is part of its build process, can affect how JSON parsing is handled. Tree shaking is a process used to remove unused code from the final compiled output. When parsing JSON in Flutter, if you're not careful about how you access JSON data, the tree shaking process might mistakenly remove parts of your code that are perceived as unused, leading to unexpected behavior.

To mitigate this, it is essential to follow best practices for parsing JSON in Flutter, such as defining model classes and accessing JSON data in a way that's compatible with tree shaking.

Spinner widget

A *spinner* widget in the context of user interface design generally refers to a visual element or control that indicates that a process is ongoing or data is being loaded. Spinners are often used to provide feedback to the user, showing that some action is in progress and they should wait for a moment.

A spinner widget is typically a circular loading indicator that spins to signify that an operation, such as data fetching or processing, is happening. The spinner provides a visual cue to the user that the app is working and not frozen.

In Flutter, you can create a spinner widget using the **CircularProgressIndicator** widget or by using custom widgets to provide additional context or information along with the spinner. The **CircularProgressIndicator** is a built-in Flutter widget specifically designed for indicating progress or loading.

Here is an example of using the **CircularProgressIndicator** widget in Flutter:

```
1.  import 'package:flutter/material.dart';
2.
3.  class MyLoadingScreen extends StatelessWidget {
4.    const MyLoadingScreen({super.key});
5.
6.    @override
7.    Widget build(BuildContext context) {
8.      return const Center(
9.        child: CircularProgressIndicator(), // Display a simple spinner
10.     );
11.   }
12. }
13.
14. void main() {
15.   runApp(MaterialApp(
16.     home: Scaffold(
17.       appBar: AppBar(
18.         title: const Text('Spinner Widget Example'),
19.       ),
20.       body: const MyLoadingScreen(),
21.     ),
```

```
22.  ));
23. }
```

Code 6.17: Spinner widget example

Passing data backwards through navigator

In Flutter, you can pass data backward through the navigator when you navigate back to the previous screen by returning the data from the destination screen. Here is how you can do it:

Sending data from the destination screen

In the destination screen, where you want to send data back to the previous screen, you can use the **Navigator.pop** method. This method allows you to return a result when you navigate back to the previous screen. For example:

```
1. // Destination screen
2. onPressed: () {
3.    // Create a result object that contains the data you want to pass
      back
4.    var dataToSendBack = 'This is the data to pass back';
5.    Navigator.pop(context, dataToSendBack);
6. }
```

Code 6.18: Passing data from destination screen

In the code above, we use **Navigator.pop** to send the **dataToSendBack** object back to the previous screen.

Receiving data in the previous screen:

In the previous screen (the screen that initiated the navigation to the destination screen), you can use await when calling **Navigator.push** to receive the data when the destination screen is popped. Here is an example of how to receive the data:

```
1. // Navigate to the destination screen
2. var result = await Navigator.push(
3.    context,
4.    MaterialPageRoute(builder: (context) => DestinationScreen()),
5. );
6.
```

```
7. // Check if a result was received
8. if (result != null) {
9.    // Handle the received data
10.   print('Received data: $result');
11. }
```

Code 6.19: Passing data to destination screen.

In this code, we use await with **Navigator.push** to receive the result returned from the destination screen. If a result is received (that is, the destination screen used **Navigator. pop** to return data), it can be accessed in the result variable.

By using this approach, you can effectively pass data backward through the navigator in Flutter from a destination screen to the previous screen. This is useful for scenarios where you need to send data back to the calling screen after a user action or other events in the destination screen.

Location service

In Flutter, you can implement location services using various plugins and packages to access the device's GPS and location data. One of the most popular plugins for handling location services in Flutter is the *geolocator* package. Here is how you can get started with location services in Flutter using the geolocator package:

1. Add the geolocator package to your **pubspec.yaml** file:

```
2. dependencies:
3.   flutter:
4.     sdk: flutter
5.   geolocator: ^8.0.1
```

Code 6.20: Geolocator package on pubspec file

Run **flutter pub get** to fetch the package.

2. Import the geolocator package in your Dart file.

3. **Request Location Permissions**:

You need to request permission from the user to access their location. To do this, add the necessary permissions to your **AndroidManifest.xml** (for Android) and **Info.plist** (for iOS).

Make sure you have the appropriate permissions added to your **AndroidManifest. xml** and **Info.plist** files. The **permission_handler** package handles the iOS **Info.plist** for you but does not modify the AndroidManifest.xml. You need to do this manually.

Android: Open **android/app/src/main/AndroidManifest.xml** and add the following permissions:

1. `<uses-permission android:name="android.permission.ACCESS_COARSE_LOCATION" />`

2. `<uses-permission android:name="android.permission.ACCESS_FINE_LOCATION" />`

Code 6.21: location permission for Android

iOS: No manual modification is required for **Info.plist** when using the **permission_handler** package, as it will manage this for you. However, make sure your app's **Info.plist** file includes the **NSLocationWhenInUseUsageDescription** key with a description of why your app needs location access.

Here is an example of how to add the **NSLocationWhenInUseUsageDescription** key with a description in your iOS **Info.plist** file:

1. Open your Flutter project's iOS directory and locate the **Info.plist** file. This file is typically found in the **ios/Runner** directory of your project.

2. Open the **Info.plist** file in a text editor or Xcode.

3. Add the following XML entry to the **Info.plist** file:

    1. `<key>NSLocationWhenInUseUsageDescription</key>`

    2. `<string>We need your location to provide location-based services and improve your experience.</string>`

Code 6.22: Location permission for iOS

4. Initialize the geolocator and get the current location:

```
1.  Position? _currentPosition;
2.
3.  void _getCurrentLocation() async {
4.    final GeolocatorPlatform geolocator = GeolocatorPlatform.
      instance;
5.    try {
6.      Position position = await geolocator.getCurrentPosition(de
        siredAccuracy: LocationAccuracy.high);
7.      setState(() {
8.        _currentPosition = position;
9.      });
10.   } catch (e) {
11.     print(e);
```

```
12.   }
13. }
```

Code 6.23: Get current position

In the code above, **_getCurrentLocation** is a function that fetches the current device location using the geolocator package. You can then use this location data as needed in your Flutter application.

Remember to handle errors and exceptions properly, such as if the user denies location permissions or if the device's location services are turned off. Always check for permission status before trying to access location data.

Depending on your app's requirements, you can also listen for location changes using the geolocator package.

Please ensure that you have the necessary permissions to access location services on both Android and iOS platforms. Additionally, consider handling location services gracefully and securely in your app, as well as checking for device location settings. This is just a basic example to get you started with location services in Flutter.

Sample app with networking call

Let us create an example application, applying the insights we have gained from the topics covered in this chapter. In this demonstration, we will initiate by retrieving location details, followed by fetching weather information and presenting the results on a screen.

So, let us start with main file.

```
1.  import 'package:flutter/material.dart';
2.  import 'package:weather_app/screens/weather_data_screen.dart';
3.
4.  void main() {
5.    runApp(const MyApp());
6.  }
7.
8.  class MyApp extends StatelessWidget {
9.    const MyApp({Key? key}) : super(key: key);
10.
11.   @override
12.   Widget build(BuildContext context) {
13.     return MaterialApp(
14.       title: 'Weather App',
```

```
15.        theme: ThemeData(
16.          colorScheme: ColorScheme.fromSeed(seedColor: const
             Color(0XFF0065FA)),
17.          useMaterial3: true,
18.        ),
19.        home: const WeatherDataScreen(),
20.     );
21.   }
22. }
```

Code 6.24: main file

This serves as the entry point of the application, where we return the **WeatherDataScreen**. Now, let's examine the code for **WeatherDataScreen**. The **WeatherDataScreen** class is a **StatefulWidget** that fetches the user's location using the **LocationService** class, and then retrieves weather data based on the obtained latitude and longitude. Once the weather data is fetched, it navigates to the **WeatherResultScreen** to display the weather information.

Before we dive into the details, let us break down the code into smaller segments. Breaking down the code into smaller segments will make it easier to understand. Let us proceed with that approach.

- **Imports**: Import necessary packages and custom classes.
- **WeatherDataScreen StatefulWidget**: Define the **StatefulWidget** for the Weather Data screen.
- **_WeatherDataScreenState Class**: Define the State class for WeatherDataScreen.
- **InitState Method**: Override the **initState()** method to initialize state.
- **_getLocation Method**: Method to get device location and fetch weather data.
- **fetchWeather Method**: Method to fetch weather data from API.
- **_navigateToWeatherResult Method**: Method to navigate to **WeatherResultScreen**.
- **Build Method**: Override the **build()** method to build the UI.

The following code represents the complete code for **WeatherDataScreen**. Considering its length, attempting to review the entire code in one go may prove challenging. It is recommended to approach it methodically, addressing each point from the breakdown.

```
1. // Imports
2. import 'dart:convert';
3. import 'package:flutter/material.dart';
4. import 'package:geolocator/geolocator.dart';
5. import 'package:http/http.dart' as http;
```

```
6.  import '../services/location.dart';

7.  import 'package:weather_app/screens/weather_result_screen.dart';

8.  import 'package:weather_app/services/weather_data.dart';

9.

10. // Define the WeatherDataScreen StatefulWidget

11. class WeatherDataScreen extends StatefulWidget {

12.   const WeatherDataScreen({Key? key}) : super(key: key);

13.

14.   @override

15.   State<WeatherDataScreen> createState() => _WeatherDataScreenState();

16. }

17.

18. // Define the State class for WeatherDataScreen

19. class _WeatherDataScreenState extends State<WeatherDataScreen> {

20.   // Instance of LocationService to get device location

21.   LocationService locationService = LocationService();

22.

23.   // Variable to store the current position

24.   Position? _position;

25.

26.   // Override the initState() method to initialize state

27.   @override

28.   void initState() {

29.     super.initState();

30.     _getLocation(); // Call method to get device location

31.   }

32.

33.   // Method to get device location

34.   Future<void> _getLocation() async {

35.     try {

36.       // Create an instance of LocationService

37.       LocationService location = LocationService();

38.

39.       // Get the current device location
```

```
40.          _position = await location.getLocation();
41.

42.          // Fetch weather data using device location
43.          final weatherData = await fetchWeather(
44.            _position?.latitude ?? 0.0,
45.            _position?.longitude ?? 0.0,
46.          );
47.

48.          // Navigate to the result screen if weather data is available
49.          if (weatherData != null) {
50.            _navigateToWeatherResult(weatherData);
51.          }
52.        } catch (e) {
53.          // Handle errors
54.          print('Error: $e');
55.        }
56.      }
57.

58.    // Method to fetch weather data from API
59.    Future<WeatherData?> fetchWeather(double latitude, double
       longitude) async {
60.      try {
61.        const apiKey = '4ed1e37e89277c79528a372962b6a980';
62.        final apiUrl =
63.            'https://api.openweathermap.org/data/2.5/weather?lat=$lat-
             itude&lon=$longitude&appid=$apiKey&units=metric';
64.

65.        // Make a GET request to fetch weather data
66.        final response = await http.get(Uri.parse(apiUrl));
67.

68.        if (response.statusCode == 200) {
69.          // Parse JSON response and create WeatherData object
70.          final jsonMap = json.decode(response.body);
71.          final weatherData = WeatherData.fromJson(jsonMap);
72.          return weatherData;
```

```
73.          } else {
74.            throw Exception('Failed to load weather data');
75.          }
76.        } catch (e) {
77.          // Handle errors
78.          print('Error: $e');
79.          return null;
80.        }
81.      }
82.
83.      // Method to navigate to WeatherResultScreen
84.      void _navigateToWeatherResult(WeatherData weatherData) {
85.        Navigator.of(context).push(
86.          MaterialPageRoute(
87.            builder: (context) => WeatherResultScreen(weatherData:
                 weatherData),
88.          ),
89.        );
90.      }
91.
92.      // Override the build() method to build the UI
93.      @override
94.      Widget build(BuildContext context) {
95.        return Scaffold(
96.          appBar: AppBar(
97.            backgroundColor: Theme.of(context).colorScheme.secondary,
98.            title: const Text("Weather Data"),
99.          ),
100.          body: Center(
101.            child: Column(
102.              mainAxisAlignment: MainAxisAlignment.center,
103.              children: <Widget>[
104.                // Display device latitude and longitude
105.                Center(
```

```
106.                    child: _position != null
107.                      ? Text(
108.                        "Latitude: ${_position?.latitude},
                           Longitude: ${_position?.longitude}",
109.                        )
110.                      : const CircularProgressIndicator(),
111.                    ),
112.                    // Display weather data if available (removed for
                       brevity)
113.                  ],
114.                ),
115.              ),
116.            );
117.        }
118.    }
```

Code 6.25: WeathereDataScreen file

Now let us look at the **LocationService** class:

```
1.  import 'package:geolocator/geolocator.dart';
2.
3.  class LocationService {
4.    Future<Position?> getLocation() async {
5.      try {
6.        Position position = await Geolocator.getCurrentPosition(
7.          desiredAccuracy: LocationAccuracy.low,
8.        );
9.        return position;
10.     } catch (e) {
11.        print("Error getting location: $e");
12.     }
13.   }
14. }
```

Code 6.26: LocationService file

The **LocationService** class is a simple class that provides a method (**getLocation**) to retrieve the user's current location using the Geolocator package. Here is a breakdown of the code:

- **Import**: The class imports the necessary geolocator package, which is used to interact with the device's location services.

- **LocationService Class**: The **LocationService** class contains a single method, **getLocation**, which is asynchronous and returns a Future<Position?>. Position is a class from the geolocator package that represents a geographical position (latitude, longitude, altitude, etc.).

- **getLocation Method**: The **getLocation** method uses the **Geolocator. getCurrentPosition** method to asynchronously retrieve the current position of the device. It specifies **LocationAccuracy.low** as the desired accuracy, which indicates a lower level of accuracy but faster response time. If the location is successfully obtained, it returns the Position object. If an error occurs during the location retrieval, it catches the exception, prints an error message to the console, and returns null.

- **Error handling**: Errors during location retrieval are caught, and an error message is printed to the console. The method then returns null to indicate that the location could not be obtained.

This class provides a convenient way to handle location retrieval in the **WeatherDataScreen**. Now let us look at **WeatherData** class, how it parses the **json** response to an object with required properties.

```
1.  class WeatherData {
2.    final double temperature; // Temperature in Celsius
3.    final String description; // Weather description
4.    final String iconUrl; // URL to the weather icon
5.    final String cityName; // Name of the city
6.
7.    WeatherData({
8.      required this.cityName,
9.      required this.temperature,
10.     required this.description,
11.     required this.iconUrl,
12.   });
13.
14.   factory WeatherData.fromJson(Map<String, dynamic> json) {
```

```
15.     final main = json['main'];
16.     final weather = json['weather'][0];
17.     final name = json["name"];
18.
19.     return WeatherData(
20.         cityName: name,
21.         temperature: main['temp'].toDouble(),
22.         description: weather['description'],
23.         iconUrl: 'https://openweathermap.org/img/
        wn/${weather['icon']}@2x.png');
24.   }
25. }
```

Code 6.27: WeatherData file

The **WeatherData** class is a data model representing weather information. It has a constructor that takes the necessary parameters (**cityName**, **temperature**, **description**, and **iconUrl**), and a factory method **fromJson** for creating an instance of **WeatherData** from a JSON map.

Here is a breakdown of the key components:

- **WeatherData Class**: It has final fields for temperature, description, iconUrl, and cityName, representing the key weather attributes. The constructor (WeatherData) initializes the fields with the provided values.

- **Factory Method (fromJson):** The fromJson factory method is responsible for creating a WeatherData instance from a JSON map. It extracts relevant information from the JSON map, such as temperature, weather description, city name, and the icon URL. The temperature is obtained from the 'main' section of the JSON, the weather description from the first element of the 'weather' array, and the city name directly from the 'name' field.

- **iconUrl**: The icon URL is constructed using the 'icon' field from the 'weather' array to build the URL for the weather icon as shown below:

  '**https://openweathermap.org/img/wn/${weather['icon']}@2x.png**'. The icon URL is constructed using the OpenWeatherMap URL format.

- **Use of the toDouble() Method**: The temperature is converted to a double using **main['temp'].toDouble()** to ensure that it is stored as a double.

Overall, this class efficiently encapsulates the structure and logic related to representing weather data. Now let us look at the **WeatherResultScreen**, this is a Flutter widget that displays weather information using the provided **WeatherData**.

```
1.  import 'package:flutter/material.dart';
2.  import '../services/weather_data.dart';
3.
4.  class WeatherResultScreen extends StatelessWidget {
5.    final WeatherData weatherData;
6.
7.    const WeatherResultScreen({super.key, required this.weatherData});
8.
9.    @override
10.   Widget build(BuildContext context) {
11.     return Scaffold(
12.       appBar: AppBar(
13.         title: const Text('Weather Result'),
14.       ),
15.       body: Center(
16.         child: Column(
17.           mainAxisAlignment: MainAxisAlignment.center,
18.           children: <Widget>[
19.             Text(
20.               'City: ${weatherData.cityName}',
21.               style: const TextStyle(
22.                 fontSize: 18, // Adjust the font size as needed
23.                 fontWeight: FontWeight.bold, // Adjust the font
                     weight as needed
24.                 color: Colors.black, // Adjust the text color as needed
25.               ),
26.             ),
27.             Image.network(
28.               weatherData.iconUrl,
29.               width: 50, // Adjust the width as needed
30.               height: 50, // Adjust the height as needed
31.             ),
32.             Text('Temperature: ${weatherData.temperature}°C'),
33.             Text('Description: ${weatherData.description}'),
```

```
34.
35.            // Add more widgets to display additional weather data
               as needed
36.        ],
37.      ),
38.    ),
39.  );
40. }
41.}
```

Code 6.28: WeatherResultScreen file

Important points to observe in the code are as follows:

- A named constructor within the class mandates a required parameter, **weatherData**, which must be of type **WeatherData**.

- To establish a fundamental structure for the screen, the widget employs a Scaffold, incorporating an AppBar to feature the title.

- Within the scaffold's body, a Column nested in the Center widget houses elements such as temperature, description, and an image.

If you run the app, you should something similar to this screen:

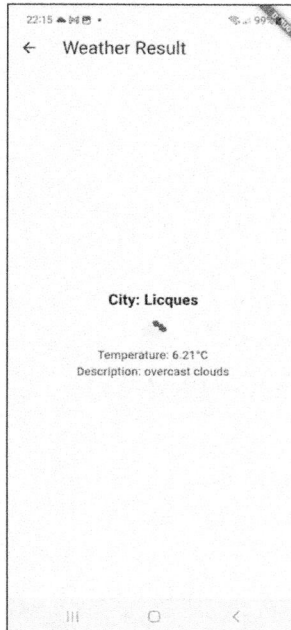

Figure 6.1: Weather result screen

If you want to enhance or customize it further, you can consider adding more widgets or formatting options based on your preferences.

Conclusion

This chapter has provided an in-depth exploration of fetching data from the internet in Flutter applications. You have learned essential concepts such as making network calls with the http library, managing asynchronous operations using futures, parsing JSON data, integrating loading indicators with the Spinner widget, passing data backward through the navigator, and utilizing location services. Armed with this knowledge, you are now well-equipped to create dynamic and responsive Flutter apps that fetch and handle data from the internet seamlessly, enhancing user experiences and functionality.

Looking ahead, the next chapter will delve into Firebase integration in Flutter applications. You will explore how to leverage Firebase's powerful features such as real-time database, authentication, cloud messaging, and more to add advanced functionalities and cloud-based services to your Flutter apps.

Multiple choice questions

1. **What is the primary purpose of the http package in Flutter?**
   a. Managing local database
   b. Making HTTP requests to external APIs
   c. Animating UI elements
   d. Handling device sensors

2. **What is a Future in Flutter?**
   a. A representation of a value that may be available in the future
   b. A constant value
   c. A widget for user input
   d. A navigation route

3. **What is the purpose of decoding JSON in Flutter?**
   a. Displaying images
   b. Handling user authentication
   c. Working with structured data
   d. Controlling animations

4. **What is the main() function of a spinner widget in Flutter?**

   a. Collecting user input

   b. Providing feedback during data retrieval

   c. Managing app navigation

   d. Controlling state management

5. **How can you pass data back to the previous screen in Flutter?**

   a. Using shared preferences

   b. Utilizing the Flutter EventBus

   c. Through the Navigator with arguments

   d. Storing data in a global variable

6. **What does the Flutter location service provide?**

   a. Real-time weather updates

   b. User's geographical location information

   c. Animations for map views

   d. Social media integration

Answers

1. a. Making HTTP requests to external APIs
2. a. A representation of a value that may be available in the future
3. c. Working with structured data
4. b. Providing feedback during data retrieval
5. c. Through the Navigator with arguments
6. b. User's geographical location information

Join our book's Discord space

Join the book's Discord Workspace for Latest updates, Offers, Tech happenings around the world, New Release and Sessions with the Authors:

https://discord.bpbonline.com

CHAPTER 7

Firebase Integration to Flutter App

Introduction

In this chapter, we will explore the integration of Firebase, a comprehensive mobile and web application development platform, with Flutter—a popular open-source UI software development toolkit. Firebase offers a set of tools and services that streamline the development process and enhance the functionality of your Flutter applications.

Structure

The chapter covers the following topics:

- Introduction to Firebase
- Setting up Firebase project
- Firebase authentication
- Cloud Firestore integration
- CRUD operations with Cloud Firestore in Flutter.
- Dart Streams
- Stream builder
- Async Snapshot
- Query Snapshot

Objectives

The chapter aims to provide a comprehensive understanding of integrating Firebase services with Flutter applications. Starting with the basics, you will learn how to set up a Firebase project and seamlessly add your Flutter apps to it. Authentication functionalities using Firebase Authentication will be explored, covering various sign-in methods. The integration of Cloud Firestore, a NoSQL cloud database, will be detailed, along with **Create, Read, Update, Delete (CRUD)** operations within Flutter apps. Furthermore, you will delve into Dart Streams, understanding their role in asynchronous programming within Flutter, and how `StreamBuilder` widgets can be employed to create dynamic UIs that respond to changes in data streams. Throughout the chapter, concepts like `AsyncSnapshot` and `QuerySnapshot` will be discussed, how to effectively manage and manipulate data retrieved from Firestore queries. By the end, you will gain the necessary knowledge to utilize Firebase services seamlessly within your Flutter projects, facilitating real-time data management and user authentication functionalities. So let's begin.

Introduction to Firebase

In the world of modern mobile and web application development, having a reliable backend infrastructure is paramount to delivering a seamless user experience. **Firebase**, a comprehensive mobile and web application development platform developed by Google, has emerged as a go-to solution for developers worldwide.

Defining Firebase

Firebase is not just a **Backend-As-A-Service (BaaS)** platform; it is a unified ecosystem that provides a variety of cloud-based services, making it easier for developers to build, scale, and maintain applications. Whether you are working on a small project or a large-scale application, Firebase offers a suite of tools to handle diverse functionalities, from real-time data synchronization to authentication and cloud storage.

Key Firebase services

Following are some key services offered by Firebase:

- **Realtime database:** Firebase's Realtime Database is a NoSQL cloud database that enables real-time data synchronization. Changes made to the database are instantly reflected across all connected clients, making it ideal for applications requiring live updates.
- **Cloud Firestore:** A scalable and flexible NoSQL document database, Cloud Firestore organizes data in collections and documents. It is designed to scale with your application and provides powerful querying capabilities.

- **Firebase authentication:** Firebase authentication simplifies the process of user authentication. It supports various authentication methods, including email/password, social logins (Google, Facebook, etc.), and anonymous authentication.

- **Cloud functions:** Firebase cloud functions allow you to run server-side logic in response to events triggered by Firebase features and HTTPS requests. It is a powerful tool for automating tasks and executing backend code.

- **Cloud storage:** Firebase cloud storage offers secure and scalable object storage for your application's media files, such as images, videos, and more.

Advantages of selecting Firebase for Flutter

In the following section, we will discuss why choosing Firebase is important for Flutter:

- **Seamless integration**: Firebase is designed to seamlessly integrate with Flutter, the open-source UI software development toolkit. This integration streamlines the development process, allowing developers to focus on building features rather than managing infrastructure.

- **Real-time updates**: The real-time nature of Firebase services aligns perfectly with Flutter's reactive UI framework, enabling developers to create dynamic and responsive applications.

- **Scalability**: Firebase scales effortlessly, making it suitable for projects of all sizes. Whether you're developing a small prototype or a large-scale production app, Firebase can grow with your needs.

In the upcoming sections, we will discuss the process of setting up a new Firebase project, integrating it with both Android and iOS platforms, and incorporating Firebase services into a Flutter application.

Firebase offers a robust foundation for building feature-rich and scalable applications, and by the end of this chapter, you will have a solid understanding of how to integrate Firebase services into your Flutter projects.

Setting up Firebase project

To enhance our grasp of Firebase, let us construct a straightforward shopping list application. In this app, individuals can view or add items to the shopping list by signing in. For instance, within a family with several members, each person can log in to a shared account and collectively manage and update the shopping list for the week, accommodating the unique items each family member wishes to include. The shopping list items can be stored either locally on the user's device or in the cloud, accessible on the internet.

To enable cloud storage functionality, our plan is to utilize Firebase. By leveraging Firebase's prebuilt methods and classes, we aim to efficiently store both user data and shopping list information in the cloud. Specifically, we will utilize Cloud Firestore for data storage and Authentication for user sign-in and access control.

Cloud Firestore and Authentication are the primary Firebase features that we will integrate into this application. However, Firebase offers a multitude of other capabilities that can enhance app development. For more detailed information, please refer to the Firebase documentation at **https://firebase.google.com/docs/engage**.

Let us begin with creating our Flutter app as shown in the figure below:

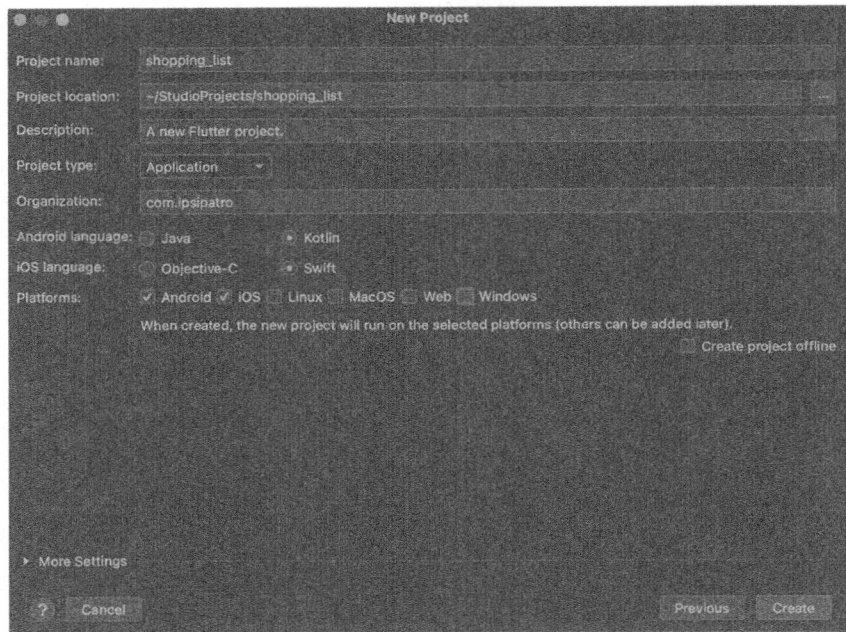

Figure 7.1: *New Flutter project creation*

Once created, just run the project once and leave it for now.

It is time to initiate the Firebase setup process, now.

1. Begin by accessing **https://firebase.google.com/** through your preferred web browser.

2. Sign into your Google account, and then proceed to the console by selecting the "**Go to console**" button.

3. Now, select add project to add a new Firebase project. New Firebase project creation is a three-step process. Let us go through it one by one:

    a. The first step is the create project step, where you need to enter your project name, which is going to be displayed in your Firebase console. Underneath the project name, you can see the unique identifier (shopping-list-43877) of the newly created project auto generated. You can edit the unique identifier, but the newly entered identifier must be unique and available so it is advised to leave it unedited. Refer *Figure 7.2*:

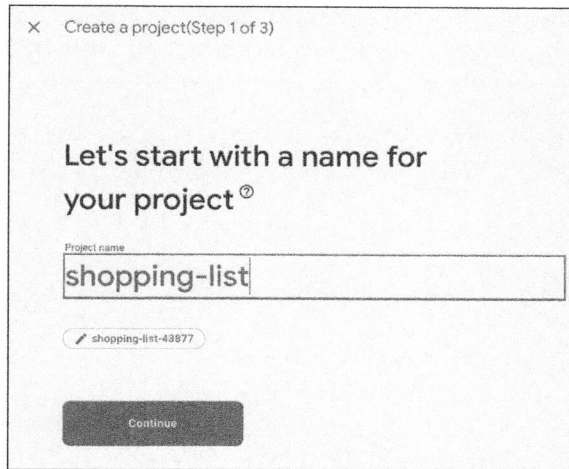

Figure 7.2: *Step 1 of creating new firebase project*

Once you are satisfied, tap continue and you are going to land on *Step 2* of this process, as shown in the figure below:

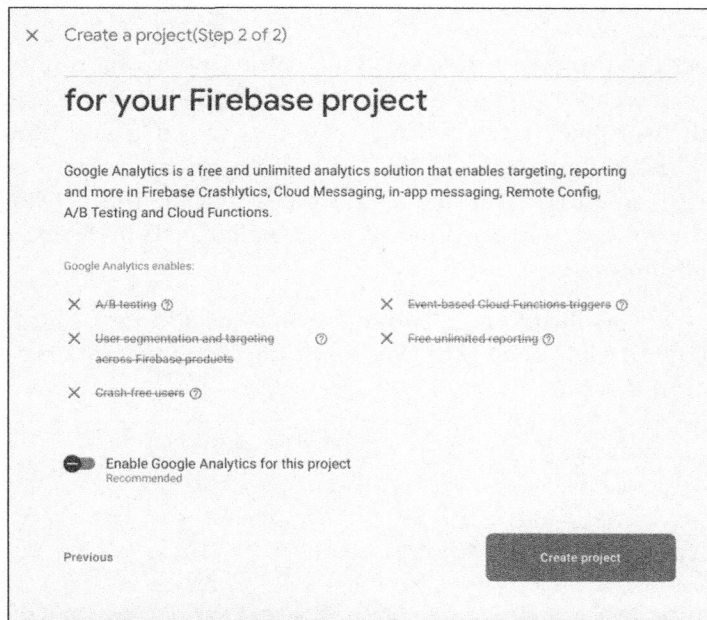

Figure 7.3: *Step 2 of creating new firebase project*

b. You can enable Google Analytics if needed for your project but in this instance, we have disabled it.

c. Tap on **Create project** to move to Step 3, which is the final step. Just tap continue in this step and in a few seconds your Firebase project will be ready.

4. Once it is ready, tap on continue and move to the Firebase console. There you should be able to see your newly created project, as illustrated below:

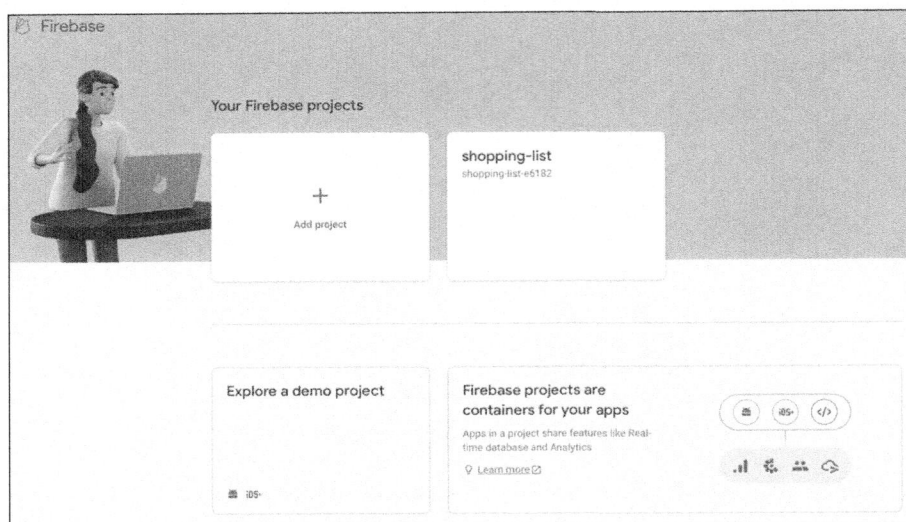

Figure 7.4: New Firebase project in console

5. Now, select the project to proceed. This is the opportune moment to set up our app within the chosen project. In the past, before Firebase offered direct support for Flutter, users were required to create separate iOS and Android projects to integrate Firebase with their Flutter apps. The process has now been streamlined, allowing for creating a Flutter app directly within the Firebase project itself. However, if desired, you can still follow the steps to add iOS and Android projects for your Flutter app.

In this guide, we will specifically go through the steps of adding a Flutter app directly to the project. To do this, simply choose the Flutter option from the project overview page, as illustrated in the figure below:

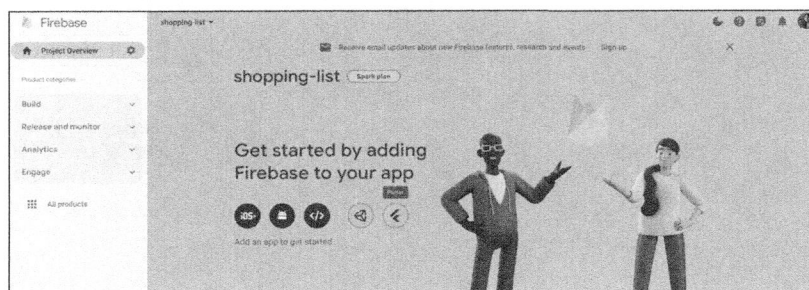

Figure 7.5: Firebase project overview

Adding Flutter app to Firebase project

This is also a three-step process.

1. The first step is to prepare your workspace, as shown in the following figure:

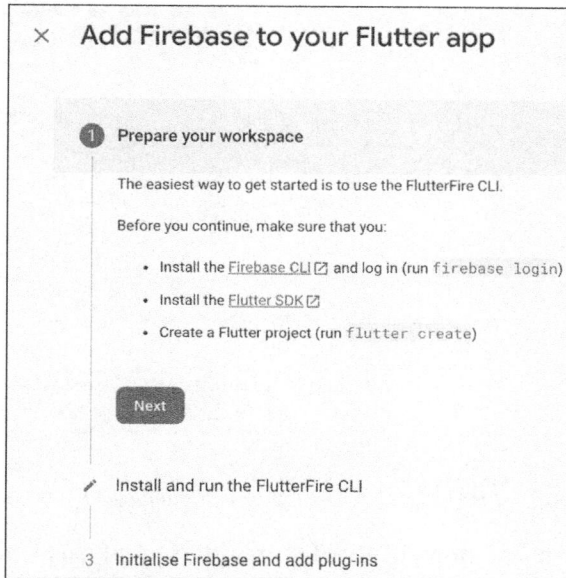

Figure 7.6: Step 1 of Flutter app setup

This step is crucial in the process. Let us proceed by clicking on the provided link to install the Firebase CLI. The Firebase CLI is a Firebase command line tool. The image below illustrates the current steps, but keep in mind that they may change by the time you consult them. Nevertheless, using it as a reference is still advantageous. When you click the link, it will redirect you to a page with instructions for installing Firebase CLI on different operating systems. Choose the operating system that matches your development machine.

Below is a screenshot for macOS, you can install it using one of the three options: auto install script, standalone binary and npm. It is recommended that the npm option is picked:

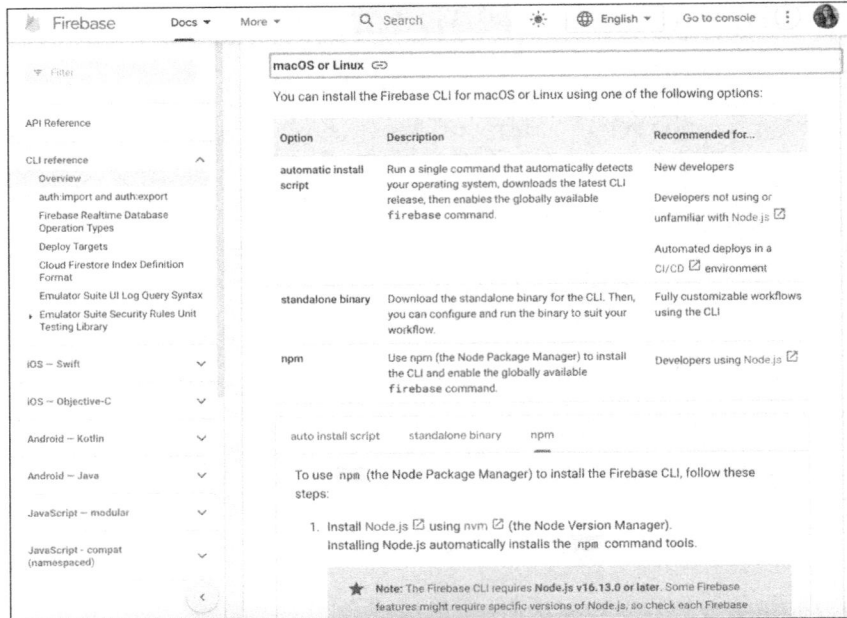

Figure 7.7: Firebase CLI installation macOS

Following the instructions in the documentation, at this stage, we are required to install Node.js to use npm for installing Firebase CLI. Please click on the provided link and follow the outlined steps to install Node.js. This is how the link will look:

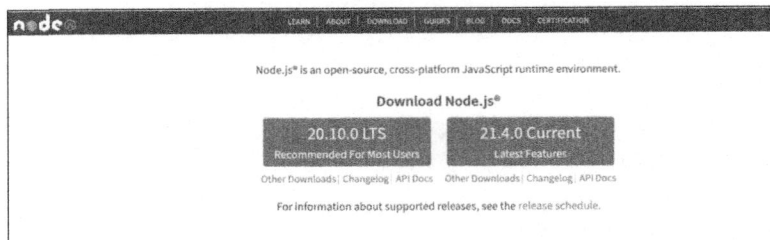

Figure 7.8: Download Node.js

Download it and double click to start the initialization process. After the successful installation of Node, you can use npm. Execute the command '`npm install -g firebase-tools`' in your terminal to install Firebase CLI via npm.

In case your installation encounters an EACCES permission error, refer to the solution provided at **https://docs.npmjs.com/resolving-eacces-permissions-errors-when-installing-packages-globally**. If you encounter any other errors, try searching for solutions, as it is likely that you are not the only one facing the issue.

After successfully installing Firebase CLI, confirm its functionality by testing it with the following commands in your terminal:

```
firebase login
firebase projects:list
```

Running "**firebase login**" in the terminal window will display a message stating "**Already logged in as your email address**" if you are already logged in. If you are not logged in, it will open a new browser window for you to log in, as shown below:

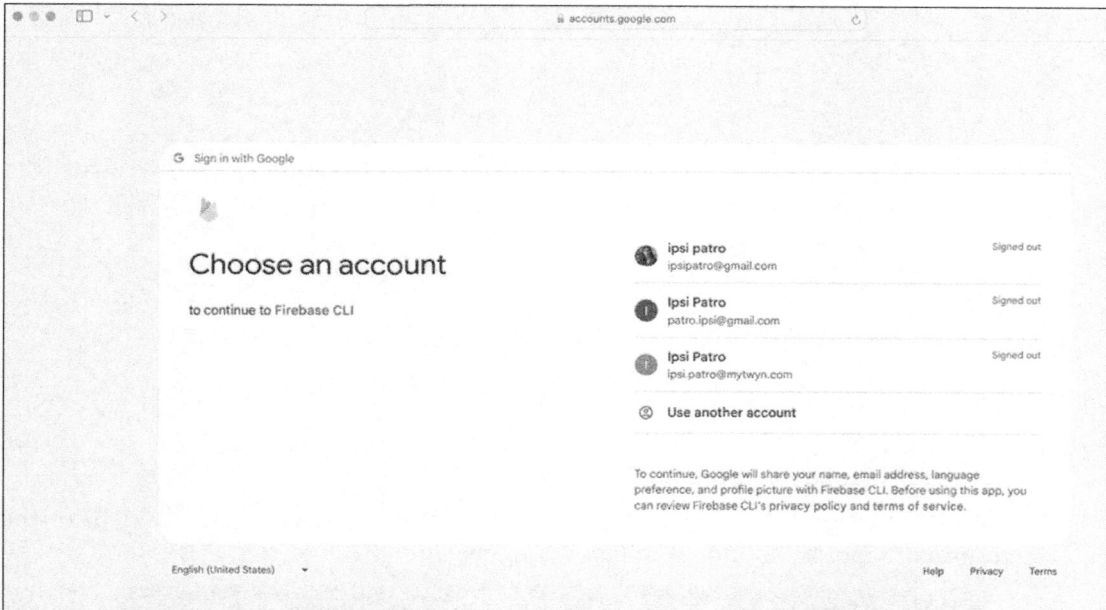

Figure 7.9: Firebase login choose account window

A successful login indicates that Firebase CLI is installed correctly, and you can proceed to the next step, which involves installing the Firebase SDK (a step you may have already completed). Nevertheless, it is beneficial to verify by running the command:

```
flutter doctor
```

Resolve any issues if detected before proceeding.

We will not be creating a project as we have already created the **shopping_list** app in the '**setting up Firebase project**' topic in the beginning (Refer to *Figure 7.1*). We are going to use that same project.

2. Let us proceed to the second step of Flutter app setup which is to install and run the FlutterFire CLI, as shown in the figure below:

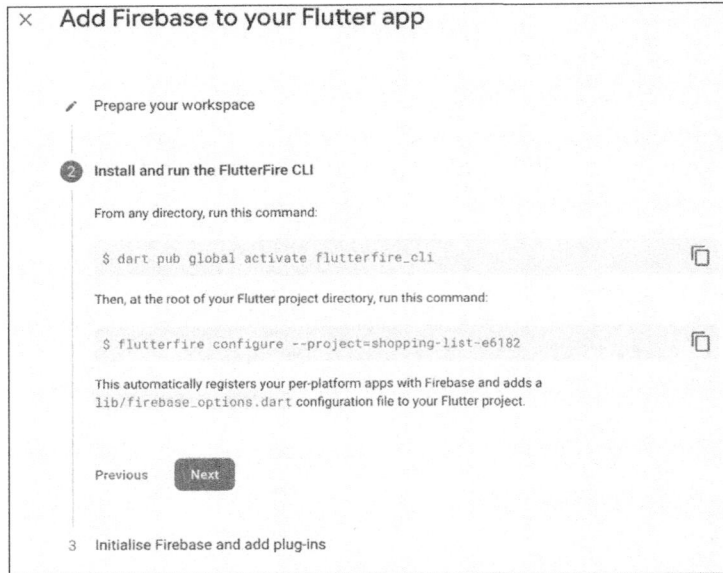

Figure 7.10: Step 2 of Flutter app setup

As the step says, from any directory, run the command:

dart pub global activate flutterfire_cli

Now let us open our **shopping_list** app and execute this command from the terminal window, as shown in below image:

Figure 7.11: Activate flutterfire CLI

Now the flutterfire is activated but to use flutterfire globally we must add the path to our default shell. If your default shell is Bash, you would typically add the path to your .bashrc or **.bash_profile** file. The exact file may depend on your specific system configuration and how Bash is set up on your machine. Here the default shell is zsh to open the file you can use a command '**open ~/.zshrc**' in your terminal. After that you can add the below PATH to the .zshrc file:

export PATH="$PATH":"$HOME/.pub-cache/bin"

Now, close and reopen Android Studio. Copy the configuration command, "**flutterfire configure --project=shopping-list-e6182**" from *Step 2*. Make sure to replace "shopping-list-e6182" with your project's unique identifier as provided by Firebase. Attempting to use a different unique identifier than the one provided by Firebase will result in a failed command. Now, execute the command in your terminal window, as demonstrated below:

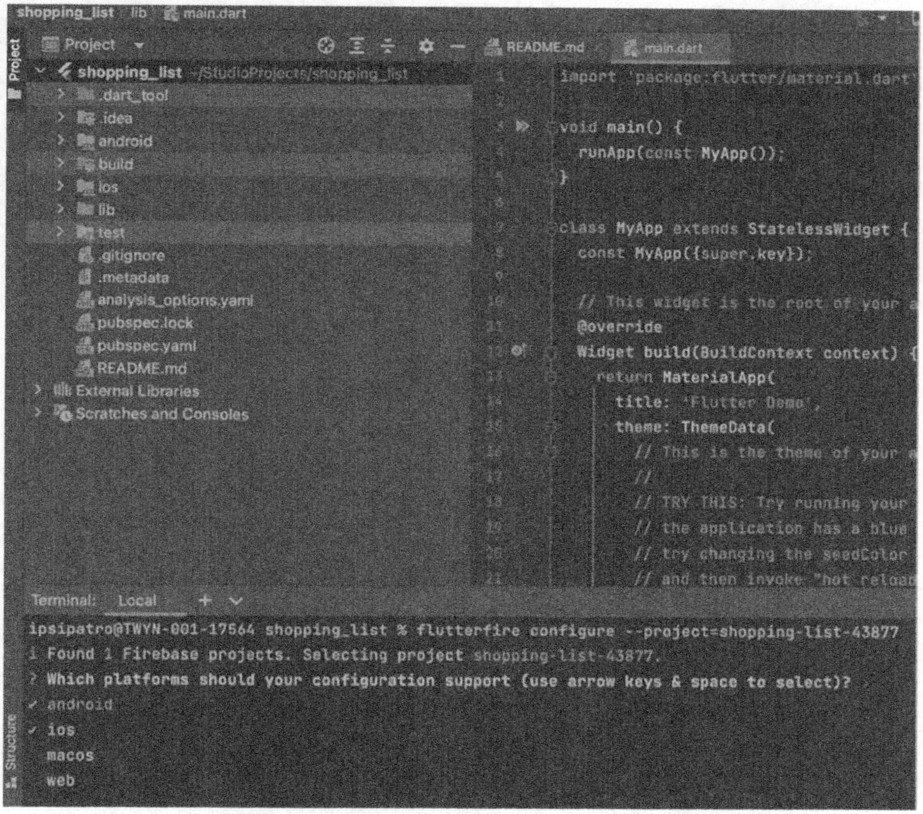

Figure 7.12: Configure command

Upon executing this command, you will be prompted to select the required platforms for support. By default, android and iOS platforms are pre-selected, and options for macOS and web are also available. You can toggle the selection of any platform using the space bar. Once satisfied, press enter. This will execute your command and prompt you with another question.

The files **android/build.gradle** and **android/app/build.gradle** will be modified to apply Firebase configuration and Gradle build plugins. You will be asked, "**Do you want to continue?**" To proceed, simply hit *enter*.

If you are content with your choices, pressing enter will successfully execute the command. You should then receive a message indicating that the Firebase configuration file, **lib/firebase_options.dart**, has been generated successfully, along with details about the Firebase apps created. This signifies the successful configuration of Firebase for your project, as depicted in the figure below:

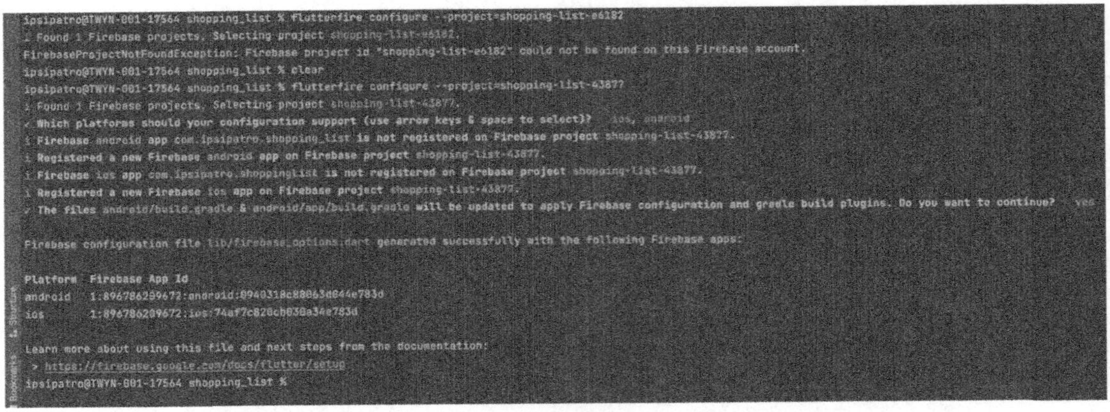

Figure 7.13: Configure command successful

You will now find a newly created file named **firebase_options.dart** within your lib folder. However, you must encounter an error like the one illustrated below:

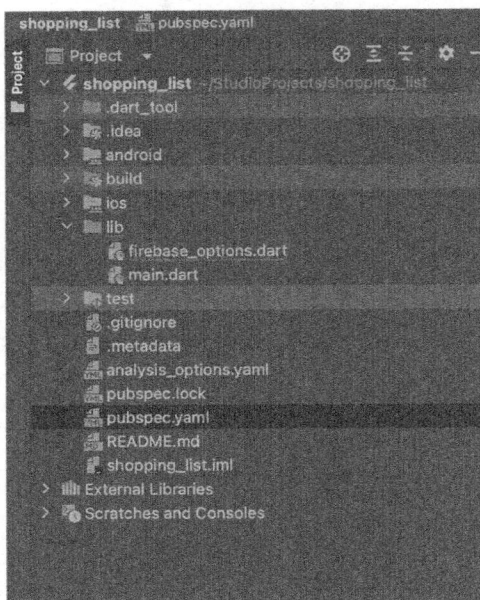

Figure 7.14: Error in Firebase_option

This occurs because the recently generated **firebase_options.dart** file is attempting to import **firebase_core**, which has not been added yet. For that open your **pubspec.yaml** file and add ' '**firebase_core: ^2.24.2**' as demonstrated below:

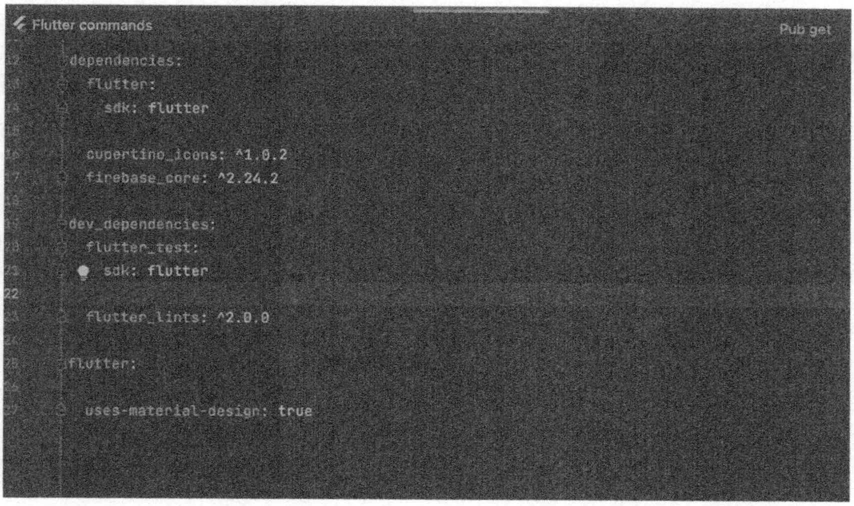

Figure 7.15: pubspec.yaml file

Afterwards, execute the command, **pub get**, which should the error present.

3. Now, proceed to the third and final step of setting up this Flutter app, which involves initializing Firebase and adding plugins. Please consult the figure below for detailed steps:

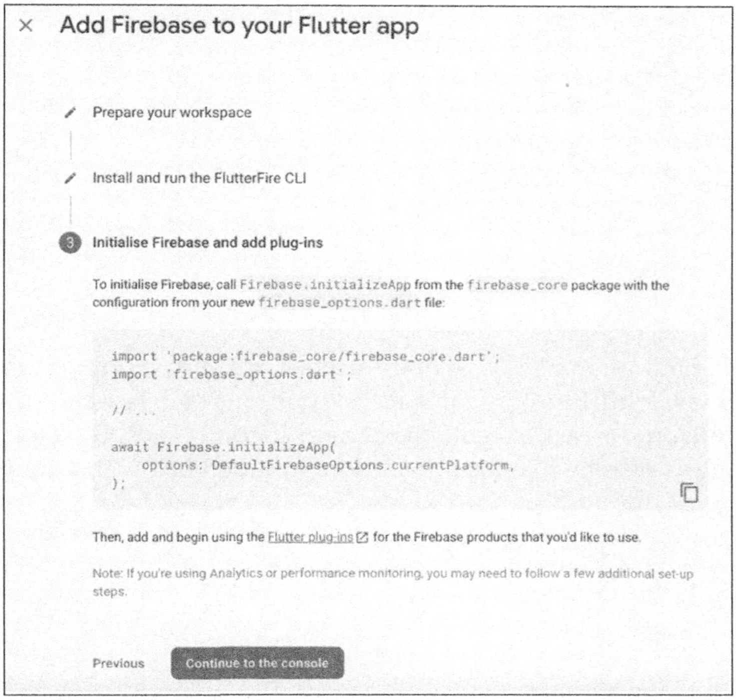

Figure 7.16: Step 3 of Flutter app setup

As indicated in the step, we need to provide options: **DefaultFirebaseOptions. currentPlatform** to **Firebase.initializeApp**, a step we have not completed yet but will shortly. The **DefaultFirebaseOptions** is located within the newly generated Firebase option file, and it automatically selects the appropriate configurations based on the platform you are using.

In line with the final step, incorporate and start utilizing the Flutter plugins for the desired Firebase products. If you click on the link and open it in your browser, you will find a comprehensive list of available Firebase plugins, as illustrated below:

Product	Plugin name	iOS	Android	Web	Other Apple (macOS, etc.)
Analytics	firebase_analytics	✓	✓	✓	beta
App Check	firebase_app_check	✓	✓	✓	beta
Authentication	firebase_auth	✓	✓	✓	beta
Cloud Firestore	cloud_firestore	✓	✓	✓	beta
Cloud Functions	cloud_functions	✓	✓	✓	beta
Cloud Messaging	firebase_messaging	✓	✓	✓	beta
Cloud Storage	firebase_storage	✓	✓	✓	beta
Crashlytics	firebase_crashlytics	✓	✓		beta
Dynamic Links	firebase_dynamic_links	✓	✓		
In-App Messaging	firebase_in_app_messaging	✓	✓		
Firebase installations	firebase_app_installations	✓	✓	✓	beta
ML Model Downloader	firebase_ml_model_downloader	✓	✓		beta
Performance Monitoring	firebase_performance	✓	✓	✓	
Realtime Database	firebase_database	✓	✓	✓	beta
Remote Config	firebase_remote_config	✓	✓	✓	beta

Figure 7.17: Firebase plugins

Out of the available plugins, only two are needed for our shopping list app. The first essential plugin is Cloud Firestore, and the second one is related to authentication. To integrate them into our project, execute the necessary commands. By selecting the options, you will encounter a display like the illustration provided below in your browser:

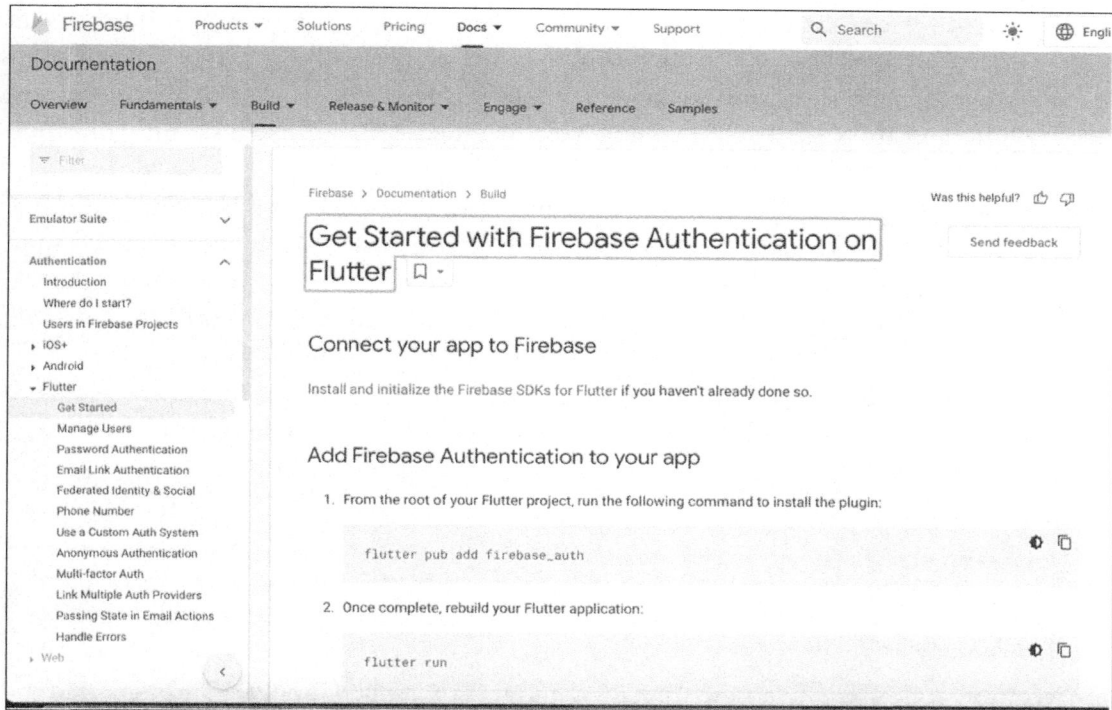

Figure 7.18: Firebase Authentication plugin

Repeat the procedure for **cloud_firestore** as well. Copy and execute the commands **'flutter pub add firebase_auth** 'and '**flutter pub add cloud_firestore**' in your project's terminal. After ensuring the successful execution of these commands, confirm the inclusion of these packages in your **pubspec.yaml file**.

The configuration of our Flutter app is now finished. Move forward by clicking the "Continue to Console" button in *Step 3*.

We have now completed the Firebase setup for our app. At this point, run your app once and verify that you can successfully launch it on your device or simulator.

Firebase authentication

Firebase Authentication allows users to sign in to the application using various authentication methods such as email/password, phone number, Google, Facebook, or other identity providers supported by Firebase.

Here are the key features of Firebase authentication:

- **Secure authentication methods**: Firebase Authentication supports various authentication methods, including email/password, phone number, Google Sign-In, Facebook Login, Twitter Login, GitHub authentication, and more.

- **Identity verification**: It allows you to verify the identity of users by sending email verification or SMS verification codes.

- **Custom authentication system**: Firebase authentication also supports custom authentication systems, enabling you to integrate with existing authentication mechanisms if needed.

- **Easy integration**: Firebase authentication provides SDKs for popular platforms, including iOS, Android, and web (JavaScript). This simplifies the integration process for developers.

- **User management**: You can manage user accounts, reset passwords, and disable or delete accounts through the Firebase console or programmatically.

- **Security rules**: Firebase allows you to define security rules to control access to your data and functions based on the authentication state and user roles.

Now let us shift our focus to our project and contemplate the app's design. This app will consist of three screens:

1. Login screen
2. Signup screen
3. Items list screen.

To accomplish this, create a new directory under '**lib**' named '**screen**' and generate the files for each screen. Now, as a challenge, try creating routes for your app without referring to the solution. Additionally, as a part of the challenge, set the initial route to the Login screen and Initialize Firebase.

Hope you have given it a go and have a something similar **main.dart** file as shown below:

```
1. import 'package:firebase_core/firebase_core.dart';
2. import 'package:flutter/material.dart';
3. import 'package:shopping_list/screens/login_screen.dart';
4. import 'package:shopping_list/screens/shopping_list.screen.dart';
5. import 'package:shopping_list/screens/signup_screen.dart';
6. import 'firebase_options.dart';
7.
8. void main() async {
9.   WidgetsFlutterBinding.ensureInitialized();
10.   await Firebase.initializeApp(options: DefaultFirebaseOptions.
    currentPlatform);
11.   runApp(const ShoppingList());
12. }
13.
```

```
14. class ShoppingList extends StatelessWidget {
15.   const ShoppingList({super.key});
16.
17.   @override
18.   Widget build(BuildContext context) {
19.     return MaterialApp(
20.       initialRoute: LoginScreen.id,
21.       routes: {
22.         LoginScreen.id: (context) => const LoginScreen(),
23.         SignUpScreen.id: (context) => const SignUpScreen(),
24.        ShoppingListScreen.id: (context) => const ShoppingListScreen(),
25.       },
26.     );
27.   }
28. }
```

Code 7.1: Main .dart file

The *line number 10* of *Code 7.1* represents a vital aspect of Firebase initialization. It corresponds to *Step 3* of the Flutter app setup for Firebase, as illustrated in *Figure 7.16*. However, we deliberately chose not to address that step at that point.

You may have observed, to eliminate any hardcoded string route names, we can adopt an approach of establishing an '**id**' variable that serves as the route name.

Now, before transitioning to the Login screen or Signup screen, it is imperative to have a designated space for saving user information, and this is precisely one of the reasons we have opted for Firebase.

To begin, return to the Firebase console and choose the project. Under the "Build" section, navigate to authentication inside your Firebase project. Here, you will find a list of options that you can enable to determine the methods through which users can sign up, as illustrated below:

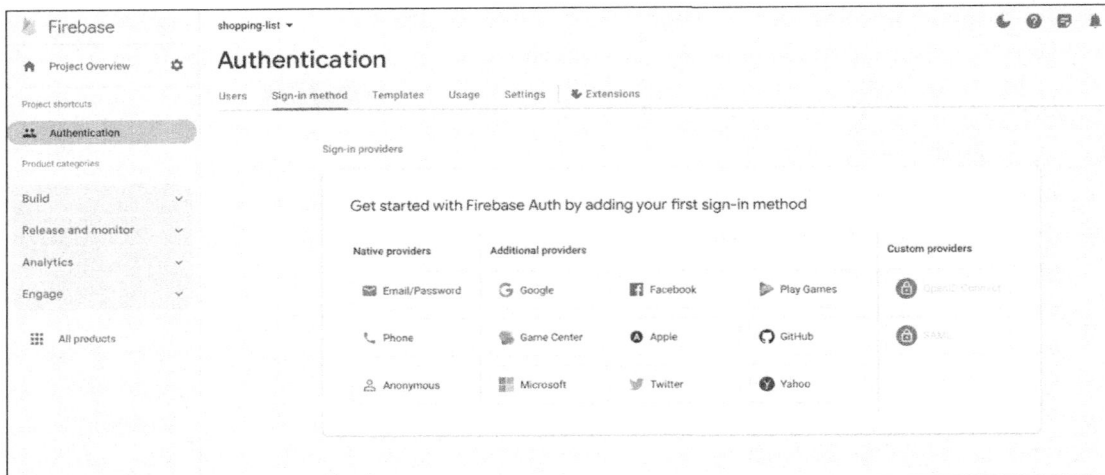

Figure 7.19: *Firebase authentication options list*

To simplify the shopping list app, you can choose to enable only the Email/Password option. This allows users to register with any email and a valid password. To implement this, select the mentioned option and enable it, as demonstrated in the figure below:

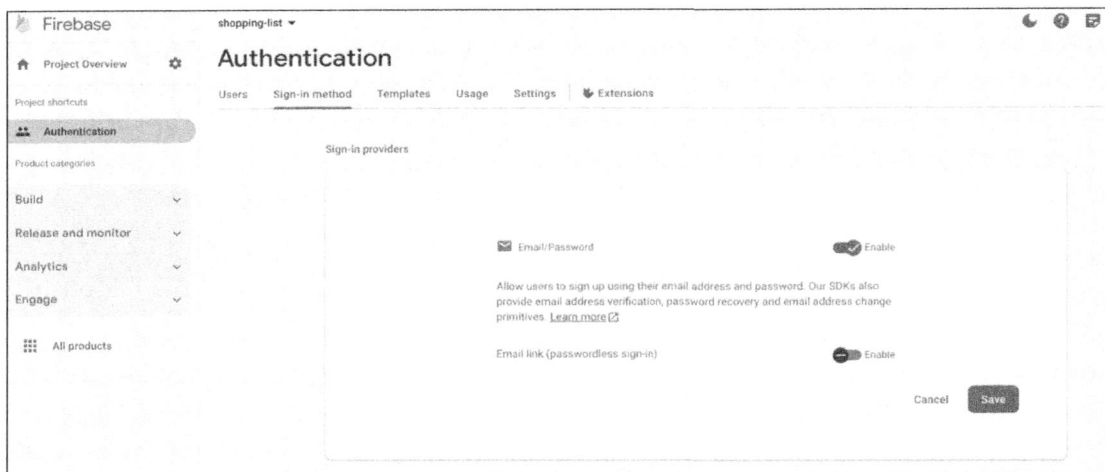

Figure 7.20: *Enabling Email/Password authentication option*

If you wish to expand the options at any point by adding a new one, you can achieve this by tapping on "**Add new Provider**" from the existing options screen, as shown below:

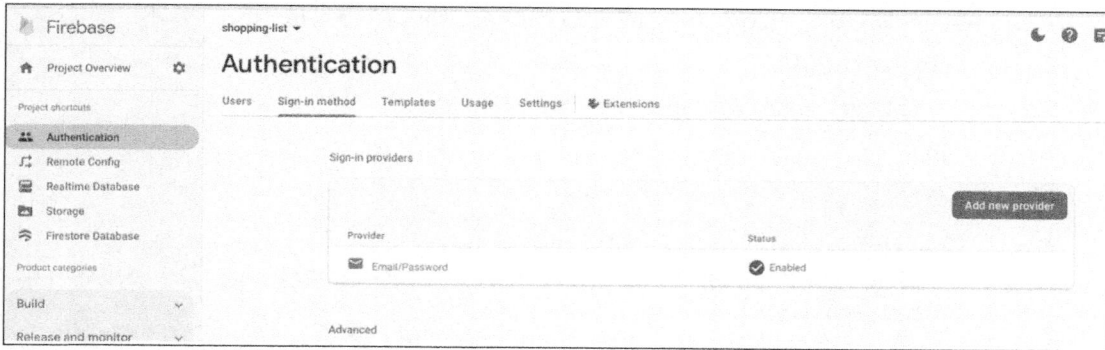

Figure 7.21: *Firebase authentication*

Now we are ready to use Firebase as our users' database. So, let us go ahead and create a simple login screen now. The resulted screen design will be as shown below:

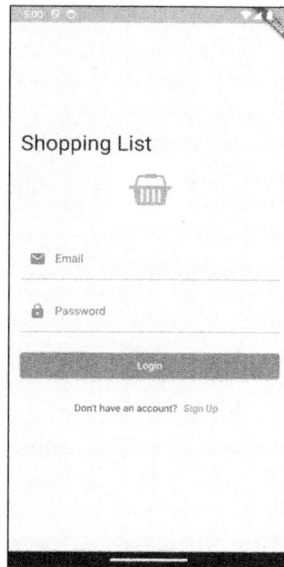

Figure 7.22: *Login screen*

Now, let us look at the solution:

```
1.  class LoginScreenState extends State<LoginScreen> {
2.    final FirebaseAuth _auth = FirebaseAuth.instance;
3.    String email = "";
4.    String password = "";
5.    bool isLoggingIn = false;
6.
```

```
7.    Future<void> _signInWithEmailAndPassword() async {
8.      setState(() {
9.        isLoggingIn = true;
10.     });
11.
12.     try {
13.       await _auth.signInWithEmailAndPassword(email: email, password:
          password);
14.       if (!mounted) return;
15.       Navigator.pushNamed(context, ShoppingListScreen.id);
16.     } catch (e) {
17.       String errorMessage = "";
18.
19.       if (e is FirebaseAuthException) {
20.         switch (e.code) {
21.           case 'user-not-found':
22.             errorMessage = "User not found. Please check your email.";
23.             break;
24.           case 'wrong-password':
25.             errorMessage = "Invalid password. Please try again.";
26.             break;
27.           case 'invalid-email':
28.             errorMessage = "Invalid email format. Please enter a
              valid email.";
29.             break;
30.           default:
31.             errorMessage = "Authentication failed. Please try again.";
32.             break;
33.         }
34.       }
35.       ScaffoldMessenger.of(context).showSnackBar(
36.         SnackBar(
37.           content: Text(errorMessage),
38.           duration: const Duration(seconds: 3),
39.         ),
```

```
40.         );
41.       } finally {
42.         setState(() {
43.           isLoggingIn = false;
44.         });
45.       }
46.   }
47.
48.   @override
49.   Widget build(BuildContext context) {
50.     return Scaffold(
51.       body: Padding(
52.         padding: const EdgeInsets.all(16.0),
53.         child: Column(
54.           mainAxisAlignment: MainAxisAlignment.center,
55.           crossAxisAlignment: CrossAxisAlignment.stretch,
56.           children: [
57.             SizedBox(
58.               width: 250.0,
59.               child: DefaultTextStyle(
60.                 style: const TextStyle(
61.                     fontSize: 30.0, fontFamily: 'Agne', color:
                        Colors.black),
62.                 child: AnimatedTextKit(
63.                   animatedTexts: [
64.                     TypewriterAnimatedText('Shopping List'),
65.                   ],
66.                 ),
67.               ),
68.             ),
69.             Image.asset(
70.               'images/logo.jpg',
71.               height: 100.0,
72.               width: 100.0,
```

```
73.            ),
74.            const SizedBox(height: 20.0),
75.            TextFormField(
76.              maxLines: 1,
77.              keyboardType: TextInputType.emailAddress,
78.              decoration: const InputDecoration(
79.                labelText: 'Email',
80.                prefixIcon: Icon(Icons.email),
81.              ),
82.              onChanged: (value) {
83.                email = value;
84.              },
85.            ),
86.            const SizedBox(height: 16.0),
87.            TextFormField(
88.              maxLines: 1,
89.              decoration: const InputDecoration(
90.                labelText: 'Password',
91.                prefixIcon: Icon(Icons.lock),
92.              ),
93.              onChanged: (value) {
94.                password = value;
95.              },
96.            ),
97.            const SizedBox(height: 24.0),
98.            ElevatedButton(
99.              onPressed: isLoggingIn ? null : _
                    signInWithEmailAndPassword,
100.               child: isLoggingIn
101.                   ? const Row(
102.                       mainAxisAlignment: MainAxisAlignment.center,
103.                       children: [
104.                         CircularProgressIndicator(),
105.                         SizedBox(width: 10),
```

```
106.                        Text('Logging In'),
107.                      ],
108.                   )
109.                : const Text('Login'),
110.              ),
111.            const SizedBox(height: 12.0),
112.            Row(
113.              mainAxisAlignment: MainAxisAlignment.center,
114.              children: [
115.                const Text("Don't have an account?"),
116.                TextButton(
117.                  onPressed: isLoggingIn
118.                      ? null
119.                      : () {
120.                          Navigator.pushNamed(context,
                               SignUpScreen.id);
121.                        },
122.                  child: const Text('Sign Up'),
123.                ),
124.              ],
125.            ),
126.          ],
127.        ),
128.      ),
129.    );
130.  }
131. }
```

Code 7.2: Shopping list app login screen

A few important points regarding the code used are as follows:

- Add **animated_text_kit** to your **pubspec.yaml** file. It is not necessary but just an opportunity to apply some animation to our project and recall what we have already learned. Go through the Flutter package documentation, it contains a collection of some cool and awesome text animations. In this instance, we have used **TypewriterAnimatedText**. In *line number 62*, one of the children is a **SizedBox** containing the animated text. You can explore other animations for experimentation or integration into your actual projects.

- At *line number 2*, we have instantiated the **_auth** variable as a **FirebaseAuth** instance. This is essential for verifying the availability of a user with the provided email and password inside the users 'database for our Firebase project.

- In *line 13*, the code invokes the **signInWithEmailAndPassword** method from Firebase Auth, providing the user-entered email and password to verify user availability with the entered details. In the event of incorrect credentials, the method throws a **FirebaseAuthException**. This exception is captured within a catch block, and the associated error message is displayed to the user through a Snackbar in *line 37*.

- For **asyn** operation, a boolean flag (**isLoggingIn**) is used to indicate whether the login process is ongoing. Use **setState** to update the state and trigger UI updates during asynchronous operations.

The user can log in only after completing the sign-up process. Once again, it is advised to attempt the implementation by leveraging the design and some of the concepts from the login screen. The process is quite analogous. Review the Firebase authentication documentation to understand how to create a new user, which is a crucial aspect of this screen. Now, let us examine the design of the sign-up screen, outlined below:

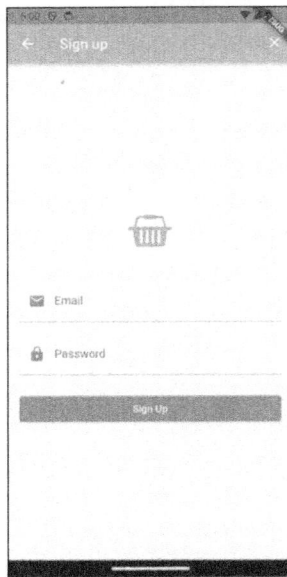

Figure 7.23: Signup screen

Now you have successfully implemented the design and created users for the application. The code for the sign-up class is almost the same as the login screen. The main difference is that we need a method to create a user rather than **signInWithEmailAndPassword**.

Let us look at the implementation of this method:

```
1.    Future<void> _createAccountWithEmailAndPassword() async {
2.      setState(() {
3.        isLoggingIn = true;
4.      });
5.      try {
6.        await _auth.createUserWithEmailAndPassword(
7.          email: email,
8.          password: password,
9.        );
10.       if (!mounted) return;
11.       Navigator.pushNamed(context, ShoppingListScreen.id);
12.     } catch (e) {
13.       String errorMessage = "An error occurred during account
          creation.";
14.
15.       if (e is FirebaseAuthException) {
16.         switch (e.code) {
17.           case 'email-already-in-use':
18.             errorMessage =
19.                 "The email address is already in use by another
                  account.";
20.             break;
21.           case 'invalid-email':
22.             errorMessage = "The email address is invalid.";
23.             break;
24.           case 'weak-password':
25.             errorMessage = "The password is too weak.";
26.             break;
27.           default:
28.             errorMessage = "Account creation failed. Please try again.";
29.             break;
30.         }
31.       }
```

```
32.
33.        ScaffoldMessenger.of(context).showSnackBar(
34.          SnackBar(
35.            content: Text(errorMessage),
36.            duration: const Duration(seconds: 3),
37.          ),
38.        );
39.      } finally {
40.        setState(() {
41.          isLoggingIn = false;
42.        });
43.      }
44.  }
```

Code 7.3: Shopping list app signup screen

The key observation lies in *line number 6*, where a new user is created by passing the user's email and password to the **createUserWithEmailAndPassword** method within the Firebase Authentication package, unless an error occurs during its execution. Call this method on tap of the Sign-up button. After a successful creation of the user, you can verify them inside the Firebase Authentication users' section, as illustrated in the figure below:

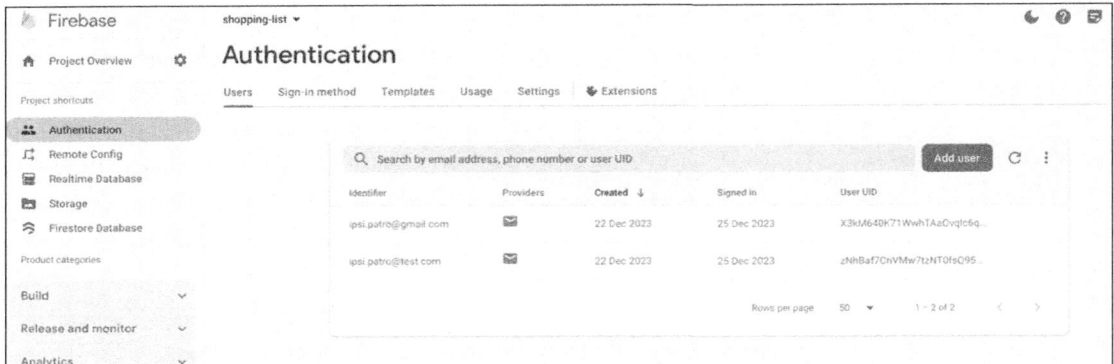

Figure 7.24: Users list in Firebase

With this, the user creation and login part is done, but the crucial element of this application is the shopping list screen. This screen allows users with identical logins to view and modify the list of items collaboratively that is yet to be covered; for that, let us move to the next topic.

Cloud Firestore integration

Cloud Firestore is a NoSQL cloud database provided by Google Firebase, offering real-time synchronization and scalability. Integrating Cloud Firestore into our application allows you to store and manage data in a flexible, scalable, and easily accessible manner. Here are the key steps to integrate Cloud Firestore into our project:

1. In the Firebase Console, navigate to "**Firestore Database**" and click on "**Create Database.**", as shown in the following figure:

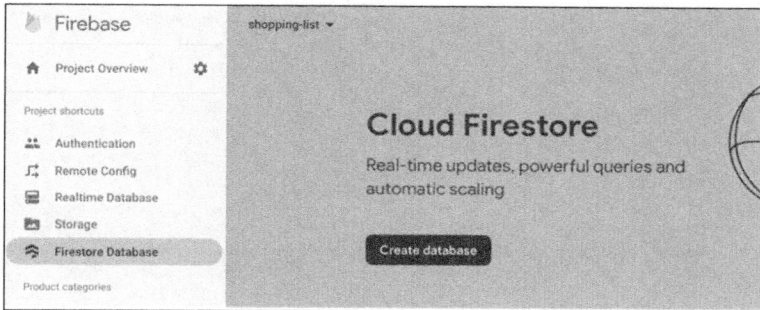

Figure 7.25: Create cloud Firestore database

2. Choose the location for your database, as illustrated using the following figure:

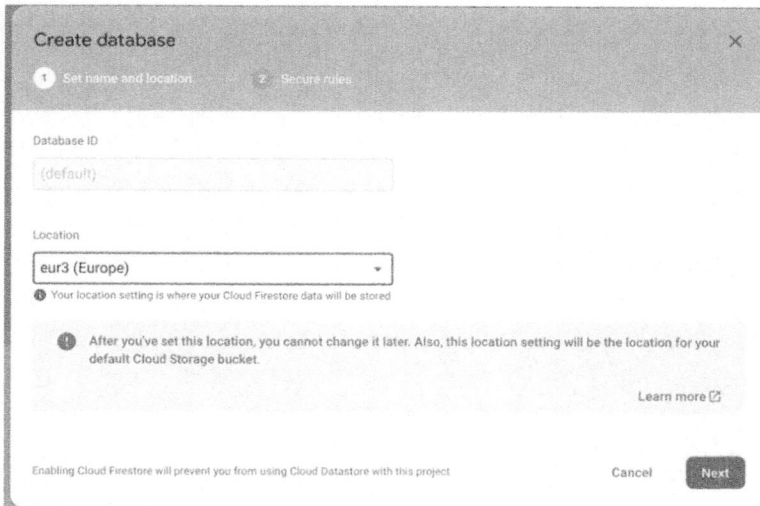

Figure 7.26: Create cloud Firestore database

3. Set the security rules. We can start in test mode as shown below and adjust rules later:

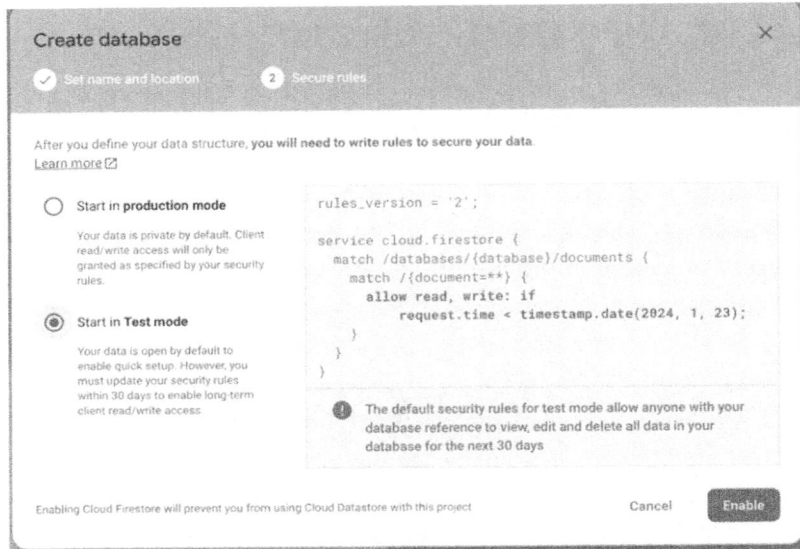

Figure 7.27: Set the security rules

Now it is time to create a collection to save items of our shopping list to firebase cloud Firestore. For that, just navigate to Firestore Database and tap on Start Collection and name your collection as shown below:

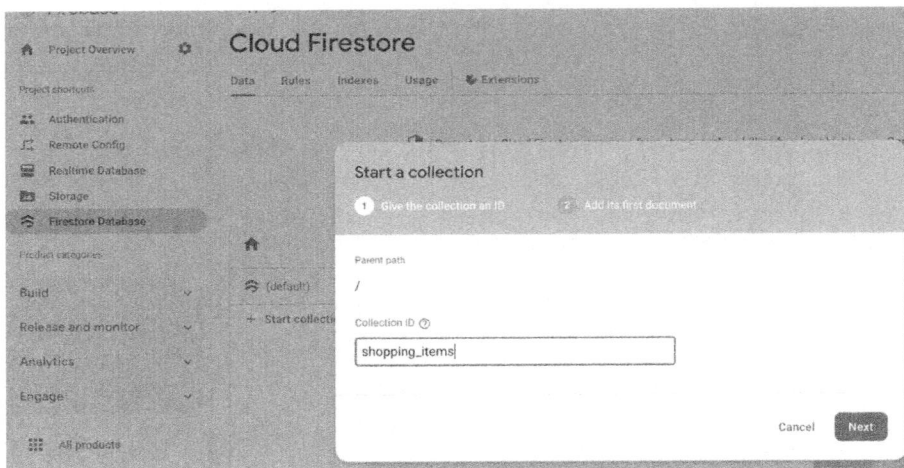

Figure 7.28: Create collection

4. The next step is to add the first document with the required fields as shown below:

Tap on Auto-Id to generate a document Id and add required fields. Here, we have chosen fields as shown below:

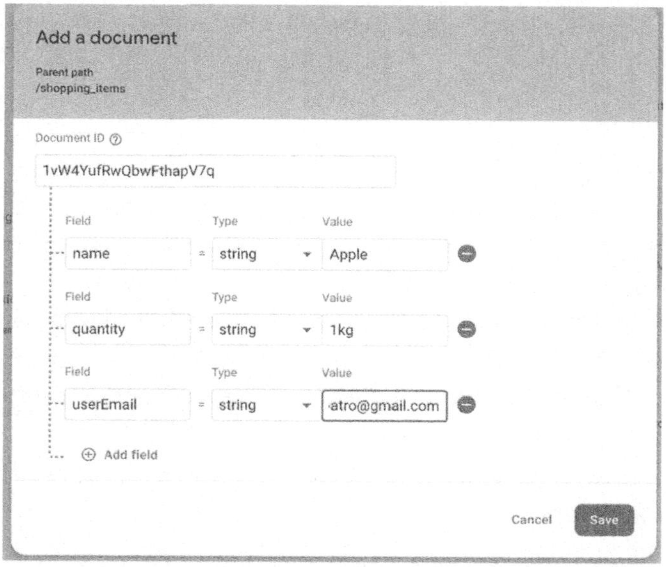

Figure 7.29: *Add required fields for your document*

After successfully adding the first item to your user's shopping list, the next important part is to learn how we can retrieve these documents inside our Flutter app.

CRUD operations with Cloud Firestore in Flutter

To implement **Create, Read, Update, Delete (CRUD)** operations in a Flutter app using Cloud Firestore, you will need to interact with the **cloud_firestore** package. Here is an example of how you can perform each CRUD operation:

- **Create data**: The following sample code shows you how you can add a new document to your Firebase collection:

```
1. import 'package:cloud_firestore/cloud_firestore.dart';
2.
3. Future<void> createData(String name, String email) async {
4.   try {
5.     CollectionReference users = FirebaseFirestore.instance.
       collection('users');
6.     await users.add({'name': name, 'email': email});
7.     print('Data added successfully.');
8.   } catch (e) {
```

```
9.       print('Error creating data: $e');
10.   }
11. }
```

Code 7.4: Add documents to Firebase collection

In this example, it is assumed that you have a collection named '**users**' with documents containing '**name**' and '**email**' fields. Adjust the collection name and fields based on your Firestore structure.

- **Retrieve data**: Use the **FirebaseFirestore** class to interact with Cloud Firestore. Here is a basic example of retrieving data:

```
1. import 'package:cloud_firestore/cloud_firestore.dart';
2.
3. Future<void> fetchData() async {
4.   try {
5.     // Get a reference to the Firestore collection
6.     CollectionReference users = FirebaseFirestore.instance.
         collection('users');
7.
8.     // Get documents from the collection
9.     QuerySnapshot querySnapshot = await users.get();
10.
11.    // Process each document in the collection
12.    querySnapshot.docs.forEach((doc) {
13.      print('User ID: ${doc.id}, Name: ${doc['name']}, Email:
           ${doc['email']}');
14.    });
15.  } catch (e) {
16.    print('Error fetching data: $e');
17.  }
18. }
```

Code 7.5: Retrieve documents from Firebase collection

- **Update data**: The following sample code shows you how you can update your document inside a collection in Firebase:

```
1. import 'package:cloud_firestore/cloud_firestore.dart';
2.
```

```
3.  Future<void> updateData(String userId, String newName, String
    newEmail) async {
4.    try {
5.      CollectionReference users = FirebaseFirestore.instance.
        collection('users');
6.      await users.doc(userId).update({'name': newName, 'email':
        newEmail});
7.      print('Data updated successfully.');
8.    } catch (e) {
9.      print('Error updating data: $e');
10.   }
11. }
```

Code 7.5: Update documents from Firebase collection

- **Delete data**: Finally, let us see how we can delete documents inside Firebase collection from the Flutter app:

```
1.  import 'package:cloud_firestore/cloud_firestore.dart';
2.
3.  Future<void> deleteData(String userId) async {
4.    try {
5.      CollectionReference users = FirebaseFirestore.instance.
        collection('users');
6.      await users.doc(userId).delete();
7.      print('Data deleted successfully.');
8.    } catch (e) {
9.      print('Error deleting data: $e');
10.   }
```

Code 7.6: Retrieve documents from Firebase collection

Now, you should have a good idea of how to handle Firebase base collection documents. So, let us proceed to our application to display the list of items inside our collection on our **shopping_list** screen and incorporate the functionality to add new items. Users should be able to retrieve items from Firebase Cloud Firestore by using a "**Cloud Download**" button on the app bar or a "**Retrieve Items from Cloud**" button on the screen.

It is time to build our shopping list screen. The resulting screen should look like the screen shot attached below:

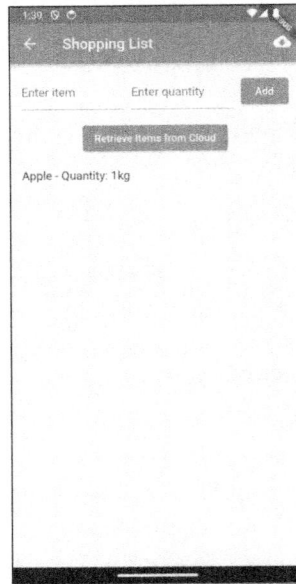

Figure 7.30: *Shopping list screen*

Now, let us examine crucial sections of the code for this screen.. Let us concentrate on the code relevant to adding and retrieving shopping items for the user first. Initially, let us review the code responsible for initializing essential objects needed to add and retrieve items from the list:

```
1.   final TextEditingController _itemController = TextEditingController();
2.   final TextEditingController _quantityController =
     TextEditingController();
3.   final _itemsCollection =
4.       FirebaseFirestore.instance.collection('shopping_items');
5.   User? _currentUser; // Variable to store the current user
6.
7.   List<Map<String, dynamic>> _shoppingItems = [];
8.
9.   @override
10.  void initState() {
11.    _getCurrentUser();
12.    _retrieveItemsFromCloud();
13.    super.initState();
14.  }
```

```
15.
16.    // Function to get the current user's information
17.    void _getCurrentUser() {
18.      FirebaseAuth.instance.authStateChanges().listen((User? user) {
19.        setState(() {
20.          _currentUser = user;
21.        });
22.      });
23.    }
```

Code 7.7.1: Shopping items list screen object initialization

Some key things to look at:

- **TextEditingController**

  Let us talk about **TextEditingController** used in *Code 7.7*. In *lines 1* and *2*, two instances of **TextEditingController** are created for the "**Item Name**" and "**Quantity**" text fields. This Flutter class is commonly employed to govern the text input of a **TextField**. Here are several advantages of using **TextEditingController**:

  o **Reading input data**: Extract the input data using **String inputValue = _ controller.text;**.

  o **Setting initial values**: Initialize the controller with an initial value using **TextEditingController _controller = TextEditingController(text: 'Initial Value');**.

  o **Handling form submissions**: When working with forms, utilize **TextEditingController** to manage form submissions. For instance, you can access form data from the controller when the user taps the submit button.

  o **Clearing or resetting the Input Field**: Clear the text input with **controller. clear();**.

  o **Listening for changes**: **_controller.addListener(() { //** execute actions when the text changes }); This feature will be beneficial if you wish to perform actions when the value changes.

  o **Avoiding rebuilds**: Creating a new instance of **TextEditingController** with each widget rebuild may result in the loss of the previous text state. By establishing the controller outside the build method, you ensure the preservation of the state across rebuilds.

  o **Memory management**: Dispose of the controller when it is no longer needed to prevent potential memory leaks. The dispose method is typically called in the widget's dispose lifecycle method.

In summary, **TextEditingController** facilitates interaction and control over text input in a Flutter application. It provides flexibility and control, particularly beneficial when working with forms, implementing dynamic UI updates, and managing user input.

- **Firestore Collection Reference:**

  Code 7.7 Line 3 initializes a variable named **_itemsCollection**, representing a reference to a specific collection in Firebase Cloud Firestore. Let us break it down now:

  - **FirebaseFirestore.instance**: This component points to the primary entry for accessing Firebase Cloud Firestore in a Flutter app, granting access to the Firestore database linked to your Firebase project.

  - **.collection('shopping_items')**: This method specifies a particular collection within the Firestore database, named '**shopping_items**'. A Firestore collection is a grouping of documents, each comprising key-value pairs.

  Consequently, at *line number 3*, a reference to the '**shopping_items**' collection is created in the Firestore database. This reference is then employed for various operations, such as adding documents to the collection, retrieving documents, or monitoring real-time updates to the collection. Now let us look at the implementation of add and retrieve items method:

```
1.  void _addItem() {
2.      String newItem = _itemController.text.trim();
3.      String quantity = _quantityController.text.trim();
4.
5.      if (_currentUser != null && newItem.isNotEmpty) {
6.        _itemsCollection.add({
7.          'name': newItem,
8.          'quantity': quantity,
9.          'userEmail': _currentUser!.email,
10.       });
11.       _itemController.clear();
12.       _quantityController.clear();
13.     }
14.   }
15.
16.  void _retrieveItemsFromCloud() async {
17.     try {
```

```
18.        if (_currentUser != null) {
19.          QuerySnapshot querySnapshot = await _itemsCollection
20.              .where('userEmail', isEqualTo: _currentUser!.email)
21.              .get();
22.          List<Map<String, dynamic>> items = querySnapshot.docs
23.              .map((doc) => doc.data() as Map<String, dynamic>)
24.              .toList();
25.
26.          setState(() {
27.            _shoppingItems = items;
28.          });
29.        }
30.      } catch (e) {
31.        print('Error retrieving items: $e');
32.      }
33.  }
```

Code 7.7.2: Shopping items list add and retrieve items

In *line number 6,* **itemsCollection** is utilized to add a document to the collection, and in *line number 19,* it is used to retrieve '**shopping_items**' for the logged-in. Now it is easy to build the UI as shown in code below:

```
1.    Widget build(BuildContext context) {
2.      return Scaffold(
3.        appBar: AppBar(
4.          title: const Text('Shopping List'),
5.          actions: [
6.            IconButton(
7.              icon: const Icon(Icons.cloud_download),
8.              onPressed: _retrieveItemsFromCloud,
9.            ),
10.          ],
11.        ),
12.        body: Column(
13.          children: [
14.            Padding(
```

```
15.              padding: const EdgeInsets.all(16.0),
16.              child: Row(
17.                children: [
18.                  Expanded(
19.                    child: TextField(
20.                      controller: _itemController,
21.                      decoration: const InputDecoration(
22.                        hintText: 'Enter item',
23.                      ),
24.                    ),
25.                  ),
26.                  const SizedBox(width: 10),
27.                  Expanded(
28.                    child: TextField(
29.                      controller: _quantityController,
30.                      decoration: const InputDecoration(
31.                        hintText: 'Enter quantity',
32.                      ),
33.                    ),
34.                  ),
35.                  const SizedBox(width: 10),
36.                  ElevatedButton(
37.                    onPressed: _addItem,
38.                    child: const Text('Add'),
39.                  ),
40.                ],
41.              ),
42.            ),
43.            ElevatedButton(
44.              onPressed: _retrieveItemsFromCloud,
45.              child: const Text('Retrieve Items from Cloud'),
46.            ),
47.            Expanded(
48.              child: ListView.builder(
```

```
49.                  itemCount: _shoppingItems.length,
50.                  itemBuilder: (context, index) {
51.                    String itemName = _shoppingItems[index]['name'];
52.                  String itemQuantity = _shoppingItems[index]['quantity'];
53.                String itemUserEmail = _shoppingItems[index]['userEmail'];
54.
55.                    return ListTile(
56.                      title: Text('$itemName - Quantity: $itemQuantity'),
57.                    );
58.                  },
59.                ),
60.              ),
61.            ],
62.          ),
63.        );
64.  }
```

Code 7.3: Shopping items list build method

Using this approach, any updates in the list become visible only when we call **retrieveItemsFromCloud method**, which may not be an ideal solution. Let us examine how we can tackle this by utilizing Firebase and employing a StreamBuilder to obtain real-time data.

Dart Streams

Dart Streams refers to the asynchronous programming model provided by Dart, a programming language used for building Flutter applications. In Dart, a stream is a sequence of asynchronous events. Streams provide a way to handle a sequence of data over time, and they are widely used for handling asynchronous operations such as user input, network requests, and more.

Here is a breakdown of key points related to Dart Streams:

- **Definition:** Dart Streams represent a functionality within the Dart language facilitating the management of sequences of asynchronous events.
- **Asynchronous events:** Streams represent a sequence of events that occur over time, where each event is processed asynchronously.

- **Publish-subscribe pattern:** Streams follow the publish-subscribe pattern. Multiple subscribers can listen to a single stream, and they will be notified whenever a new event occurs.

- **Stream Controller:** A `StreamController` is often used to manage a stream. It acts as both a source of events (sink) and a stream itself.

- **Creating Streams:** Dart provides various ways to create streams, including using the Stream class directly or using convenience methods like `StreamController` and async* functions.

- **Listening to Streams:** Subscribers can listen to a stream using the listen method. The `onData`, `onError`, and `onDone` callbacks can be used to handle events, errors, and stream completion, respectively.

- **Handling Stream data:** Dart provides methods like map, where, take, and others to transform and manipulate stream data.

- **Async/Await with Streams:** Asynchronous functions and the await keyword can be used with streams to handle asynchronous operations in a more readable and sequential manner.

- **Built-in Dart Streams:** Dart includes built-in streams for handling asynchronous tasks, such as Future and `StreamController`.

- **Flutter and Dart Streams:** In Flutter, streams are commonly used for handling user input, animations, and asynchronous operations like fetching data from APIs.

- **Hot and cold Streams:** Streams can be categorized as hot or cold. Hot streams broadcast events regardless of whether there are subscribers, while cold streams only produce events when a subscriber is actively listening.

- **Dispose function:** In Dart, especially when working with streams, the dispose function is commonly used to clean up resources, including closing streams. This is particularly important to prevent memory leaks and ensure efficient resource management, especially when dealing with long-lived streams.

Understanding Dart Streams is crucial for effective asynchronous programming in Dart and is especially useful in Flutter for managing UI updates and handling asynchronous tasks without blocking the main thread. Here is a simple example of creating a stream:

```
1. import 'dart:async';
2.
3. void main() {
4.   // Create a stream controller
5.   var controller = StreamController<int>();
6.
7.   // Create a stream from the controller
8.   var stream = controller.stream;
```

```
9.
10.  // Listen to the stream
11.  var subscription = stream.listen((data) {
12.   print('Data: $data');
13.  });
14.
15.  // Add data to the stream
16.  controller.add(1);
17.  controller.add(2);
18.  controller.add(3);
19.
20.  // Close the stream when done
21.  controller.close();
22. }
```

Code 7.8: Dart stream

StreamBuilder

In Flutter, the **StreamBuilder** widget is used to build UI components based on the latest snapshot of interaction with a stream. It is particularly useful for handling asynchronous operations, such as fetching data from a network or responding to user input. Here are a few examples where you can use the snapshots provided by the **StreamBuilder** widget in Flutter:

- **Real-time Data Display**: **StreamBuilder** is commonly used to display real-time data fetched from a stream, such as live updates from a database, sensor data, or messages from a chat room. You can use the snapshot's data to update UI components dynamically as new data arrives.

- **Form Validation**: **StreamBuilder** can be used for real-time form validation, where the input data is validated asynchronously. You can use the snapshot's data to display validation errors or success messages based on the validation result.

- **Authentication State**: **StreamBuilder** is often used to display UI components based on the authentication state of the user. For example, you can show different screens or widgets based on whether the user is logged in or not.

Here is an example of using **StreamBuilder** to display data in a Flutter widget:

```
1.  import 'package:flutter/material.dart';
2.
```

```
3. void main() {
4.   runApp(MyApp());
5. }
6.
7. class MyApp extends StatelessWidget {
8.   final StreamController<int> controller = StreamController<int>();
9.
10.   @override
11.   Widget build(BuildContext context) {
12.     return MaterialApp(
13.       home: Scaffold(
14.         appBar: AppBar(
15.           title: Text('StreamBuilder Example'),
16.         ),
17.         body: StreamBuilder<int>(
18.           stream: controller.stream,
19.           builder: (BuildContext context, AsyncSnapshot<int>
              snapshot) {
20.             if (snapshot.hasError) {
21.               return Text('Error: ${snapshot.error}');
22.             }
23.
24.             if (!snapshot.hasData) {
25.               return Text('No data available');
26.             }
27.
28.             return Text('Data: ${snapshot.data}');
29.           },
30.         ),
31.         floatingActionButton: FloatingActionButton(
32.           onPressed: () {
33.             // Add data to the stream when the button is pressed
34.             controller.add(42);
35.           },
```

```
36.            child: Icon(Icons.add),
37.          ),
38.        ),
39.      );
40.   }
41. }
```

Code 7.9: Stream builder example

Now let us update our shopping list screen to use stream builder to get real-time updates. In your code for **ShoppingListScreen** just update the Expanded widget as shown in code below:

```
1.  // The StreamBuilder is connected to the stream of snapshots from the
    _itemsCollection Firestore collection,
2.  // and it updates the UI whenever new data is available.
3.            Expanded(
4.              child: StreamBuilder<QuerySnapshot>(
5.                stream: _itemsCollection
6.                    .where('userEmail', isEqualTo: _currentUser?.email)
7.                    .snapshots(),
8.                builder: (context, AsyncSnapshot<QuerySnapshot>
                  snapshot) {
9.                  if (snapshot.hasError) {
10.                   return Text('Error: ${snapshot.error}');
11.                 }
12.
13.                 if (snapshot.connectionState == ConnectionState.
                  waiting) {
14.                   return const Text('Loading...');
15.                 }
16.
17.               List<Map<String, dynamic>> items = snapshot.data!.docs
18.                   .map((doc) => doc.data() as Map<String, dynamic>)
19.                   .toList();
20.
21.               return ListView.builder(
```

```
22.                     itemCount: items.length,
23.                     itemBuilder: (context, index) {
24.                       String itemName = items[index]['name'];
25.                       String itemQuantity = items[index]['quantity'];
26.
27.                       return ListTile(
28.                       title: Text('$itemName - Quantity: $itemQuantity'),
29.                         );
30.                     },
31.                   );
32.                 },
33.               ),
34.             ),
```

Code 7.10: Shopping list screen with stream builder

Async Snapshot

The **AsyncSnapshot** class in Flutter is part of the **dart:async** library and is commonly used in conjunction with the **StreamBuilder** widget to represent the latest asynchronous interaction with a data source. It provides information about the state of an asynchronous computation, including whether it is still loading, has completed with data, or if an error has occurred.

Here is a brief overview of **AsyncSnapshot**:

- **Snapshot states: AsyncSnapshot** has three primary states:
  - **ConnectionState.none**: No asynchronous operation has been performed.
  - **ConnectionState.waiting**: The asynchronous operation is in progress.
  - **ConnectionState.done**: The asynchronous operation has been completed.
- **Accessing data:** You can access the data returned by the asynchronous operation using the data property. This property is null if the operation is still in progress or has encountered an error.
- **Error handling:** The error property contains the error (if any) that occurred during the asynchronous operation. It is null when there is no error.
- **has Data:** The **hasData** property is a boolean indicating whether the snapshot has data.
- **has Error:** The **hasError** property is a boolean indicating whether an error occurred.

- **Common use with StreamBuilder:** `AsyncSnapshot` is often used with the `StreamBuilder` widget. The builder function of `StreamBuilder` receives an `AsyncSnapshot` as a parameter, allowing you to conditionally build your UI based on the state of the asynchronous operation.

QuerySnapshot

The `QuerySnapshot` class in Flutter is part of the `cloud_firestore` package and represents a snapshot of query results from a Firestore database. It contains a list of `QueryDocumentSnapshot` instances, each representing a document in the result set.

Here are some key points about `QuerySnapshot`:

- **Query documents:** A `QuerySnapshot` contains a list of `QueryDocumentSnapshot` instances, each representing a document returned by a query.

- **Iterable interface:** `QuerySnapshot` implements the Iterable interface, allowing you to iterate over its documents using methods like **forEach**.

- **Document changes:** You can access the list of documents using the docs property. Additionally, you can get the documents that were added, removed, or modified in a query result using the **docChanges** property.

- **Empty snapshot:** A `QuerySnapshot` may be empty if the query does not match any documents in the collection.

- **Example usage:** When working with a **StreamBuilder** and Firestore, a `QuerySnapshot` is often used to represent the data received from a stream. For example, when using **snapshots()** to listen to changes in a collection.

Here is a simple example of using **AsyncSnapshot** and **QuerySnapshot** with **StreamBuilder**:

```
1.  StreamBuilder<QuerySnapshot>(
2.    stream: FirebaseFirestore.instance.collection('example_
      collection').snapshots(),
3.    builder: (BuildContext context, AsyncSnapshot<QuerySnapshot>
      snapshot) {
4.      if (snapshot.hasError) {
5.        return Text('Error: ${snapshot.error}');
6.      }
7.
8.      if (snapshot.connectionState == ConnectionState.waiting) {
9.        return Text('Loading...');
10.     }
11.
```

```
12.      if (snapshot.data == null || snapshot.data!.docs.isEmpty) {
13.        return Text('No documents found.');
14.      }
15.
16.      // Accessing the documents
17.      List<QueryDocumentSnapshot> documents = snapshot.data!.docs;
18.
19.      // Process the documents as needed
20.      // ...
21.
22.      return ListView.builder(
23.        itemCount: documents.length,
24.        itemBuilder: (context, index) {
25.          // Build UI using documents[index]
26.          return ListTile(
27.            title: Text('Document ${index + 1}'),
28.          );
29.        },
30.      );
31.    },
32. );
```

Code 7.11: AsyncSnapshot and QuerySnapshot example

In this example, **snapshot.data!.docs** is a list of **QueryDocumentSnapshot** instances, allowing you to access the individual documents returned by the query. Adjust the code according to your specific requirements and document structure in Firestore.

Now, let us enhance our **shopping_list** screen code by incorporating the use of **AsyncSnapshot** and **QuerySnapshot**. To achieve this, simply modify the code within the Expanded widget, specifically at *line 73*:

```
1.    Expanded(
2.      child: StreamBuilder<QuerySnapshot>(
3.        stream: _itemsCollection
4.            .where('userEmail', isEqualTo: _currentUser?.email)
5.            .snapshots(),
6.        builder: (context, AsyncSnapshot<QuerySnapshot> snapshot) {
```

```
7.              if (snapshot.hasError) {
8.               return Text('Error: ${snapshot.error}');
9.              }
10.
11.             if (snapshot.connectionState == ConnectionState.waiting) {
12.              return const Text('Loading...');
13.              }
14.
15.             List<Map<String, dynamic>> items = snapshot.data!.docs
16.               .map((doc) => doc.data() as Map<String, dynamic>)
17.               .toList();
18.
19.             return ListView.builder(
20.               itemCount: items.length,
21.               itemBuilder: (context, index) {
22.                String itemName = items[index]['name'];
23.                String itemQuantity = items[index]['quantity'];
24.
25.                return ListTile(
26.                  title: Text('$itemName - Quantity: $itemQuantity'),
27.                );
28.               },
29.             );
30.            },
31.          ),
32.        ),
```

Code 7.12: AsyncSnapshot and QuerySnapshot in shopping list screen code

Here are a few key points:

- **StreamBuilder** widget (*Lines 2*): The **StreamBuilder** widget is used to rebuild the UI based on the latest snapshot of data from a stream. In your case, the stream is coming from Firestore.

- Stream (*Line 3*): The stream property is set to _itemsCollection. where**(...).snapshots()**, meaning it's listening to changes in the Firestore collection where the **'userEmail'** field is equal to the current user's email.

- Builder function (*Lines 6*): The builder function is called whenever new data is available or when an error occurs. It receives an `AsyncSnapshot<QuerySnapshot>` named snapshot.

- Error handling (*Lines 7-8*): If there is an error in fetching data, it displays an error message using a Text widget.

- Loading state (*Lines 11-12*): If the data is still loading, it displays a 'Loading...' message using a Text widget.

- Accessing documents (*Lines 15-17*): If there is no error and the data is not in a loading state, it extracts the documents from the `QuerySnapshot` using `snapshot.data!.docs` and converts them to a list of `Map<String, dynamic>`.

- ListView builder (*Lines 19-29*): It then uses a `ListView.builder` to build a list of `ListTile` widgets based on the items retrieved from Firestore. Each `ListTile` displays the name and quantity of an item.

By concluding this section, we complete the shopping list app. However, you can expand the app further by incorporating options to delete or update items, utilizing the knowledge you have gained from the CRUD Operations topic.

Conclusion

This chapter provided a comprehensive exploration of Firebase integration in Flutter app development. We covered the setup of a Firebase project, authentication methods, and the integration of Cloud Firestore for NoSQL data storage. The implementation of CRUD operations in Flutter, along with a detailed examination of Dart Streams, Stream Builder, Async Snapshot, and Query Snapshot, offers a solid foundation for building reactive and dynamic user interfaces. With this knowledge, you're well-equipped to leverage Firebase's capabilities for seamless data management and real-time updates in your Flutter applications.

As we look ahead to the next chapter, anticipate diving into more advanced topics that will elevate your Flutter skills. It includes an introduction to the Provider package, exploration of Flutter versions, discussions on design patterns such as BLoC, insights into unit testing and debugging methodologies, and a comprehensive guide on publishing your app to both the App Store and Google Play Store.

With these upcoming topics, you will deepen your expertise and gain practical insights into building robust and scalable Flutter applications. Stay tuned for an enriching exploration into the intricacies of Flutter development.

Multiple Choice Questions

1. **Firebase overview: What is Firebase primarily known for in the context of mobile app development?**
   a. Database management
   b. Machine learning
   c. Cloud storage
   d. Backend as a Service

2. **Firebase Authentication: Which method is used to register a user with Firebase Authentication in Flutter?**
   a. createUserWithEmailAndPassword
   b. authenticateUser
   c. registerUser
   d. addUserToFirebase

3. **Cloud Firestore: What type of database is Cloud Firestore?**
   a. Relational database
   b. Graph database
   c. NoSQL document database
   d. SQLite database

4. **CRUD Operations: Which operation is used for updating data in Cloud Firestore?**
   a. create
   b. read
   c. update
   d. delete

5. **Dart Streams: What is the main purpose of Dart Streams?**
   a. Synchronous data handling
   b. Asynchronous data handling
   c. File input/output
   d. Static data manipulation

6. **Stream Builder: What widget is used for building dynamic UI components based on data streams?**
   a. FutureBuilder

b. StreamBuilder

c. DataBuilder

d. ReactiveWidget

7. **Async Snapshot: What role does Async Snapshot play in handling asynchronous data?**

a. Captures a snapshot of the entire app state

b. Manages asynchronous function calls

c. Holds the current state of asynchronous data

d. Synchronizes data between Firebase and the app

8. **Query Snapshot: What does Query Snapshot enable in Cloud Firestore?**

a. Real-time data updates

b. Data encryption

c. Data compression

d. Historical data tracking

Answers

1. d. Backend as a Service
2. a. createUserWithEmailAndPassword
3. c. NoSQL document database
4. c. update
5. b. Asynchronous data handling
6. b. StreamBuilder
7. c. Holds the current state of asynchronous data
8. a. Real-time data updates

Join our book's Discord space

Join the book's Discord Workspace for Latest updates, Offers, Tech happenings around the world, New Release and Sessions with the Authors:

https://discord.bpbonline.com

CHAPTER 8
Miscellaneous

Introduction

As we embark on the final chapter, we will discuss the advanced aspects of Flutter development, exploring the powerful Provider package for state management. We will navigate through Flutter's evolving versions, unravel essential design patterns such as **Model-View-ViewModel (MVVM)**, **Model-View-Presenter (MVP)**, and **Model-View-Controller (MVC)**, and talk about the efficiency of **Business Logic Component (BLoC)** patterns. Additionally, we will sharpen our skills in unit testing and debugging, concluding our journey by demystifying the process of publishing a Flutter app on the App Store. This culmination encapsulates the comprehensive toolkit needed to elevate your Flutter development expertise to new heights.

Structure

The chapter will cover the following topics:

- Introduction to the Provider package
- Riverpod
- Flutter versions
- Design patterns in Flutter
- BLoC design patterns

- Unit testing
- Debugging:
- Publishing app in app store and
- Publish your flutter app on the play store:

Introduction to the Provider package

In Flutter, the term *provider package* refers to the *provider* package, which is a state management solution commonly used in Flutter applications. The provider package helps manage the state of your application and facilitates the sharing of data between different parts of your widget tree.

Here is a brief overview:

- **Provider package:** The provider package is a Dart package that offers a simple and efficient way to manage state in Flutter applications. It follows the provider pattern and is built on top of the **InheritedWidget** to provide a clean and easy-to-use API.
- **State management:** In Flutter, managing the state is crucial for building responsive and dynamic user interfaces. The provider package helps in managing state by allowing widgets to access and listen to changes in the state without having to pass the state explicitly through the widget tree.
- **Usage:** To use the provider package, you typically create a **ChangeNotifier** or a class that extends **ChangeNotifier** to represent your application's state. After this, you can use Provider widgets to provide this state to the parts of your widget tree that need it.

Here is a simple example:

```
1. import 'package:flutter/material.dart';
2. import 'package:provider/provider.dart';
3.
4. void main() {
5.   runApp(MyApp());
6. }
7.
8. class MyModel with ChangeNotifier {
9.   int _count = 0;
10.
11.   int get count => _count;
12.
```

```
13.   void increment() {
14.     _count++;
15.     notifyListeners();
16.   }
17. }
18.
19. class MyApp extends StatelessWidget {
20.   @override
21.   Widget build(BuildContext context) {
22.     return ChangeNotifierProvider(
23.       create: (context) => MyModel(),
24.       child: MaterialApp(
25.         home: MyHomePage(),
26.       ),
27.     );
28.   }
29. }
30.
31. class MyHomePage extends StatelessWidget {
32.   @override
33.   Widget build(BuildContext context) {
34.     final myModel = Provider.of<MyModel>(context);
35.
36.     return Scaffold(
37.       appBar: AppBar(
38.         title: Text('Provider Package Example'),
39.       ),
40.       body: Center(
41.         child: Text('Count: ${myModel.count}'),
42.       ),
43.       floatingActionButton: FloatingActionButton(
44.         onPressed: () => myModel.increment(),
45.         child: Icon(Icons.add),
46.       ),
```

```
47.    );
48.  }
49.}
```

Code 8.1: Provider package example

Riverpod

Riverpod is a state management library for Flutter that provides a more intuitive and declarative way to manage application states compared to other solutions like Provider or Redux. It is built on top of Flutter's provider package and offers several advantages, such as:

- **Provider independence**: Riverpod promotes a more modular and independent approach to managing the state by decoupling the providers from the UI widgets. This makes it easier to refactor and test code, as providers can be defined independently of the UI.

- **Scoped providers**: Riverpod allows you to define providers within specific scopes, such as at the application level, within a widget subtree, or even within a specific lifecycle. This enables more fine-grained control over where and how the state is accessed and managed.

- **Dependency injection**: Riverpod supports dependency injection out of the box, making it easy to inject dependencies into your application's components without relying on global variables or singletons.

- **Asynchronous state handling**: Riverpod provides built-in support for handling asynchronous state, such as fetching data from APIs or performing background tasks. It seamlessly integrates with Flutter's async/await syntax, making it easy to work with asynchronous operations.

- **Immutable state management**: Riverpod encourages the use of immutable data structures for managing states, which helps prevent common pitfalls associated with mutable states and makes it easier to reason about application behavior.

Here is a simple example of how you can use Riverpod to manage the application state:

```
1. import 'package:flutter/material.dart';
2. import 'package:flutter_riverpod/flutter_riverpod.dart';
3.
4. // Define a provider for storing and managing a counter state
5. final counterProvider = StateProvider((ref) => 0);
6.
7. void main() {
```

```
8.    runApp(ProviderScope(child: MyApp()));
9. }
10.
11. class MyApp extends StatelessWidget {
12.   @override
13.   Widget build(BuildContext context) {
14.     return MaterialApp(
15.       home: Scaffold(
16.         appBar: AppBar(title: Text('Riverpod Counter')),
17.         body: Center(
18.           child: Consumer(builder: (context, watch, _) {
19.             final counterState = watch(counterProvider);
20.             return Text('Counter: ${counterState.state}');
21.           }),
22.         ),
23.         floatingActionButton: FloatingActionButton(
24.           onPressed: () {
25.             // Increment the counter state when the button is pressed
26.             context.read(counterProvider).state++;
27.           },
28.           child: Icon(Icons.add),
29.         ),
30.       ),
31.     );
32.   }
33. }
```

Code 8.2: Riverpod example

In this example, we define a provider called **counterProvider** to manage the state of a counter. We then use the Consumer widget to access and listen to changes in the counter state within the UI. When the floating action button is pressed, the counter state is incremented using **context.read(counterProvider).state++**.

Overall, Riverpod provides a powerful and flexible solution for managing state in Flutter applications, with an emphasis on simplicity, modularity, and performance.

Flutter versions

Flutter continues to evolve with regular releases. The Flutter framework is developed by Google and the latest stable version is usually found on the official Flutter website or on their GitHub repository.

Here is a general guide on how to check for the latest Flutter version:

- **Using the Command Line:**

  1. Open your terminal or command prompt.

  2. Run the following command to check the Flutter channel and version:

     `flutter -version`

     This will display information about the Flutter framework, Dart SDK version, and other relevant details.

  3. To check for updates, you can run:

     `flutter upgrade`

     This command will update your Flutter installation to the latest stable version.

- **Flutter release channels:**

  Flutter has several release channels, which are as follows:

  o Stable channel: This channel provides the most stable Flutter version.

  o Dev channel: Developers can use this channel to get early access to features and fixes.

  o Beta channel: This channel offers a more stable preview of upcoming releases.

- **Checking Flutter's official channels:**

  You can also visit Flutter's official channels, such as:

  o **https://github.com/flutter/flutter**: Check the releases section for the latest stable version.

  o **https://flutter.dev**: The website often provides information on the latest stable release.

Remember that the information provided here might become outdated, and it is always a good idea to check the official channels for the most up-to-date information. If there have been new releases or changes, you can find the details on the official Flutter channels mentioned above.

Design patterns in Flutter

Design patterns are general reusable solutions to common problems encountered during software development. Flutter, being a UI toolkit for building natively compiled applications, allows developers to apply various design patterns to create scalable, maintainable, and efficient code. Here are some commonly used design patterns in Flutter:

- **Singleton pattern**
  - o **Purpose**: Ensure a class has only one instance and provide a global point of access to it.
  - o **Example in Flutter**: Using a singleton pattern for managing a global state, such as an authentication service.

- **Provider pattern**
  - o **Purpose**: Manage and share the state across the widget tree efficiently.
  - o **Example in Flutter**: Using the provider package to handle state management and provide data to widgets.

- **BLoC pattern**
  - o **Purpose**: Separate the business logic from the UI layer, making the code more maintainable and testable.
  - o **Example in Flutter**: Using the BLoC package to implement a business logic component and manage the state.

- **Observer pattern**
  - o **Purpose**: Define a one-to-many dependency between objects so that when one object changes state, all its dependents are notified and updated automatically.
  - o **Example in Flutter**: Implementing observers to listen for changes in a data model and update the UI accordingly.

- **Command pattern**
  - o **Purpose**: Encapsulate a request as an object, thereby allowing users to parameterize clients with queues, requests, and operations.
  - o **Example in Flutter**: Using the Command pattern to encapsulate UI actions and execute them on demand.

- **Decorator pattern**
  - o **Purpose**: Attach additional responsibilities to an object dynamically. Decorators provide a flexible alternative to subclassing for extending functionality.
  - o **Example in Flutter**: Decorating widgets with additional features or behaviors without modifying their existing structure.

- **Strategy pattern**
  - o **Purpose**: Define a family of algorithms, encapsulate each one, and make them interchangeable. Strategy lets the algorithm vary independently from clients that use it.
  - o **Example in Flutter**: Implementing different strategies for handling data fetching, such as using a local cache or making a network request.

- **Factory method pattern**
  - o **Purpose**: Define an interface for creating an object, but let subclasses alter the type of objects that will be created.
  - o **Example in Flutter**: Using factory methods to create different types of widgets based on certain conditions.

- **Builder pattern**
  - o **Purpose**: Separate the construction of a complex object from its representation, allowing the same construction process to create various representations.
  - o **Example in Flutter**: Using a builder pattern to create complex widget trees with a clear and readable syntax.

These design patterns can be applied in various combinations to solve different challenges in Flutter development. The choice of pattern depends on the specific requirements of your application and the problem you are trying to solve.

MVVM, **MVP**, and **MVC** are classic architectural patterns that have been widely used in software development. Each pattern defines a way to organize the code and separate concerns to achieve maintainability, scalability, and testability. Here is a brief overview of each pattern and how they can be applied in the context of Flutter:

Model-View-ViewModel

Let us now understand various components of MVVM:

- **Model**
  - o Represents the data and business logic of the application.
  - o Manages data access, validation, and transformation.

- **View**
  - o Represents the UI elements and structure.
  - o Responsible for presenting the data and capturing user input.

- **ViewModel**
    - o Acts as an intermediary between the Model and View.
    - o Holds the presentation logic and exposes data and commands to the View.
    - o Does not have a direct reference to the View, promoting better testability.
- **Example in Flutter**

    The provider package or Riverpod can be used for state management, with separate classes for the Model, View, and ViewModel.

Model-View-Presenter

Let us now understand each component of MVP in detail now:

- **Model**
    - o Manages the data and business logic, similar to the MVVM pattern.
- **View**
    - o Represents the UI elements.
    - o Sends user input to the Presenter for handling.
- **Presenter**
    - o Acts as an intermediary between the Model and View.
    - o Handles user input, updates the Model, and updates the View accordingly.
    - o Promotes a separation of concerns by keeping the View as passive as possible.
- **Example in Flutter**

    The BLoC or provider package can be used for state management, with the Presenter handling business logic.

Model-View-Controller

Let us discuss each component of MVC in detail now:

- **Model**
    - o Represents the data and business logic, like MVVM and MVP.
- **View**
    - o Represents the UI elements.
    - o Observes the Model for changes and updates accordingly.
- **Controller**
    - o Handles user input, modifies the Model, and updates the View.
    - o Acts as an intermediary between the Model and View.

Flutter's own architecture is somewhat inspired by MVC, where Widgets act as both the View and Controller, and state management solutions like provider or *Riverpod* can be used for handling the Model.

Flutter-specific considerations:

In Flutter, there is often a focus on using widgets as the building blocks of UI, and certain patterns may be adapted or combined based on the specific needs of the application.

State management solutions like provider, BLoC, or *Riverpod* can be used to implement the business logic and manage the state in Flutter applications, aligning with the principles of these architectural patterns.

Ultimately, the choice between these patterns depends on factors such as the complexity of the application, team preferences, and the specific requirements of the project.

Business Logic Component design patterns

Business Logic Component is a state management pattern and library for Flutter that helps manage the state of an application in a clear and efficient way. BLoC separates the business logic from the UI layer, making the code more maintainable and testable. The core idea behind BLoC is to have components responsible for managing the state and emitting streams of output.

Here is a high-level overview of the key concepts in the BLoC pattern:

- **Business Logic Component**: The BLoC is a class or a set of classes responsible for managing the state and handling business logic. It typically exposes input sinks and output streams to interact with the UI layer.

- **Sink and stream**

  o **Sink:** A sink is an input that allows the UI layer to send events or data to the BLoC.

  o **Stream:** A stream is an output that emits a sequence of events or data to which the UI layer can subscribe.

- **Events and states**

  o **Events:** Actions or occurrences triggered by the UI layer (e.g., button clicks, user input).

  o **States:** Represent the different states of the application at a given point in time.

- **BlocProvider:** A widget provided by the bloc package that helps manage the lifecycle of the BLoC and provides it to the widget tree.

- **BlocBuilder and BlocListener:** Widgets provided by the bloc package to build UI components based on the current state of the BLoC or to react to state changes.

- **Immutability:** BLoC encourages the use of immutable data structures to represent state changes.

Here is a simple example of a counter app using BLoC in Flutter:

```dart
1.  import 'package:flutter/material.dart';
2.  import 'package:flutter_bloc/flutter_bloc.dart';
3.
4.  // Events
5.  abstract class CounterEvent {}
6.
7.  class IncrementEvent extends CounterEvent {}
8.
9.  class DecrementEvent extends CounterEvent {}
10.
11. // States
12. class CounterState {
13.    final int count;
14.
15.    CounterState(this.count);
16. }
17.
18. // BLoC
19. class CounterBloc extends Bloc<CounterEvent, CounterState> {
20.    CounterBloc() : super(CounterState(0));
21.
22.    @override
23.    Stream<CounterState> mapEventToState(CounterEvent event) async* {
24.      if (event is IncrementEvent) {
25.        yield CounterState(state.count + 1);
26.      } else if (event is DecrementEvent) {
27.        yield CounterState(state.count - 1);
28.      }
29.    }
30. }
31.
```

```
32. // UI
33. class CounterApp extends StatelessWidget {
34.   @override
35.   Widget build(BuildContext context) {
36.     return MaterialApp(
37.       home: BlocProvider(
38.         create: (context) => CounterBloc(),
39.         child: CounterScreen(),
40.       ),
41.     );
42.   }
43. }
44.
45. class CounterScreen extends StatelessWidget {
46.   @override
47.   Widget build(BuildContext context) {
48.     final CounterBloc counterBloc = BlocProvider.
        of<CounterBloc>(context);
49.
50.     return Scaffold(
51.       appBar: AppBar(
52.         title: Text('BLoC Counter App'),
53.       ),
54.       body: BlocBuilder<CounterBloc, CounterState>(
55.         builder: (context, state) {
56.           return Center(
57.             child: Column(
58.               mainAxisAlignment: MainAxisAlignment.center,
59.               children: <Widget>[
60.                 Text('Count: ${state.count}'),
61.                 SizedBox(height: 16),
62.                 Row(
63.                   mainAxisAlignment: MainAxisAlignment.center,
64.                   children: <Widget>[
```

```
65.                        FloatingActionButton(
66.                    onPressed: () => counterBloc.add(IncrementEvent()),
67.                        child: Icon(Icons.add),
68.                      ),
69.                    SizedBox(width: 16),
70.                    FloatingActionButton(
71.                    onPressed: () => counterBloc.add(DecrementEvent()),
72.                        child: Icon(Icons.remove),
73.                      ),
74.                  ],
75.                ),
76.              ],
77.            ),
78.          );
79.        },
80.      ),
81.    );
82.  }
83. }
84.
85. void main() {
86.    runApp(CounterApp());
87. }
```

Code 8.3: BLoC example

In this example, the **CounterBloc** manages the state of the counter, and the UI is built using the **BlocBuilder** widget to react to changes in the BLoC's state. The **CounterScreen** widget dispatches events to the BLoC when the user interacts with the buttons.

Remember that there are various state management solutions in Flutter, and the choice depends on the specific needs of your application. BLoC is just one option and is widely used for its clarity and scalability.

Unit testing

Unit testing is an essential part of the software development process, including Flutter development. In Flutter, you can use the built-in testing framework, known as **flutter_**

test, to write and run unit tests for your Dart code. Unit tests are designed to test individual units of code in isolation, ensuring that each unit works as expected.

Here is a basic guide on how to perform unit testing in Flutter:

1. **Setting up the test environment**

   Make sure your Flutter project has the necessary dependencies for testing by checking your **pubspec.yaml** file. Ensure that you have the following dependencies:

   ```
   1. dev_dependencies:
   2.   flutter_test:
   3.     sdk: flutter
   ```

   Code 8.4: Unit testing setup

   Then, run flutter pub get to fetch the dependencies.

2. **Writing unit tests**

   Create a new file for your unit tests, typically named **example_test.dart** inside the test directory. Here is an example of a simple unit test:

   ```
   1. // Import necessary packages
   2. import 'package:flutter_test/flutter_test.dart';
   3.
   4. // Import the code you want to test
   5. import 'package:your_flutter_project/example.dart'; // Replace with your actual file path
   6.
   7. void main() {
   8.   test('Addition test', () {
   9.     // Arrange
   10.    int result = add(2, 3);
   11.
   12.    // Assert
   13.    expect(result, 5);
   14.  });
   15.
   16.  test('Subtraction test', () {
   17.    // Arrange
   ```

```
18.     int result = subtract(5, 2);
19.
20.     // Assert
21.     expect(result, 3);
22.   });
23. }
```

Code 8.5: Unit testing example

3. **Running unit tests**

   Use the following command in your terminal to run the unit tests:

   flutter test

   This command will discover and run all the tests in your project. If the tests pass, you will see an output indicating success. If there are failures, the output will provide details about which tests failed and why.

   The **testing coverage pyramid** also emphasizes the distribution of test coverage across the different levels. While the exact percentage allocation may vary depending on factors such as project requirements, team preferences, and the nature of the application, a commonly suggested guideline is to aim for the following approximate percentage distribution:

   a. **Unit Tests:** These should ideally comprise the majority of the test suite, covering around 70-80% of the overall test coverage. Unit tests provide granular coverage of individual units or components and are typically faster to write and execute compared to higher-level tests.

   b. **Integration Tests:** Integration tests should cover around 15-20% of the test coverage. They focus on verifying the interactions and integration points between different units or modules of the system. While integration tests are broader in scope than unit tests, they are still more targeted and faster than end-to-end tests.

   c. **End-to-End Tests:** End-to-end tests should constitute the remaining 5-15% of the test coverage. These tests simulate real user interactions and validate the entire application workflow from start to finish. End-to-end tests are slower to execute and can be more complex to set up and maintain compared to unit and integration tests.

It's important to note that these percentages are guidelines and may vary depending on the specific requirements and characteristics of each project. The goal is to achieve a balanced testing approach that provides adequate coverage across different layers of the application while optimizing test effectiveness, efficiency, and maintainability.

Tips for writing unit tests

Below are some points to be kept in mind while writing a unit test:

- **Arrange-Act-Assert (AAA):** Organize your tests into three sections - arrange, act, and assert. This helps in making your tests more readable.

- **Mocking:** Use mock objects or test doubles to isolate the unit of code being tested from its dependencies.

- **Grouping tests:** You can group related tests together using the group function from the **flutter_test** package.

- **Test coverage:** Aim for high test coverage to ensure that most of your code is tested.

Remember that unit tests are just one part of a comprehensive testing strategy. In addition to unit tests, you may also want to consider integration tests and widget tests for a more thorough testing approach in Flutter.

Debugging

Debugging is the process of identifying and fixing errors, bugs, or issues within a software application. It involves systematically investigating the behavior of the program, tracing the source of the problem, and making necessary adjustments to correct it. Debugging techniques may include examining log messages, using breakpoints to pause execution and inspect variables, stepping through code line by line, and employing tools such as debuggers or logging frameworks. Effective debugging is an essential skill for software developers, as it helps ensure the reliability, stability, and functionality of their applications.

Let us look at some commonly used debugging techniques that we can be used when debugging Flutter applications:

- **Logging**:
  - Use logging statements strategically to print information about the program's state.
  - Leverage tools like the logger package to manage logging levels.

- **Flutter DevTools**:
  - Familiarize yourself with Flutter DevTools, a set of performance and debugging tools.
  - Use DevTools to inspect the widget tree, debug layout issues, and analyze performance.

- **Breakpoints and stepping**:
  - Set breakpoints in your code to pause execution and inspect variables.

     o   Use the debugging tools in your IDE to step through code execution.

- **Flutter inspector**:
  - o   Utilize the Flutter Inspector to inspect and interact with the widget tree.
  - o   Identify and fix layout issues and UI glitches.

- **Hot reload**:
  - o   Leverage Flutter's hot reload feature to quickly see the effects of code changes without restarting the entire application.

- **Exception handling**:
  - o   Implement appropriate exception handling to catch and log errors gracefully.
  - o   Use the **try-catch** mechanism to handle exceptions and provide meaningful error messages.

- **Logging libraries**:
  - o   Explore logging libraries like logger or logging to manage and filter logs effectively during development and debugging.

- **Flutter driver tests**:
  - o   Use Flutter Driver tests for end-to-end testing and UI automation.
  - o   Flutter Driver allows you to interact with your app as a user would and verify expected behavior.

Remember that effective debugging and testing are ongoing processes. Regularly revisit and update your tests as your codebase evolves and utilize debugging tools to quickly identify and resolve issues during development. Additionally, encourage collaboration within your team to share insights and collectively improve the quality of your Flutter application.

Publishing app in an app store

Publishing an app on the app store involves several steps, and the process can change over time as Apple updates its guidelines and requirements. Here is a general overview of the steps you need to follow to publish a Flutter app on the App Store:

1. **Prepare your Flutter app**
   a. **Update and optimize**: Ensure your app is stable, performs well, and follows Apple's design guidelines. Optimize your app for different iOS devices and screen sizes.
   b. **App icons and screenshots**: Provide high-quality app icons and screenshots that showcase your app's features.

   c. **App name and description**: Choose a unique and descriptive app name. Write a compelling app description that highlights its key features.

2. **Create an Apple developer account**

   a. Enroll in the Apple developer program:

   b. Visit the Apple developer program website and enroll in the program. Follow the enrollment steps, which may include paying an annual fee.

3. **Set up Xcode and Flutter**

   a. **Install Xcode**: Download and install Xcode from the Mac App Store. Open Xcode and sign in with your Apple ID.

   b. **Set up Flutter for iOS**: Ensure your Flutter app is configured to build for iOS. Follow Flutter's official documentation for setting up your Flutter app for iOS deployment.

4. **Generate App ID and provisioning profiles**

   a. **Create an App ID**: In the Apple developer center, create an App ID for your app.

   b. **Generate provisioning profiles**: Create provisioning profiles for distribution and associate the provisioning profiles with your App ID.

5. **Configure App Store Connect**

   a. **Create an App in App Store Connect**: Go to App Store Connect and create a new app and fill in the required details.

   b. **App version and build number**: Set the version number and build number in your Flutter project. Update the pubspec.yaml file accordingly.

6. **Build and Archive Your App**

   a. In Xcode, select "**Generic iOS Device**" as the build target.

   b. Choose "**Product**" | "**Archive**" to build an archive for distribution.

7. **Submit your app for review**

   a. **Submit to app store connect**: Open the Organizer in Xcode and find the archive you just built. Click "**Distribute App**" and follow the prompts to submit your app to App store connect.

   b. **Complete App Store Connect Submission**: In App Store Connect, complete the required information, including adding screenshots, app descriptions, etc. Submit your app for review.

8. **Await app review and release**

   a. **App review process**: Apple will review your app to ensure it meets their guidelines. This process may take some time.

   b. **Release your app**: Once your app is approved, you can set its release status to make it available on the App Store.

Publish your Flutter app on the Play Store

Below mentioned are the steps to be followed to publish your app on the Play Store:

1. **Prepare your flutter app**

   a. **Update and optimize**: Ensure your app is stable, performs well, and follows Google's design guidelines (Material Design). Optimize your app for different Android devices and screen sizes.

   a. **App icons and screenshots**: Provide high-quality app icons and screenshots that showcase your app's features.

   b. **App name and description**: Choose a unique and descriptive app name. Write a compelling app description that highlights its key features.

2. **Create a Google Play Developer Account**

   a. Visit the Play Console: Go to the Google Play Console. Sign in with your Google account.

   b. Set up a developer account: Pay a one-time registration fee to set up a Google Play Developer account.

3. **Set up google play console**

   a. Create a new app: In the Play Console, click on "Create App" to set up a new app. Fill in the required information, including the app's title, default language, and the app's content rating.

   b. App version and build number: Set the version number and build number in your Flutter project. Update the **pubspec.yaml** file accordingly.

4. **Generate a signing key**

   a. **Generate a Keystore**: Create a keystore file for signing your Android app.

   b. Follow Flutter's official documentation for setting up your Flutter app for Android deployment.

5. **Build an APK or app bundle**

   a. **Build for release**: Run the following command to build a release APK:

   bashCopy code

   ```
   flutter build apk --release
   ```

   b. You can also build an **Android App Bundle (AAB)**

   bashCopy code

   ```
   flutter build appbundle
   ```

6. **Upload your app Google Play Console:**

   To upload an .aab file to Google Play, you can follow these steps:

   a. **Sign in to Google Play Console:** Go to the Google Play Console website (**https://play.google.com/console/**) and sign in with your Google account.

   b. **Create a new release:** Select the app you want to release from the list of apps in your console. Then, click on the "**Release**" tab in the left menu and select "**Production.**"

   c. **Upload your .aab file:** Click on "**Create Release**" and then select the option to upload your .aab file. Drag and drop your .aab file into the designated area, or click on "Browse Files" to select the file from your computer.

   d. **Fill in release details:** Once the .aab file is uploaded, you'll need to fill in some release details, such as the release name, release notes, and any other required information. Make sure to review and verify all the details before proceeding.

   e. **Review and rollout:** After filling in the release details, review the information carefully to ensure accuracy. You can also configure the rollout options, such as staged rollout percentages and release tracks, if desired.

   f. **Confirm and rollout:** Once you're satisfied with the release details and configuration, click on the "**Review**" button to review everything one last time. If everything looks good, click on "**Confirm rollout**" to proceed with the release.

   g. **Monitor the release:** After the release is confirmed, you can monitor its progress in the "Release dashboard" section of the Google Play Console. Keep an eye on user feedback, crash reports, and other metrics to ensure a successful rollout.

Your .aab file should now be uploaded and released on Google Play. It may take some time for the release to be fully processed and available to users worldwide.

Conclusion

As we reach the end of this book, you have journeyed from the fundamentals to advanced concepts, building a robust skill set for Flutter development. From UI design and widget composition to state management with Provider, navigating design patterns, understanding BLoC architecture, and mastering unit testing and debugging — each chapter has enriched your proficiency.

In closing, remember that Flutter's dynamic ecosystem constantly evolves. Stay curious, explore new features, and embrace emerging best practices. As you embark on your own projects, may this book serve as a valuable companion, providing insights and solutions to propel your Flutter development endeavors.

Thank you for joining this Flutter exploration. May your coding adventures be exciting, your applications innovative, and your Flutter journey filled with continuous growth and success. Happy coding!

Join our book's Discord space

Join the book's Discord Workspace for Latest updates, Offers, Tech happenings around the world, New Release and Sessions with the Authors:

https://discord.bpbonline.com

Index

Printed in Great Britain
by Amazon

46078458R00190